Consumer Behaviour in the Food Industry

...erworth
Heinemann, 1995   0750t

Consumer Behaviour in the Food Industry:
A European Perspective

Jonathan Bareham

University of Brighton Business School

Butterworth-Heinemann Ltd
Linacre House, Jordan Hill, Oxford OX2 8DP

 A member of the Reed Elsevier plc group

OXFORD LONDON BOSTON
MUNICH NEW DELHI SINGAPORE SYDNEY
TOKYO TORONTO WELLINGTON

First published 1995

© Butterworth-Heinemann Ltd 1995

British Library Cataloguing in Publication Data
Bareham, J. R.
    Consumer Behaviour in the Food Industry:
    European Perspective
    I. Title
    647.950688

ISBN 0 7506 1931 7

Composition by Genesis Typesetting, Laser Quay, Rochester, Kent
Printed in Great Britain

Contents

Preface

This book is an introduction to the study of consumer behaviour. In each chapter there is an exploration of one of the many factors which can influence why people buy particular products.

As an introduction it differs from other texts in that there is a concentration on one set of products, food and drink, with a European perspective and examples.

The organizing framework of the book and the rationale for inclusion of the different topics in each chapter is outlined in Chapter 1. The book is arranged in five parts, in turn examining the political, economic and technical influences, cultural and social influences, psychological influences and marketing influences which can have an impact on purchase behaviour.

Food is an interesting commodity in that, unlike many products, we have to consume it in order to survive. However, there is also a physiological limit on how much and how often we can consume.

What people buy is obviously affected by availability. Many products vary in seasonality and hence price both within one country and in different parts of Europe. However, the relationship between price and purchase behaviour is not a simple one. Consumption does not always decrease in a one to one ratio as price increases. Consumers may, for example, substitute one product for another, such as cheaper cuts of meat for more expensive ones, or continue their purchase pattern despite price changes. The price itself may be manipulated as a result of trade barriers or the operation of cartels. The availability and price of bananas in European shops, for instance, is heavily influenced by trade agreements between Caribbean suppliers and the European Union. Many food products have only become available in recent years because of technological innovations to improve shelf life or storage in the freezer cabinet.

Chapters 2–5 of this book explore the political, economic and technological influences on what food and drink products are made available to the consumer.

People buy food not just because they are hungry or because it is available at an economic price but also because of cultural and social reasons. The Turkish immigrant living in Germany or the Moroccan in Paris will not eat the same as the indigenous population. Consumption is affected by a person's cultural, religious and historical roots. Food acquires meaning in the anthropological sense. Only certain foods may be eaten by certain people on certain occasions. The changing demographic profile with a growing population of older people throughout Europe and an increase in those living alone also means that consumption patterns are changing. The influence of the family as a social unit is diminishing, although at a lesser rate in the predominantly Catholic countries of southern Europe versus northern Europe.

Over the past fifty years diet has changed, with a move away from fats, sugar and some dairy products but with vast regional and national differences. There are also longer term changes in people's diet due to a combination of growing prosperity and the impact of varying cultural and social norms.

Chapters 6–12 consider a range of cultural and social influences on consumers. This includes an exploration of the impact of culture, history, religion, demography, social class and the family and household unit.

Putting to one side the influence of culture and the more immediate pressure of family or acquaintances, the consumer's personal image is invested in what they buy. The values and attitudes, and hence the lifestyle, of one group of consumers will mean they have very different purchase patterns from another group. Interest in the quality or naturalness of food products has recently been a growing area of concern for some consumers. They tend to buy more expensive products which they perceive to have these attributes. At the same time there are many consumers who are totally and only concerned with price, which has fuelled the growth of discount food chains throughout Europe.

In Chapters 13–15 individual psychological variables are explored. This includes the discussion of values, personality, lifestyle, attitudes and behaviour.

What consumers buy is affected by what products they know about, what they know about them and whether those products are in front of them when they are deciding what to buy. The media help to shape the perceptions of consumers and to inform them. What is made available is crucially dependent on what retailers choose to make available. In most European countries food retailing has become more and more dominated by fewer and fewer operators whose power base in exerting an influence on manufacturers has strengthened. In poorer countries such as Greece and Portugal the small specialist food shop persists but in most European countries food is primarily sold in supermarkets and hypermarkets, although the rapid rise of discounters started in Germany.

Elements of the marketing mix are explored in Chapters 16 and 17 with particular attention to the effectiveness of communications and to changes in the food retailing environment.

A large part of the book is therefore concerned with different ways of analysing consumers into different categories or segments. The final chapter is somewhat of an antidote to this approach. It discusses the work of Ehrenberg which concentrates more on the pattern of purchase by populations of consumers without getting too concerned with individual or group differences.

Overall, the book is concerned with who buys what food and drink products, where they buy them, why and how. It takes the classical approach to consumer behaviour which in itself brings together an eclectic mix of disciplines and part disciplines; anthropology, sociology, psychology, economics and politics.

The approach taken here covers some of the subject matter in seminal works such as Engel, Blackwell and Miniard's *Consumer Behaviour* (1993), now in its seventh edition. Much is owed to the inspiration of Foxall's *Consumer Behaviour: a Practical Guide* (1980). However, the link between theory and practice in his and his co-author's most recent work (Foxall and Goldsmith, 1994) illustrates better the intention with this text. Since the study of food is at its core it also refers extensively to more specialist texts such as Ritson's *Food Consumer* (1986) and anthropological and sociological work such as Mennell *et al.* (1992) on *The Sociology of Food* and Murcott (1986) on *The Sociology of Food and Eating*. However, in preparing this book an effort has been made to include European material and information derived from market research and news media. In particular, the latter is intended to give the book a topicality and relevance by the inclusion of short illustrative cases to supplement or elaborate a theoretical point. Not as much of the European data was to hand as had first been hoped, although much more than is here is bound to exist, thereby setting a challenge for a further edition or another author! Not the least of the problems was that the definition of Europe was changing as the book was being written. The pragmatic decision made was to include reference only to members of the European Union in 1993.

The text is intended for students studying an introduction to consumer behaviour, particularly on courses with a food orientation such as food marketing, retailing, consumer studies, home economics and hospitality management. It is hoped the book will also be of interest to undergraduate and postgraduate students concerned with consumer behaviour as part of a marketing course. Questions appear at the end of each chapter to help the reader reflect on the material provided or to trigger exploration of related issues. The reader will hopefully find the opening chapter helpful in giving an organizing framework for the book.

The book was prompted by a fruitful experience of teaching undergraduates at what is now Sheffield Hallam University and more recently at the University of Brighton. In particular I am grateful for the help given by Jayam Dalal who searched for relevant information, for advice given on early drafts by my wife, Jan, and to marketing colleagues at Brighton. Jo Baker did the majority of the word processing in a highly efficient and effective manner. I am also grateful to my publishers and employers for their patience and support.

I take full responsibility for any inaccuracies and deficiencies in the text which I hope will provide an interest and stimulus to the reader in the growing field of consumer behaviour.

Jonathan Bareham
Brighton

1 *An introduction – models of buyer behaviour and food choice*

Introduction

Maria Gonzales shops with her friend and neighbour Dorita at the market in Teulada, a small town near the coast in the Alicante region of Spain. She goes twice a week to buy fresh vegetables and fruit, and chat with her friends. She usually buys what she wants from the same stall although she always looks around the market first to see if there are any particularly cheap offers. Most of her other groceries are bought once a week on a shopping trip to Pepe la Sal's, a small supermarket in the high street. A lot of what she buys is fairly similar from week to week with some increase in luxury items before Christmas or for a special celebration. Every day Maria or one of her children go to the local bakers to buy fresh bread.

Irene and Derek Jones invariably shop at Marks & Spencer's food hall in the centre of Brighton, on the south coast of England; they usually go together on a Saturday when both are off work. They like the quality of what is available and the fact that pre-prepared meals can be bought and 'fluffed up' for dinner parties without too much trouble. When their teenage children are at home from university during holidays then the children sometimes go off to Asda, one of the larger supermarkets, to load up with shopping. Late at night they may creep down to the local Circle K to get stocked up with crisps and drink.

These two examples represent part of the food purchase behaviour of people in different parts of Europe. The purchase of food is only part of the sequence of events from first conceptualizing what to buy followed by actual selection, preparation and consumption. Nevertheless, these examples give enough of an indication that for different people on different occasions a variety of factors can have an influence on what they buy, when, where and how. Some of those which can be identified in these two examples include cultural differences, the impact of other family members and friends, the type of retail environment and hence what products are available, and the reason for the purchase.

This book is concerned with an exploration of these different influences looked at in detail and one at a time. This first chapter is concerned with a general overview of how the different influences are interrelated. In some ways it is easier to read this chapter after rather than before other chapters. The most helpful strategy might be to read it now to get the overview and plan of the book and then come back to it later as well.

The purpose of this chapter is to do three things: first to describe general models of consumer behaviour and second, those which are concerned to identify factors that influence food choice in particular. The third aim is to describe a particular model of factors influencing food purchase which simultaneously provides a framework for the remainder of the book.

The purpose of models

If a new supermarket were to open on the other side of town and I decided to drive to visit it I would not at that instant have had the direct experience of having been there before. My ability to get there would depend on either a mental or an actual map. Either in my head or on paper I have a model of where I need to go which in turn guides my behaviour.

If the price of the tomatoes I usually buy in the market were to go up by 10 per cent I might still buy them. However even before getting to the market I will probably have decided that if the price has risen by 50 per cent then I will do without tomatoes or choose something cheaper. Again, I have a mental model, a link between hypothetical prices and my purchase behaviour.

Models in the field of consumer behaviour are similar to maps. They attempt to give a simplified version of the relationship between factors that influence behaviour. In doing so they attempt to demonstrate the variable relationship between factors, as in the tomato example. As one factor, price, changes then so does behaviour towards both this product and others.

These two rather different analogies also demonstrate that just as it is possible to have very different maps of the same town it is possible to have very different models of the same phenomenon, consumer behaviour. Each can add something to our understanding as long as the variety does not lead to confusion.

The objective of a model is two-fold. First, the intention is to enable description, explanation, prediction and ultimately control of consumer behaviour. Second, models help researchers in developing better hypotheses and theories about the relationship between factors that have an influence on consumer behaviour. Models of consumer behaviour are a long way from fulfilling either of these objectives; most models are simply descriptive. Some do allow a degree of prediction if used carefully. Mostly their use is in appreciating the variety of factors that can have an influence on even simple purchase decisions.

Consumer behaviour models

A variety of different types of model exist in the consumer behaviour literature. These are briefly described here.

Black box models

For some years a colleague and I taught a course on a food marketing degree. His background was in economics, mine was in applied psychology. He would argue that people were rational, I would argue that life was more complicated than that. He was interested in what to me were simplistic assumptions about the behaviour of a mass of people. If the price of butter goes up people in general buy less of it. His model was about the behaviour of populations of people and he was not too worried about why they behaved like that. I was and am more interested in individuals, sets of individuals and the processes which affect their reaction to a price change.

The economic model is explored in more detail in Chapter 4. Essentially it is a black box approach. A change is made to one or more inputs and the effect on outputs is examined. The concern is not with the processes within the box, which therefore remains a mystery or 'black box' (see Figure 1.1).

Figure 1.1 *The black box model*

However, I have learned to be more tolerant of his approach. It is obviously possible and useful to consider this simple model of consumer behaviour. If one of the inputs is changed, such as price or the amount of advertising, and it can be shown this has a consistent effect on purchase behaviour, then that is valuable information. The limitations with this sort of model lie in the fact it does not explain or predict behaviour.

Decision-making models

These models are concerned with the stages consumers go through in reaching a decision (see Figure 1.2). The emphasis is on internal cognitive processes, in other words what goes on within the black box.

Consider the simple proposition of someone buying a new cooker. It is unlikely they would simply go to the shop and buy one. First, they would need to have decided they wanted one. Either they were setting up house for the first time or else the old one was worn out. Then they would look around to see what was available, ask friends, and perhaps respond to adverts they had previously ignored. On the basis of information about price, features, size and so on they would make a decision, buy a cooker, have it installed and then keep evaluating it once it was purchased. This would determine whether they ever bought the same make again or what they said to their friends about it. This chain of events is obviously more likely and lengthy in the case of the purchase of an expensive item bought infrequently. In the case of a daily or weekly purchase of food the process is much shorter, unconscious or non-existent.

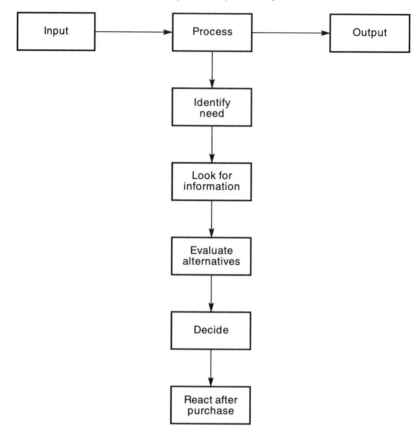

Figure 1.2   *An outline decision-making model*

This type of model is considered in greater depth in the chapter on persuasive communications (Chapter 17).

Mathematical models

Some models attempt to define mental constructs in measurable terms and then relate one to another in order to enable prediction.

The classic example is that of Fishbein, which is explained more fully in Chapter 15. This model attempts to predict behaviour by first measuring two components of attitudes; beliefs and evaluations. By use of a mathematical formula, the measure of attitude, and a measure of the influence of other people, are combined to predict behaviour. As another example, Ehrenberg has used a mathematical model explained in great detail by East (1990) and in greater depth in Chapter 18. By use of simple measures of purchase frequency and the proportion of people who have bought a particular product in a particular period, Ehrenberg has successfully predicted purchase behaviour which mirrors the actual behaviour of people recorded from audits.

Comprehensive models

There are many varied models in the consumer behaviour literature, all intended to encompass the many variables or factors which can have an influence on consumer behaviour. Perhaps the most classic was first introduced in 1968 by Engel, Kollatt and Blackwell (see Figure 1.3). It has been updated and modified since then but the EKB model is still the basis of the seventh edition of the main American text on consumer behaviour (Engel *et al.*, 1993). What follows is an abbreviated version of the model dissected in such a way as to show how it is essentially a combination of a decision-making model and a model which recognizes a range of influences on purchase behaviour. In essence it is descriptive rather than predictive and mainly applies to purchase of major items which are expensive or with a high degree of risk if the wrong thing is bought. The main core of the model has already been identified in the section on decision-making models above.

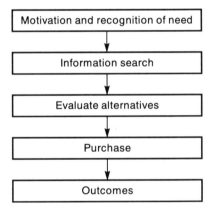

Figure 1.3 *Main stages in the EKB model*

Stage 1: need recognition

This is the start of the process. A person needs to buy a new cooker or to visit a supermarket because they are running out of food. There are obviously differences between people in their individual circumstances and background which will affect when and to what degree a particular need arises. There will also be pressures from friends or relations.

Engel, Blackwell and Miniard (1993) recognize three key determinants of need which they identify as:

- Individual differences.
- Environmental influences.
- Information stores in the memory.

Within the first two of these three categories are a variety of cultural, social and individual factors which will have an influence on the level of need as identified in Figure 1.4.

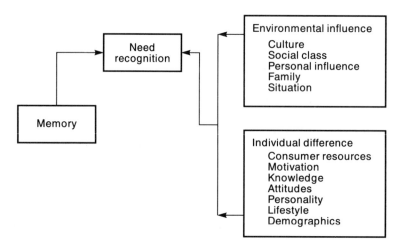

Figure 1.4 *Need recognition in the EKB model. (Based on Rice, 1993)*

Stage 2: information search

The next stage is the search for information about available purchase options (see Figure 1.5). For unimportant or cheap purchases this may not be necessary but for more important or expensive purchases it may take time and effort to find out what the options are. The sources might be the media, friends, relations or other significant people. Word of mouth information is particularly important here as identified in the chapter on opinion leadership (Chapter 11).

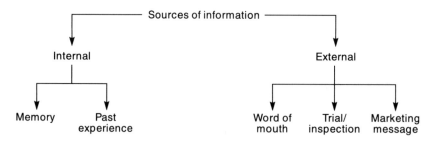

Figure 1.5 *Sources of information in the EKB model. (Based on Rice, 1993)*

The external messages are dominated in number by marketing sources such as sales people, point of sale devices, advertising etc. If these are attended to and accepted they become retained as an important influence on purchase behaviour.

Grafting together stages 1 and 2 the complete model in simplified form is illustrated in Figure 1.6.

Stage 3: alternative evaluation

Having found out about new cookers, or what new supermarkets are about to open, the prospective purchaser would weigh up the pros and cons of each. Naturally, the criteria

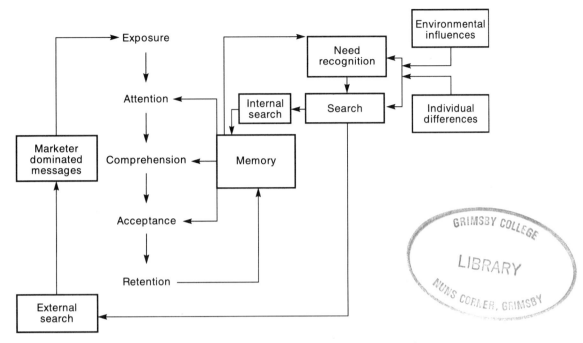

Figure 1.6   *Need recognition and information search. (Based on Rice, 1993)*

chosen on which to base the judgement are important. In the case of the cooker it may be price, ease of cleaning, whether it fits in the space in the kitchen, colour, type of heating and so on. The criteria stem from beliefs, attitudes and intentions (see Figure 1.7), a topic explored in more depth in Chapter 15.

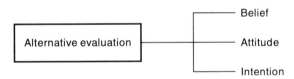

Figure 1.7   *Alternative evaluation. (Based on Rice, 1993)*

Stage 4: purchase and outcome

Having decided what to buy the consumer buys it and is either satisfied or dissatisfied. The level of satisfaction may change after purchase. The individual may come to emphasize to themselves the good features of whatever is bought in order to justify why it was bought. The total model is outlined in Figure 1.8.

In the case of buying baked beans as opposed to a new cooker the stages to do with external search and alternative evaluation are obviously much truncated.

The model has been criticized. It is complex. Although it identifies environmental and social influences it does not define relationships specifically. The predictive power is limited, essentially it is a descriptive model with lines and arrows linking concepts

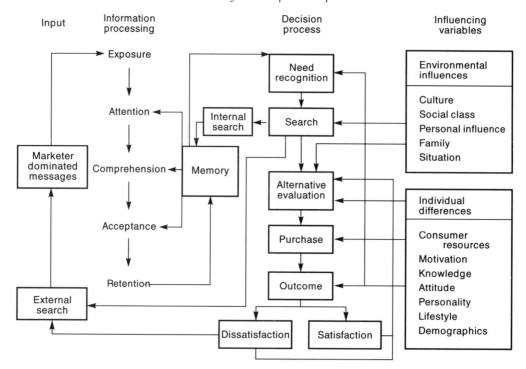

Figure 1.8   *The EKB model of consumer choice. (Based on Rice, 1993)*

which are assumed to be related. On the positive side it does emphasize the internal decision processes involved in purchase of a major product. It does demonstrate the complex range of influences on purchase and link them in one overview.

Food preference and choice models

So far the consideration has been of generalist consumer behaviour models. Various authors have focused on the set of variables which have an effect on food choice as opposed to generalized models which may be applied to the purchase of any product or service.

   Yudkin (in Shepherd, 1989) first listed a range of factors which can influence food choice in three categories:

1 Physical   Geography, season, economics, food technology
2 Social   Religion, social custom, social class, advertising, education in nutrition
3 Physiological Heredity, allergy, therapeutic diet, acceptability, nutritional need

Since that time a variety of models have been put forward with many similarities between them. Shepherd (1989) summarized these as shown in Figure 1.9. In brief these identify two major sets of influences to do with individual differences and the food

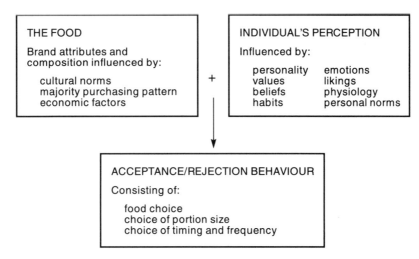

Figure 1.9   *Generalized models of food choice. (After Shepherd, 1989)*

itself, which in turn combine to have an influence on acceptance or rejection behaviour.

Shepherd (1989) also refers to two other models which link a variety of factors that have an influence on food preference (Figures 1.10 and 1.11).

A number of these models have common features. These include the identification of cultural and socio-economic factors, personal or individual characteristics such as age, sex, mood or personal circumstance, and then factors which are intrinsic to the food itself such as the method of preparation, taste, appearance, and how the food is promoted.

Although not specific to food the concept of two clusters of factors which influence purchase behaviour is categorized most simply by Foxall, 1980 (Figure 1.12), who identified aspects of social structure and individual difference.

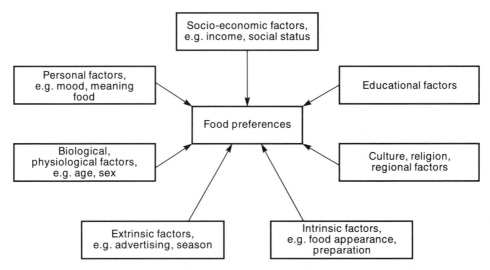

Figure 1.10   *Khan's model of food preferences, 1981. (After Shepherd, 1989)*

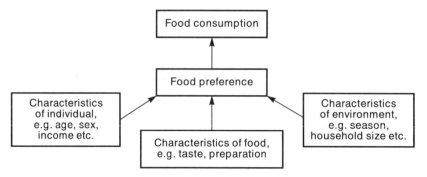

Figure 1.11   *Randall and Sanjur's model of food preference, 1981. (After Shepherd, 1989)*

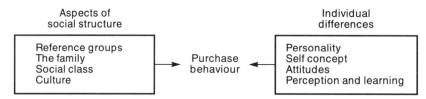

Figure 1.12   *Foxall's model of purchase behaviour. (After Foxall, 1980)*

All of these models are descriptive and essentially list a variety of factors affecting purchase behaviour. Hence the same criticism can be levelled at them as at the EKB model earlier.

The organizing model for the book

A characteristic of the models examined in this chapter is the attempt first to identify the range of factors which can have an influence on purchase behaviour and then to clump these together into a reduced set. Most of the models provide a descriptive framework, and while they allude to relationships between variables there is little evidence for the links referred to in diagrammatic representations of the models. Only the models of authors such as Fishbein and Ehrenberg give any predictive power, although here again there are limitations. This book is organized on the basis of a descriptive model, which is closest to those proposed by Foxall and Khan.

The following chapters consider in detail and one at a time specific factors which have an influence on consumer choice. These are organized into four clusters, identified as:

- Political, economic and technical
- Cultural and social
- Psychological
- Marketing

and briefly elaborated in the following sections.

Political, economic and technical influences

Most governments have developed food policies which have an effect on food availability. In the main in Western Europe these are not interventionist but more subtle in the form of advice or control via legislation on topics such as additives, diet, descriptions, labelling. This is explored in Chapter 2.

Clearly within Europe the policies of the European Union have affected the supply of food. There has been clear intervention and fixing of the market to ensure adequate supplies and keep out products from the remainder of the world. The impact of the Common Agricultural Policy is examined in greater depth in Chapter 3.

Food is a frequently purchased commodity because consumers have a continuous need. Consumers' incomes have an influence on what type of food is bought although there is not a consistent relationship with the amount bought, which is limited physiologically. The relationships between income, price and quantity and quality of food bought are explored in Chapter 4.

The changing technology involved in the production and preparation of food has an influence on what is available in the shops and how it can be presented to the consumer. This is examined in Chapter 5.

Cultural and social influences

There are long-term trends of what is acceptable in Western European society and within that, national and regional variations which can influence purchase and consumption patterns. This is considered in Chapter 6. A related phenomenon is the mythology and symbolism related to food which can have religious or historical origins. It can affect for instance the acceptability of what food will be eaten and whether new food products will become part of a consumer's diet. These phenomena are discussed in Chapters 7 and 8.

The changing population structure and with it family and household size and composition, and the structure of the work force will have an influence on consumption. This is considered in Chapter 9. Individual behaviour will be significantly influenced by social norms. Of particular influence are reference groups and important others who have a strong impact as opinion leaders. A particular group, the family, is still a significant influence on purchase behaviour. These influences are considered further in Chapters 10–12.

Psychological influences

A range of individual differences can have an impact on consumer behaviour by affecting the internal processes in decision-making. A key dimension is the value system adopted by individuals or sets of individuals. This is tied up with their personality although a more useful and predictive concept in consumer research is lifestyle. Groups of individuals can be segmented according to their psychographic or lifestyle profile. This is explained in more detail in Chapters 13 and 14.

The ultimate behaviour of consumers is heavily related to their attitudes. The attitude–behaviour equation has been one of the most heavily explored areas in social psychology. It is considered in Chapter 15.

Marketing influences

A full treatment of all elements of the marketing mix would consider in detail the location of food outlets, pricing and promotion strategies, point of sale influences and so on. This is left to more comprehensive texts to deal with in detail. However material on the location and layout of supermarkets and the changing profile of what stores or other outlets are available is considered in Chapter 16. The issue of what effect promotion strategies have is dealt with by an examination of communications research which has looked at persuasiveness and influence (Chapter 17).

Outcomes

The final part of the book is concerned with the outcomes of all these influencing factors; whether or not a purchase is made and, if so, with what frequency. It draws on much research by Ehrenberg (Chapter 18). The overall relationship between these elements used in this text is outlined in Figure 1.13.

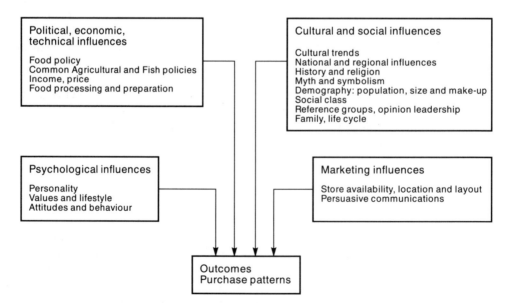

Figure 1.13   *A model of consumer choice with respect to food*

Conclusion

The purpose of consumer behaviour models is to provide description, explanation and prediction of purchase behaviour. At the same time the models provide a conceptual framework and so help researchers to set up and test new ideas so as to give even better explanations and predictions of behaviour.

Most of the models examined in this chapter provide no more than a description of the range of factors which can influence choice. Some of those which are concerned with food enable the set of factors to be specified more exactly.

On the positive side these models do help to organize research results and to demonstrate the complexity of decision processes involved in even a simple purchase, such as a can of soup at the local supermarket.

On the negative side most of the models can be criticized as providing no more than a description of a range of influencing variables. There is the danger that the mere drawing of boxes and arrows which show links between variables may imply causal relationships which in fact do not necessarily exist. Nevertheless, some organizational framework is required in order to arrange discussion of the complex topic of consumer decision-making.

The approach chosen in this book is to identify four clusters of factors – political, economic and technical; cultural and social; psychological; and marketing influences – which will have an effect on purchase behaviour. The remainder of the book is a more detailed discussion under these headings.

Questions

1 What is a model of consumer behaviour and why is it useful?
2 Describe in outline any consumer behaviour model of your choosing. Why do you consider the model you have chosen gives the best understanding of consumer behaviour?
3 What problems or deficiencies are there with all models of consumer behaviour?
4 What factors do you think are significant as an influence on the food you buy to prepare yourself?
5 How do the decisions about which butter to buy differ from decisions about which supermarket to visit?
6 Invent your own model to identify the factors which influence the purchase of a meal out.
7 Consider whether a model of consumer behaviour designed to describe food purchases by Spaniards is equally applicable in relation to food purchase by British people. Where might there be differences?

References

East, R. (1990) *Changing Consumer Behaviour*, Cassell, London
Engel, J. F., Blackwell, R. D. and Miniard, P. W. (1993) *Consumer Behaviour*, 7th edn, Dryden, Fort Worth, Texas
Foxall, G. (1980) *Consumer Behaviour*, Croom Helm, London
Shepherd, R. (1989) Factors influencing food preferences and choice. In *Handbook of the Psychophysiology of Human Eating* (ed. R. Shepherd), Wiley, Chichester

Part One

Political, Economic and Technical Influences

An important influence on what consumers buy and eat is what is made available in the market place. In most countries of Western Europe, but to a lesser extent in countries of Eastern Europe until recently controlled by centralized government, the supply of food is mainly the result of private sector enterprise, restricted only by climate, season and distribution systems. Except in periods of war, famine or major fluctuations in supply, governments tend not to interfere in the supply and distribution of food. However, the history and development of the Common Agricultural and Fisheries policies outlined in Chapter 3 show that within the European Union (EU) threshhold pricing and quota systems have had an effect on both the supply and price of foodstuffs within the EU. This has caused both overabundance and restrictions on supply and has forced up the price of goods coming into the EU from elsewhere in the world.

However, the primary aim of European governments has been to make sure that food made available to the customer is safe and that the customer has a certain amount of information on which to base purchase decisions. Hence there is an 'arms length' intervention by government between the manufacturer and consumer. This has shaped EU legislation on public health protection and more specific initiatives by individual governments in the areas of food description, labelling and preservation and more recent initiatives on nutritional advice to consumers. These are outlined in Chapter 2.

Clearly a major influence on purchase behaviour is the prevailing economy within which consumers live. Since the Second World War the economies of members of the EU have grown at approximately 3 per cent per annum. There has been a move away from centralized economies to those which are market-dominated. The poorer countries of the EU such as Greece and Portugal have caught up but not yet reached the standard of living in other parts of Europe. These changes are reflected in expenditure on food which has risen fast in the poorer countries of Europe but expenditure on food still represents a higher proportion of income than for consumers in richer countries. These differences are also reflected in typical diets of different nationalities with less spent on higher valued categories of food such as meat and cheese in poorer communities. A consumer's income, the economy in which they live, and the prices of different foodstuffs are an obvious influence on purchase behaviour. The interrelationships between these factors are briefly explained in Chapter 4.

A large proportion of the food we eat is cooked from the raw state but increasingly consumers seek convenience, which has resulted in increased sales of processed or frozen foods. This option would not have been available to the consumer without considerable technological innovation in terms of food production and storage.

In future new developments such as functional foods, new sources of protein or production of fat free foods may lead to further product innovation. It may be possible in future to shop from home or use more gadgets to help in food preparation. At the same time retailers, often in partnership with manufacturers, are becoming more sophisticated in assessing customer demand and setting up distribution systems to react to it.

Chapter 5 is concerned with a range of technological innovation in terms of food manufacture, the retail environment and methods of home storage and preparation.

Overall, Part One is therefore concerned with a variety of influences external to the consumer but which nevertheless can shape what products are made available.

2 *Food policy*

Introduction

Food policies are intended to inform decisions about who gets what food, when, how and with what effect. Public and often heated debate about food policy is nothing new. Last century modern food science began with independent chemists helping to expose how foods were being routinely adulterated by the addition of worthless or sometimes poisonous substances to increase their bulk. In the UK the Food Act drafted in 1875 has remained at the core of the law covering food ever since and basically says that food should not be adulterated. Recent legislation from the European Parliament has much the same purpose.

In most countries of the world governments do not directly intervene in what people eat, yet all to some extent have policies towards food. This is partially because a nation's diet is intimately related to issues and hence policies to do with health and education. Recent data on causes of death show considerable variation throughout Europe, some of which is postulated as linked to diet (Table 2.1). Scotland, for instance, has a mortality rate from cardiovascular disease which is more than three times that in France. Put at its basic level, an inadequately fed nation can result in economic and health problems of considerable concern to any government. On the other hand, it is rare except in times of war or famine for a government to perceive the supply and distribution of food as a public sector responsibility, in the way that is the case with respect to housing, defence or education. In the main most governments allow the private sector to supply food and only intervene in the sense of setting up supervisory legislation to make sure that what is supplied is not harmful. In addition, governments do play a part in controlling the supply and price of food as outlined in the chapter on the European Union.

Intervention by government has often been associated with war periods. The massive evidence of malnutrition in the 1930s combined with the siege economy of the Second World War led to the creation of a Ministry of Food in the UK which established rationing but also paradoxically improved the diet and health of the nation.

Following the war the monitoring and control of food law passed from central to local government in the UK. Central government replaced the Ministry of Food with a Ministry of Agriculture, Fisheries and Food which some argue has become more attuned to the needs and pressure of food manufacturers, farmers and agrochemical companies (Lang *et al.*, 1989). In recent years public concern has risen over how food is produced and preserved.

Table 2.1   *European mortality rates from selected causes*

Country	Cardio-vascular diseases	Cancers	Diseases of respiratory system	Injury and poison	All causes
Scotland	516	451	84	46	1223
N. Ireland	505	433	111	33	1194
Denmark	262	431	54	65	948
England and Wales	359	417	72	32	928
W. Germany	246	345	26	43	798
Belgium	236	312	28	68	784
Finland	291	282	31	43	745
Sweden	204	330	35	48	709
Netherlands	206	316	18	30	677
Greece	235	246	30	26	673
Norway	210	304	26	29	665
France	141	275	19	53	635

[a]Rates per 100 000 total population.
Source: Wright, 1988.

Governments have reacted with policies which have shaped legislation on how food is described, labelled and preserved. The general thrust has been to create more emphasis on food safety by the creation of a Food Safety Directorate in the UK and to give more information to the consumer (Figure 2.1). The primary aim of EU legislation has also been to ensure a high standard of public health protection. This chapter briefly outlines some recent development in these areas.

Governments have also responded to the rising evidence of a link between health and diet by taking a more active role in giving advice to consumers on nutrition so they are more informed about what foods to buy and consume. This is also considered in this chapter.

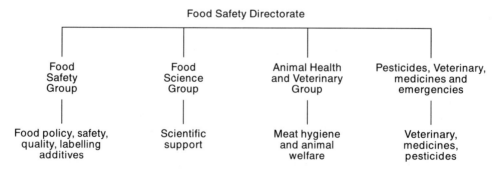

Figure 2.1   *Structure of the UK Food Safety Directorate. (After MacLean, 1991)*

Descriptions

When a person buys orange juice this is different from 'orange crush', 'orange squash', 'orange drink' or 'real orange'. Legislation is in place to define the ingredients contained in particular products so that the consumer can differentiate between what might otherwise all be referred to by the same name. EU directives insist that foodstuffs

---

Illustration 2.1 The politics of seaweed

Carrageenan (E407) is a chemically processed seaweed extract sometimes known as Irish Moss. It is used by the food industry as a gelling agent and to add bulk in a wide range of products including desserts, fillings, jellies, confectionery, meat and dairy products, soft and alcoholic drinks, preserves and sauces. It adds 'mouth feel' and fat to these processed foods and is popular because it can be called natural since it comes from seaweed.

Philippine Processed Eucheuma Seaweed (PES) differs from refined carrageenan and has not been adequately tested for safety but has the same properties in food manufacture. For years the Philippine government has been lobbying hard to have PES accepted as a food grade additive and not differentiated from carrageenan even though it does so. In 1990 the USA authorities approved PES. It was clear this was related to the desire to appease the Philippines after withdrawal of US armed forces from that country. Subsequently the US navy was granted a 3-year extension on its naval base in the Philippines. EC approval of PES has not yet been given and the EC's Scientific Committee for Food has requested further toxicity tests.

The Codex Alimentarius Commission which develops international food standards has currently referred back a decision on whether to classify carrageenan and PES as different. This had a lot to do with Philippine lobbyists who claimed 450 000 impoverished workers in the Philippines would lose employment if PES were not classified as carrageenan. It is not the first time Codex has been accused of responding more to commercial pressure than to food safety.

In 1991 Codex refused a recommendation for more stringent controls on the additive gum arabic allowing cheaper, inferior gums, not tested for safety, to be passed off as gum arabic. This followed an international campaign by gum arabic trading companies.

Codex is a joint UN World Health Organisation/Food and Agriculture Organisation body with membership of 130 governments worldwide. It is being given an increasingly important role as, under GATT agreements, it is the international body whose standards will be the basis of harmonizing food safety measures affecting human health.

The examples of seaweed extract and gum arabic have raised some questions about political manipulation in Codex decisions.

Based on N. Avery and M. Drake (1993) *Cracking the Codes: An Analysis of Who Sets World Food Standards*, National Food Alliance, London

are sold under the name by which they are customarily known in a particular member state or with sufficient description to inform the consumer of their nature. For example, with regard to alcoholic drinks there is a compulsion to indicate alcoholic strength on drinks with more than 1.2 per cent alcohol by volume.

Illustration 2.1 refers to the case of an additive used as a gelling agent where strong political pressure has been brought to bear to include substitutes which have similar nutritional properties but different origins because of the benefits to the manufacturer of two different additives being referred to as the same thing. It serves to illustrate the tremendous political pressures which can influence whether and in what form a food product is made available to the consumer.

Labelling

Nutrition labelling listing calories, protein, carbohydrates, fats, sugar, fibre and salt is voluntary except in the case of a health or nutrition claim, where an EU Food Labelling Directive came into force in October 1993 which required the most basic nutritional

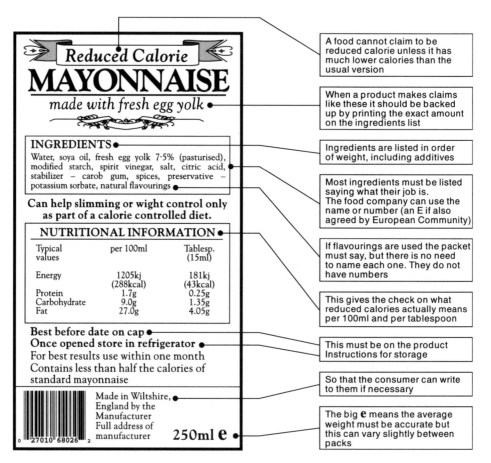

Figure 2.2   *What's on a label? (After* Food Sense, *PBO549, MAFF, London)*

labelling with a listing of these ingredients and related energy values. Medical claims such as 'cures cancer' or 'prevents heart disease' are banned for all foods or food supplements but health claims such as 'low fat' or 'high fibre' are permitted as long as the foodstuff meets certain specifications. Labelling of normal health foods may not use the words 'dietary' or 'dietetic'. Under present UK law only ingredients listed by weight must be declared on labels. The current information required on UK food labels is indicated in Figure 2.2.

One of the recent innovations in labelling is the use of 'E' numbers intended to tell consumers who want to know what additives have been used and also to let them know that the additive has been subject to exhaustive evaluation by authorities of the European Union. There are also strict conditions produce would have to meet before it could bear the 'organic farming EEC Control System' label.

As from May 1993 the Americans have introduced much stricter food labelling. Comprehensive, easy to read nutritional labels will be compulsory on every food. Sugar must be separated from total carbohydrates and saturated fats distinguished from less harmful varieties. Fibre, salt, cholesterol and protein are also listed. Crucially all the amounts relate to average serving sizes and show how much of the daily recommended intake would be provided by that serving. The words 'healthy' and 'fresh' will have to conform to strict definitions. Foods will be allowed to claim illness prevention in seven categories if they meet strict criteria laid down by US authorities. For instance, it will be possible for sellers of high fibre fruits and vegetables to claim they help reduce coronary heart disease and cancer. In effect American consumers will be given much more complete information on the food label to help them select a more healthy diet. Despite recent improvements the European consumer is unlikely to be in this position for some time because of the blocking power of food manufacturers (Erlichman, 1993), even though similar draft directives do exist (Young, 1992).

Food hygiene

The majority of food hygiene legislation is aimed at making sure the consumer does not get sick or killed by what they eat. After harvesting, all foods, whether animal or vegetable in origin, start to decay. The two main processes are the catalytic influence of enzymes leading to breakdown of food constituents, and the deterioration caused by micro-organisms which are present in all food. The traditional approach to microbiological deterioration is to change the condition of the food so that even if the microbes are present they are not able to grow and multiply. In essence, this is the basis of ancient techniques such as salting, drying, smoking, pickling and curing which are largely unchanged in modern food processing even though there are now improved techniques for achieving the same end.

The alternative is to leave the constitution of the food unchanged but to kill the micro-organisms, usually by heating and then to store the food in such a way that no more micro-organisms can get at the food, hence canned food and UHT milk. Avoidance of the chemical deterioration of food is more difficult but in essence is what is intended by canning, drying or freezing food. Drying works because micro-organisms cannot grow without water. Freeze drying has the same effect by removing water from the food stuff and turning it into the frozen state. Freezing results in water being turned into ice and so is not available to support microbial growth and the low temperature slows down all the processes of chemical deterioration.

More contentious is the process of food irradiation. In medicine irradiation has been used for a long time to sterilize medical instruments. With respect to food the process superficially offers a mechanism to extend the shelf life of foods and reduces the risk of food poisoning by killing pathogenic bacteria such as salmonella. However, against this the process damages vitamins and essential fatty acids and is suspected to cover up high bacterial counts found when food is 'going off'. This has given the process a poor reputation and generated antagonism from consumer groups and medical bodies. (Lang *et al.*, 1989).

Illustration 2.2 indicates the different stances towards irradiation taken by different member governments of the EU.

Illustration 2.2 Danish views on irradiation

A three-day conference was set up under the auspices of the Danish Technology Board to advise the Danish Parliament of what position it should take in relation to the draft European Commission directive on food irradiation. Expert witnesses were brought to Copenhagen from all over the world to be questioned by a fifteen-person lay panel chosen by a cross-section of the Danish population. The document went to the Parliament with considerable status.

In contrast the UK government set up an expert panel, many of them linked to food manufacturing and with interests in irradiation. The report favoured irradiation which after three years of wrangles was then implemented by the Ministry.

Based on T. Lang, S. Dibb, I. Cole-Hamilton and T. Lobstein (1989) 'This food business', *New Statesman and Society*, 10

Quality of diet

Recently government concern has shifted to try to persuade people of the benefits of a so-called healthy diet. This has with it at the policy level two difficult implications; the degree to which a government should wait for evidence to mount up before declaring that certain foods are better for consumers and others worse for them, and the limitations indirectly imposed on the consumer's freedom of choice.

A particular government can be caught in a bind. If there is mounting scientific evidence that particular foodstuffs are bad for the health of the nation, then the government has to be very sure of this evidence before making public declarations. The farming and food processing lobby is very strong and may tie the hands of government. The second issue of constraining freedom of choice is difficult. On the one hand a government is expected to legislate to make sure people do not get poisoned or killed by the food they eat. On the other hand, people do not like to be told what they may or may not eat.

However, in some countries inroads into consumer freedom have been made. The Norwegian government controls consumption of foodstuffs with high fat and sugar content by a pricing policy. By default the EU does the same thing. The effect of the UK

Table 2.2 *UK government recommended intakes of nutrients*

	Wartime	BMA, 1950	DHSS, 1969	DHSS, 1979
Calcium (mg)	800	80	500	500
Vitamin C (mg)	75	20	30	30
Vitamin D (mg)	10	0	2.5	0

Per day for adult males.

adopting the Common Agricultural Policy (CAP) has been to reduce butter and sugar consumption in the UK.

A variation of the same idea is for a government to recommend nutritional intakes rather than to legislate. As an example, Table 2.2 illustrates the UK government recommended intakes of various minerals and vitamins which have varied at different points in history.

More recently the UK government has taken the approach of trying to advise people on a healthy diet as a result of reports of two committees, NACNE and COMA (National Advisory Committee on Nutritional Education, and Committee on Medical Aspects of Food Policy) (see Table 2.3). From these reports and from other surveys there

Table 2.3 *Summary of recommendations of the NACNE report, 1983, and the COMA report, 1984*

The NACNE report:

Fat	Should provide no more than 30% total energy
Saturated fat	Should provide no more than 10% total energy
Polyunsaturated fat	No specific recommendations are made to increase consumption, but the polyunsaturated : saturated ratio is expected to increase if other recommendations are complied with
Sugar	Average sucrose intake should be reduced to 20 kg per head per year
Salt	Should fall by an average of 3 g per head per day
Dietary fibre	Should increase to an average of 30 g per head per day

The COMA report:

Fat	Should provide no more than 35% total energy.
Saturated fat	Should provide no more than 15% total energy
Polyunsaturated fat	No specific recommendation, but consumption is expected to increase if other recommendations are complied with
Sugar	Present intake should increase no further. The need to restrict intake on other health grounds is noted
Salt	Consideration should be given to ways of reducing intake

is mounting evidence that the type of diet that is least likely to cause disease is one that provides a high proportion of calories in whole grain cereals, vegetables and fruit; provides most of its annual protein as fish and poultry; limits the intake of fats, and if oils are used gives preference to vegetable oils; includes very few dairy products, eggs and little refined sugar (Lang *et al.*, 1989).

Linked to this, the UK government has set targets intended to reduce plasma cholesterol which is an important risk factor in coronary heart disease. Plasma cholesterol is higher in people who eat a high proportion of saturated fatty acids or who are overweight and obese. Hence one target in the Health of the Nation Strategy (HMSO, 1992) is to 'reduce the average percentage of food energy derived by the population from saturated fatty acids by at least 35% by 2005, i.e. from 17% in 1990 to no more than 11%'.

Additives

All food is a mix of chemicals. The main ones are fat, proteins and carbohydrates but there are lesser amounts of vitamins, minerals, colours, emulsifiers and antioxidants. The term additive is reserved for anything added by a food manufacturer even if it is the same as a chemical which occurs naturally.

Illustration 2.3 Is Brussels colourless?

Would you cry into your drink if you were deprived of a vivid red cocktail cherry?

In a recent debate about a new directive on food colourings British MEPs were given a spirited dislay of emotion about food colouring. Conservative MEPs brandished sticks of Blackpool rock claiming they would no longer be available if the directive went through. It was proposed two controversial red colours should be banned because of their possible toxic side-effects. These are E127 Erythrosine, used in Blackpool rock, liquorice all-sorts and glace cherries, and E128 Red 2G, used in British sausages and luncheon meats. These two colours are already banned in countries such as Denmark.

The European Parliament also supported restrictions on a number of other colours currently permitted. The substance that gives Red Leicester or Double Gloucester their colour would be reduced by 80 per cent and most basic foodstuffs such as meat, fish, poultry, fruit, vegetables and cereals would be colour-free. It would mean an end to coloured milk and yoghurt and yellow dyed haddock. Ultimately the decision about what colourings to allow hinged on whether a food had 'traditionally' been a particular colour. Kippers dipped in dye to make them brown have become 'traditional' even though the original colour came from smoking over wood chips. The Danes are likely to continue to colour their lumpfish roes and the people of Strasbourg to put canthaxanthin, a colour banned in fishfeed, into Strasbourg sausages.

Based on J. Blythman, 'We'll fight them on the beaches of Blackpool', *The Independent*, 17 April 1993

Additives are added to food for a variety of reasons. It may be necessary as part of the processing of food and is not intended to have any effect on the final taste or consistency of the food. It may be required for some specific technical reason, such as to make a food set or change consistency, e.g. pectin added to make a jam set because there is not enough in the natural fruit. It may be added to enhance the flavour or look of a product. In fact most additives, such as colourings, are for purely cosmetic reasons. Sausages are a case in point. People in the meat industry argue that without its characteristic pink colour consumers would not be able to tell a beef sausage from a pork one. Colour may trick a consumer into thinking a sausage has more meat than it does, and could conceivably give the product a longer shelf life because it looks fresher. However a good honest butcher would not be too worried if colourings were not available.

There are extensive regulations throughout the EU about what may or may not be added to food, the labelling of flavourings and additives and directives specifying how the word 'natural' can be used in labelling. Like any legislation to do with food, civil

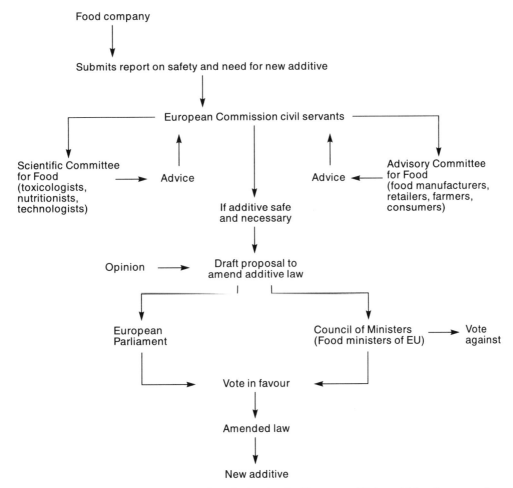

Figure 2.3 *The process of additive legislation in the European Union. (After Lang et al., 1989)*

Illustration 2.4 Food additives

Ministers on the EC Internal Market Council agreed in September 1993 to amend an EC law concerning food additives. The debate over food additives has raged since May 1992, particularly over the issue of protecting traditional foodstuffs.

The compromise agreed makes it possible to accept derogations from the general rules to protect national production of traditional foodstuffs.

Member states can continue to apply national regulations which will allow certain additives in foodstuffs which they consider as traditional, providing the situation already existed on 1 January 1992 and the foodstuffs concerned are produced in that country.

The list of foodstuffs they consider traditional had to be sent to the Commission before 1 July 1994. The Council will decide, using legislation to be adopted before 1 April 1996 whether or not a member state's claim for protection of traditional products is justified.

At the same time the Council also agreed on a directive concerning sweetness, which includes a list of twelve permitted sweeteners and the conditions covering their use. In general, sweeteners must not be used in foods for young children.

A common position on food colourings was also agreed. There will be a positive list of forty-three substances which are permitted colourings and a list of over 100 categories of foodstuffs or products in which those colours may be used. In meat products the directive requires that only natural colours are used. Colouring of white cheeses would be prohibited.

Based on *Supermarketing*, 'Food additives', 22 October 1993, p. 8

---

servants of the European Commission who receive proposals to place new additives on the approved list seek advice from expert committees. On the strength of what they are told they will advise the European Parliament and the Council of Ministers. Only if both agree will a change in legislation occur (Figure 2.3).

On balance, therefore, additives ought to be entirely safe. The problem is that some can cause allergic responses. It is also of course true that many naturally occurring foods cause allergies and some are very toxic. However, additives generate an emotional response because they are additional to what is provided by nature. Were it the case that naturally occurring foodstuffs were all tested for allergenic or toxic effects in the same way additives have then many might be ruled out. Potatoes, for instance, contain the toxin alkaloid solamine, rhubarb contains toxic oxalic acid, and many legumes contain cyanide. All are in small amounts and are filtered out by the body.

Illustrations 2.3 and 2.4 give examples of recent directives on additives approved by the European Parliament but also show the strong passions aroused by attempts by the EU to legislate against the traditional foodstuffs found in different member states.

Conclusion

The view taken in this chapter is that government intervention in the supply and distribution of food is rare amongst members of the EU. The intricacies of the European

Common Agricultural Policy do have an impact on the price and supply of some foodstuffs but this is considered in greater detail in Chapter 4.

Governments of the EU are, however, concerned about the standard of public health protection and this has translated into legislation about how food is described, labelled and preserved. European and national government directives restrict what can be included in foodstuffs and how these are described to consumers.

Consumers have a growing concern with what is in food. In particular there is a fear about the physiological effect of some food additives and methods of preserving food such as irradiation. Reports which link nutrition and health have also prompted the call for clearer and more explicit information on food labels.

So, although governments have comparatively little direct influence on the supply of food, they are concerned, in the interests of public health, with food quality. Efforts have been made to ensure that consumers can be certain a foodstuff contains what it says it does and that in particular it is not harmful. Consumers' concerns with the healthiness and nutritional value of what they eat has translated into legislation and directives from the EU to control additives and methods of preservation.

Questions

1 What is the current state of European legislation with respect to food additives?
2 Analyse the information on a jar of jam or a yoghurt pot.
   What information is on it and why?
3 What are E numbers and what do they communicate about a product?
4 What are NACNE and COMA?
   Is there any evidence that these reports have had any influence on people's diet?
5 Do you consider that governments should give nutritional advice to the population?
6 In what way do governments of the European Union influence through their policies the food available in your local supermarket?
7 What is Codex?
   Give an example, if possible from your own research, of how the lobbying power of a national government has had an influence on the additives which are endorsed for use in food manufacture.

References

COMA (1984) 'Diet and cardiovascular disease', *Report on Health and Social Subjects No. 28*, DHSS, London

Erlichman (1993) 'What's in a name?', *Guardian*, 27 March

HMSO (1992) *The Health of the Nation*, Dd839860910/92C100051–1111, HMSO, London

Lang, T., Dibb, S., Cole-Hamilton, I. and Lobstein, T. (1989) 'This food business', *New Statesman and Society*, special issue provided with Channel 4 to accompany *This Food Business*, first broadcast August 1989

MacLean, D. (1991) *Food Policy and the National Food Survey. Fifty Years of the National Food Survey 1940–1990* (ed. J. M. Slater), HMSO, London

NACNE (1983) *Proposals for nutritional guidelines for health and education in Britain,* Health Education Council, London

Wright, G. (1988) Consumer reaction to food and health. Unpublished PhD thesis, University of Bradford

Young, C. (1992) EC packaging and labelling law. *Croner's European Bulletin*, November, 3–14

3 *The European Union*

Introduction

The major proposition in Chapter 2 was that governments do not generally intervene to legislate on what food is made available to the consumer. However, looked at more closely there has been considerable intervention in Europe to manipulate supply and prices with the impact that has on what products are available to consumers and hence the degree of choice they experience. It is necessary briefly to explain European agricultural policy in order to understand what choice the consumer has and why they have to pay the prices they do.

Even though agriculture accounts for only 2.7 per cent of the gross domestic product (GDP) of the European Union and 7.7 per cent of its employment (Nugent, 1991) it has a disproportionate significance in the affairs of the Union. This is for a variety of reasons. The policy initiatives taken in the EU in relation to agriculture are amongst the most complete and wide-ranging of any in the history of the EU. The Common Agricultural Policy (CAP) is a major policy initiative within the EU intended to control the supply and prices of farm produce. Grown up around it are a large number of policies and decisions which affect farmers and consumers in every member state. A second reason why agriculture has attracted disproportionate attention is that it is a major beneficiary of EU funds and hence attracts attention both because of the large spend and because of the restrictive effect this has on spends on other initiatives.

Third, there is a greater institutional presence and bureaucracy surrounding agriculture compared with other sectors of the economy. DG6 (agriculture) is the second largest of the twenty-three Directorates General in the European Commission. There are more working parties, advisory groups and lobby groups in this sector than any other.

The existence of the CAP has periodically generated concern and ridicule. It is felt by critics to lead to the subsidization of wealthy farmers, high prices for consumers and periodic surpluses of farm goods. However, notwithstanding these assertions there is a general view from most member states that the CAP is one of the few examples of genuine Union policy and has worked in the sense of reducing the often wild fluctuations in commodity prices which can happen in world markets.

In this chapter the evolution, purpose and workings of the Common Agricultural and Fisheries policies are explored with a focus on the impact on food supply and prices of goods made available to the consumer.

Evolution of the Common Agricultural Policy

In modern times nearly every developed country has treated agriculture as a special case deserving of special policy measures. In the early days of the EU, agricultural workers made up a large proportion of the population, nearly 20 per cent. In addition they were poor, generating only 10 per cent of national income. A large community of poor workers therefore created a group which could not be ignored politically. At the same time farmers have always exerted a strong political lobby even though their numbers have now decreased to around only 8 per cent of the EU workforce.

Currently there are over 150 lobby groups established at a European level covering virtually every product group and every stage of the agricultural process. Their message is clear; to press for comprehensive market regimes to allow as high a production as possible at the highest prices possible.

The CAP evolved in the late 1950s and early 1960s mainly because the six member states at the time recognized that agriculture required special assistance. There are particular economic problems which afflict agriculture, unlike any other industry. There is a short-term problem of price instability. This is due, first, to the variability in output due to natural catastrophies such as weather and disease and, second, to the long time lag between planting or breeding and products coming to market.

As a simplified example, in bad weather the supply of potatoes will fall. This will lead to a price rise because it is not possible to draw on stocks as would be the case in manufacturing. The lowered supply forces up prices. When the next planting season comes around farmers plant more of the crop hoping to get the new higher price, but this results in over supply and hence a lowered price. These see-saws of supply and price therefore are common.

The long-term problem is that foodstuffs are relatively unaffected by alterations in both price and income. So as incomes rise there is not a corresponding increase in consumption because people can only eat so much. So farmers cannot go on increasing supply because all it will do is force down prices. The only way in which the agricultural sector can respond is to make farming more efficient, i.e. to increase output per worker rather than increase overall output.

These two sets of problems, the short-term one of price instability and the long-term one of increasing efficiency, were the driving forces behind the establishment of the CAP.

One way of reacting to the short-term problem would have been to give subsidies to individual farmers. This was what happened in the UK prior to EU membership but was far too complicated to administer in the rest of the EU, particularly France, with a very large number of very small farms. The second best solution therefore chosen was a blanket policy intended to support farm incomes through high prices, and maintaining those prices through tariffs to keep out potentially cheaper imports. Consumers therefore pay higher prices than would otherwise have been the case but governments do not have to set up complicated machinery for determining subsidies. The extra dimension which is required with this policy is a mechanism to intervene if, as has happened, farmers produce more than consumers can eat.

The long-term problem has proved much more difficult to solve. What it involves is persuading farmers to give up farming, to let some land lie fallow ('set aside' scheme) or to buy more efficient machinery.

The purpose and workings of the CAP

The purpose

The treaty of Rome which sets out the basis of the EU is in two parts. The whole of the second part is devoted to agriculture in which there are five main policy objectives:

1 To increase agricultural productivity.
2 To ensure a fair standard of living for agricultural workers.
3 To stabilize markets.
4 To guarantee regular supplies of farm products.
5 To ensure 'reasonable' prices to consumers.

How the CAP works

The mechanism chosen at the Stresa conference in 1958 to action these policies was a system which was to be common to all EU members rather than one left to individual governments. It meant there was to be one market for all community products, a barrier to imports from the rest of the world and a common fund to support the policy (FEOGA, Fond Européen d'Orientation et de Garantie Agricole). For something over 90 per cent of Community farm products, there was to be established a minimum price agreed on an annual basis below which the market price would not be allowed to fall.

In or about April of each year the Council of Ministers representing each EU member state meets to determine guaranteed prices for the approaching season. The first thing they do is fix the target price, that is the theoretical price to which they hope the market price will tend. From the target price is determined the guaranteed or intervention price. This is typically 12–20 per cent below the target price. If the market price is above this level then nothing need happen. However, if the market price falls below the guaranteed price then EU intervention agencies will be required to buy up any of the products offered to it at the intervention price using FEOGA funds.

If the target price is higher than the world price for equivalent foodstuffs, as is often the case, then the problem arises of preventing EU prices being forced down by low cost foreign imports. The solution is to subtract the transport costs from the target price. The result is the threshold price. If the threshold price is still low then a variable tax is applied by the EU. The effect is that after paying transport costs and the levy no importer could sell profitably at less than the target price.

Hence the price support system means that demand is first met from local supplies. Any unsatisfied demand is then met from supplies from other Union members. Imports can really only compete if Union demand outstrips supply so as to force the market price above the target price, but the latter tends to be fixed so as to make this very unlikely. The effect is to have a strong restrictive effect on the import of foodstuffs into the EU, even though these may be available at much lower prices on world markets.

Illustration 3.1 Going bananas

The men from Del Monte, Chiquita and Dole cannot understand where they went wrong. When the EU announced it would introduce a single market they thought it meant their bananas would compete on an equal basis with any other fruit. Already the three big multinationals control 70 per cent of the world trade in bananas and they looked forward to grabbing the rest. In fact the EU introduced new regulations covering the export of bananas to the EU from July 1993.

In the aftermath of the Second World War, Britons were craving the bananas that long years of food rationing had denied them. The government soon encouraged bananas to flood in from Jamaica and the Windward Islands providing the growers there with an alternative to sugar production.

With the advent of the single European market, and in particular the Common Agricultural Policy, it was clearly going to be difficult for the previous trade in bananas to continue. Britain wanted to continue to protect its Caribbean suppliers, France wanted to do the same for Martinique and Guadeloupe and Spain was not prepared to sacrifice its own producers in the Canaries. Germany, on the other hand, had enjoyed duty free access to unlimited quantities of cheap 'dollar' bananas from Latin America and became the biggest banana guzzler in the Community.

An alliance of France, Spain and the UK pushed through the new arrangements which will give some continued protection to their traditional suppliers while upsetting everyone else. Since July 1993 imports of dollar bananas are limited to two million tons and subject to 20 per cent duty. Imports above this tonnage are subject to 170 per cent duty.

Now the EU will still regulate the market, the producers are stuck with overproduction and falling prices. The government of Honduras believes the real victims of EU banana quotas will be the poor of Latin America.

Based on J. Pettifer, 'Going bananas', *The Guardian*, 23 March 1993

One example of the impact is given in Illustration 3.1, which shows the restriction on the import of cheap bananas to the EU. It also shows there are agreements whereby products, particularly from underdeveloped countries come into the EU without levies, although these are generally tropical products which do not compete with EU produce.

The effect of the CAP in practice

From its early days the net effect of the CAP has been to raise food prices. Prices in the UK prior to it joining the EU were 40 per cent less than those in the EU. Within the EU there was also variation, with prices in Germany some 20 per cent higher than those in France. It followed that for political reasons no member of the EU could agree to prices for any product which were less than had previously been the case. This meant prices were driven up. In its first year of operation of the CAP agricultural prices in the then six EC countries were two to three times higher than world prices. The result was fairly obvious, production in the EU increased and imports were blocked.

It also put pressure on the use of intervention funds. By 1986, FEOGA expenditure was ECU 23 bn, which was 70 per cent of the community budget. Of this huge total 36 per cent was devoted to export subsidies, that is a refund given to producers by the EU of the difference between the high EU price and the lower price they would otherwise obtain in world markets. About 19 per cent was spent on maintaining stocks of surpluses. In 1987 it was estimated the wheat held in store throughout the Community would make enough loaves to create a wall 75 feet high stretching from one end of the UK to the other.

The CAP is expensive to finance because effectively what it does is guarantee to farmers a high price, certainly one higher than what would be obtained in world markets. As a result many goods were produced in surplus. Between 1974 and 1987 the EU moved to a position of overproduction of butter, cereals, beef and sugar. Partly this was because of guaranteed high prices, but also because of better production techniques and technology. At one time, any amount of a product produced was guaranteed to be paid for at the intervention price agreed. However, after a run of surpluses which created butter mountains and wine lakes, restrictions were applied in the 1980s to limit supplies.

Success of the CAP

The EU carried out a general review of the success of the CAP in 1980. As far as consumers are concerned it can be said they have experienced relatively stable food markets. Food prices have never fallen since 1967 but they have generally risen more slowly than other prices. The emergence of over-supply has resulted in persistent surpluses and widescale dumping at knockdown prices which has upset the world market. Supplies have increased, although a system which results in 18 per cent over-supply is not exactly an unlimited success. Prices have generally been much higher to consumers than would have been the case in world markets. This money has mainly lined the pockets of big farmers.

In 1984 Community farmers were gaining ECU 52 bn as a result of the CAP. Consumers were losing ECU 48 bn through having to pay food prices well in excess of world prices, and losing ECU 20 bn in tax contributions to Community budgets.

In the late 1970s and early 1980s the defects in the CAP leading to over supply resulted in the introduction of levies or taxes in order to reduce supply. A second device was to introduce quotas. In 1988 it was agreed there would be a maximum quantity for every product on which guaranteed prices were paid. A third scheme, indicated in Illustration 3.2, was to 'set aside' land by taking it out of production of farm produce.

The CAP has certainly resulted in much modernization and rationalization of production although it has to be said there is still much overproduction prompted by high price guarantees. Markets have been stabilized in the sense that food supply in the EU is plentiful with only occasional shortages. There has also been greater price stability compared with the situation in world markets.

The CAP has led to self-sufficiency in all products which can be grown in the EU but the policy has led to the problem of over-supply which is expensive to deal with. The

Illustration 3.2 CAP in action

Some of the fields in Norfolk, as in other parts of Britain, are now 'set aside'.
Farms are paid to take about 15 per cent of their arable land out of production.
This policy developed because the effect of the CAP was to boost farm
productivity in the 1970s and 1980s. Between 1973 and 1988 agriculture
productivity rose by 2 per cent a year, while consumption rose by only 0.5 per
cent. In the rest of the world that brought consumer prices down; but in Europe
intervention prices stayed high – in large part due to the political clout of farmers.
By 1991 intervention payouts, which had also become a happy hunting ground
for fraudsters, were costing £9 bn a year.

The central aim of the recent reforms to the CAP was to slash intervention
stocks by reducing production. The guaranteed price of cereals is being cut by 29
per cent over three years and farms of more than 20 hectares are having to take
15 per cent of their land out of production.

Subsidies for livestock production will also be restricted. At the moment there
is a 'headage' payment for all suckler cows, breeding ewes and young male
animals. Under the new regime, only 90 cattle and 1750 sheep will qualify. The
number of livestock units per hectare of pasture is being reduced from 3.5 to 2 by
1995. (In the wonderful world of Brussels, a cow is one unit, a sheep 0.15 and a
10-month old calf 0.6 of a unit.)

It may not be enough if the Gatt agreement, due to be ratified at the end of 1993,
restricts the ability of the EC to export surplus.

In 1992 the British prime minister told farmers they should try to become more
like businesses and produce food for which there was growing demand; organic
produce and traditional English apples. Farmers say that demand is too limited
and what they have to respond to is the whims of Brussels and the Ministry of
Agriculture rather than to consumer demand.

They say they do respond to consumer demand as best they can. Lambs are
grown to a standard 18 kg size so their chops will fit into polystyrene trays in the
supermarket.

Based on D. Bowen, 'Growing pains', *Independent on Sunday,* 7 February 1993

---

exclusion of cheaper produce from outside the EU has definitely not benefited the
consumer and has incurred the wrath of other trading nations such as the USA, as
witnessed in the protracted round of the General Agreement on Trade and Tariffs
(GATT) negotiations which were completed in 1993.

The mechanism established as part of the CAP to subsidize agricultural exports from
the EU in the case of over-supply was altered in November 1992. The world trade
agreements negotiated as part of the GATT resulted in the Blair House accord under
which the EU was obliged to cut export subsidies on farm produce by 21 per cent over
six years. This was in addition to a 20 per cent reduction in internal farm price
supports.

After seven years of talking, the Uruguay round of the GATT talks were completed
just a few hours before the deadline in December 1993. French farmers were finally
bought off by a reallocation of EU funds in order to continue a subsidy of their

Illustration 3.3 The Blair House agreement

This is a deal between the USA and the EU, the world's two largest food trading blocs. It is designed to ensure that liberalization of trade will lead to minimum damage to the USA and EU internal markets. This is intended to leave both of them in a strong enough position to share domination of world trade. The agreement includes restrictions on how much farmers will be supported by their governments as follows:

- 21 per cent cuts by volume in EU subsidized food exports.
- Value of exports cut by 36 per cent.
- Internal supports cut by 20 per cent.
- Ten per cent of land used for growing oil seeds taken out of production and industrial oil seed use limited to 1 million tonnes.
- Compensation of EU farmers taking land out of production ('set aside' scheme).
- Curb on EU beef exports to Asia.
- US to cut wheat exports from 19.7 million to 14 million tonnes.
- A six-year peace clause which prevents the EU or USA taking unilateral action against each other.

There are various problems with this agreement. Although signed by the European Commission, there is very strong antagonism from member states, particularly France. France has lost 4 million farmers since the 1950s and in the EU as a whole farmers have declined from 17 million in 1970 to 9 million in 1990. Public opinion is mounting and is against further job losses. Second, there is no evidence the agreement will result in reduced food mountains, since the efficiency of agriculture is improving all the time.

Finally many in the EU believe the USA got the better end of this agreement and anti-American feeling is beginning to run high.

Based on 'The Blair House agreement', *Living Earth and Food*, November 1993, 9

---

agricultural products. Some of the debates and agreements leading up to the final signing are indicated in Illustrations 3.3 and 3.4. However, the paring down of agricultural and export subsidies will mean European consumers gain from having to provide less subsidy to farmers. The GATT organization was replaced in 1995 by the WTO, the World Trade Organization, to oversee trade agreements between the nations of the world.

Common Fisheries Policy (CFP)

As with general agriculture, an EU agreement also applies to fish stocks.

With unusual speed, the Commission agreed a common fisheries policy in 1970 just before the UK, Ireland and Denmark were to join the EU. This was fairly obviously to

---

Illustration 3.4 GATT negotiations

In the final stages of the GATT negotiations the EU negotiators tried to renegotiate the Blair House agreements just before the deadline was reached on 15 December 1993.

The Blair House agreement split the EU. In particular, it was flatly denounced by the French government and provoked rebellion amongst French farmers.

Convoys of French farmers on tractors sealed off city centres. They left tonnes of potatoes and other produce on town roads and blocked high speed TGV rail lines and main roads with burning straw and tyres. Sixty-eight per cent of people in a large sample taken for *Le Monde* believe France should veto the GATT talks.

The United States refused point blank to reopen negotiations which had previously been agreed to reduce export subsidies for EU products and reduce internal subsidies. In the end the French were bought off by changes in EU funding so that the GATT agreement could be signed just in time.

Based on *The Guardian*, 28 September 1993/*Daily Telegraph*, 22 September 1993

---

fix the rules before new members joined who in fact had 80 per cent of territorial waters in the Atlantic and North Sea.

The two main ingredients of the policy were an annual limit on the number of fish that could be caught – the Total Allowable Catch (TAC) – and, second, a price guarantee system similar to the CAP.

New members joining the EU were not too happy with the other principle embodied in the CFP, which was that all members could fish in the territorial waters of all other member states, up to 200 miles offshore.

When it first joined, the UK was given sole right for its fishermen to fish in the zone up to 6 miles off its coast. However, the main argument has been over how the annual TAC should be divided up amongst member states. In addition, as outlined in Illustration 3.5, national governments have introduced restrictions on the activities of their own fishing fleets both for reasons of general conservation and to meet EU quotas. Periodically this has led to fish wars and blockades. A recent example was the blockade of ports by Spanish fishermen complaining about other nations fishing for tuna in their territorial waters using superior technology.

Conclusion

The Common Agricultural Policy and the Common Fisheries Policy have been evolved by the EU to try to control the supply and price of foodstuffs. At the same time, the purpose has been to guarantee income to the agricultural community which traditionally has had a strong lobbying power within the EU. The policies have been successful in creating an effective supply of food but by the early 1980s they led to over-supply of many commodities because of the high price guaranteed to producers. The

---

Illustration 3.5 Fish wars

Owners of French and British fishing boats have fought a sporadic guerrilla war for several weeks, claiming the dramatic reduction in prices of fish has been caused by cheap imports from Russia and Iceland. The latest protests have brought to the surface frustrations which have simmered throughout the 10-year history of the EU's Common Fisheries Policy. Almost from the start British fishermen were aggrieved at a quota system which gave them 30 per cent of the catch from seas which produce the lion's share of the EU fish production. Despite the annual haggle over quotas the EU has failed to maintain fish stocks, with cod down to a quarter of 1970 levels and haddock down to one-sixth. British fishermen claim this is because EU quotas have not been effectively reinforced in other countries.

But the main haggle, which caused the blockade in Plymouth Sound, is over fishermen's fury at the Sea Fish (Conservation) Act which will allow the UK government to restrict the number of days they can go to sea. It is designed to reduce the scale of UK fishing operations in line with EU agreements. 'They wonder why the hell British fishermen should be tied up and stopped from going out making a living while their EU cousins are out there whooping it up', said a spokesman for the National Federation of Fisheries Organisations.

British boat owners want the size of the fishing fleet reduced by large scale decommissioning schemes like the ones in Denmark and Holland. Under these schemes the EU meets 70 per cent of the cost of compensating owners prepared to give up fishing.

Based on I. Katz, 'My boat will be worth £100,000 less at the stroke of a pen', *The Guardian*, 27 March 1993

---

consequence of import levies applied by the EU has been to restrict the supply of foodstuffs from other parts of the world.

The Americans, in particular, were very keen to break down the EU price support system and subsidization of exports. This was achieved via the Blair House agreement and despite concerns of some EU member states, particularly France, these changes were incorporated in the 1993 GATT agreements. In any case, the EU was taking action to reduce subsidies to farmers by setting production quotas and taking land out of production. The early years of the CAP may have helped to ensure stable supplies of food to consumers but at higher prices than applied in world markets. The net effect of the GATT agreements should be to offer consumers a wider range of products from both the EU and world markets at lower prices than might have been before these negotiations were concluded.

Questions

1 What led to the evolution of the CAP?
2 What particular economic problems affect agriculture, and hence food production, as opposed to any other sector of industry?

3   Explain how minimum prices for foodstuffs are fixed within the CAP on an annual basis.
4   Why have there been surpluses of foodstuffs within the EU and what changes have been made to correct for this?
5   What is the effect of the CAP on food prices in your local supermarket?
6   What was the Blair House accord and how did this eventually lead to the GATT agreement?
7   What is 'set aside' land?
8   In your view what differences would there be in the price and range of food commodities in European food retail outlets if (a) the CAP and (b) the 1993 GATT agreement did not exist?

Reference

Nugent, N. (1991) *The Government and Politics of the European Community*, Macmillan, London

4 *Economic influences*

Introduction

Of all the factors that can influence purchase behaviour, it is obvious that a person's income and the price of goods in the shops will be of major importance. The economic context will also be significant; whether for instance the person lives in an economy with stable prices and increasing prosperity or one with rampant inflation and declining standards. An economic analysis of consumers takes a rather different perspective from others in later chapters. The emphasis is on the similarities and patterns of aggregate behaviour of whole nations or groups of people rather than individuals. The assumption is that sets of individuals are entirely rational in their behaviour, intent on pursuing the one clear-cut objective of maximizing utility. Such hypothetical people gather information, digest it in rational, mechanistic manner and in almost robotic fashion make decisions about what or what not to buy. Even though there may be a myriad of other influences on consumption such as taste, mood, or age, an economic analysis tends to be restricted to the impact of a limited and particular set of factors. The main economic influences on food purchase are the general economic environment, but very specifically price and income. The essential focus of this chapter is therefore the way in which the quantities and types of food bought by consumers is a consequence of changes in income and prices. Brief mention is made of the economic climate in the EU member states.

Engel's Law

The relationship between income and food consumption was first investigated by Ernst Engel in the 1850s. Put simply, he showed that the poorer people are, the higher the proportion of their income they spend on food. People with more money to spend can buy more food although, of course, this does not necessarily follow because there is a limit on how much food any person can eat. Hence the relationship that the share of food in total household expenditure decreases with increasing income appears to hold in a variety of circumstances and has become known as Engel's Law (see Figure 4.1). The relationship between income and expenditure also holds across countries in the EU.

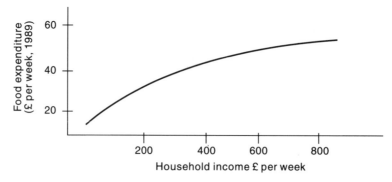

Figure 4.1   *Relation of UK food expenditure and household income. (After Chesher, 1991)*

Data in Table 4.1 show results from two different analyses of the relationship between income per capita and the percentage of that income spent on food. In richer countries of the EU, with higher per capita income, the percentage spent on food is between 11 and 18 per cent. In poorer countries, with a lower average income, such as Greece and Portugal, the percentage spent on food ranges from 22 to 42 per cent.

Put more simply and represented graphically, the data in Table 4.2 show that as income per capita rises (GDP), then the proportion of consumer expenditure on food declines roughly in a proportionate way (Figure 4.2)

Extrapolations of GDP produced by Blythe (1993) suggest that GDP will continue to grow, and that the differences in GDP between member states will continue to decrease

Table 4.1   *The relationship between income per capita and food expenditure in the European Union*

	GDP[a]	% food[b]	% food[a]
Belgium (B)	20.5	17.7	16.0
Denmark (DK)	25.0	16.4	14.8
France (F)	20.9	16.8	15.1
Germany (D)	24.5	12.7	17.3
Spain (E)	13.5	24.5	24.4
Greece (G)	6.5	33.3	41.8
Ireland (IRL)	12.2	24.5	22.3
Italy (I)	19.7	24.5	18.8
Luxembourg (L)	21.2	14.9	13.7
The Netherlands (NL)	18.9	14.8	15.1
Portugal (P)	5.6	33.4	34.6
United Kingdom (UK)	17.7	13.6	11.1

[a]*Euromonitor*, 1992.
[b]Cathro, 1992.

Table 4.2 *Gross Domestic Product of countries of the European Union (income per capita in £'000s)*

	1983	1988	1992[a]	2012[b]
Belgium	11.1	15.9	20.5	25.8
Denmark	11.9	17.2	25.0	27.7
France	12.1	17.2	20.9	27.2
Spain	7.8	11.8	13.5	19.8
Greece	6.1	8.6	6.5	13.7
Ireland	6.9	11.3	12.2	17.1
Italy	11.0	16.4	19.7	27.3
Luxembourg	12.8	19.1	21.2	31.8
The Netherlands	11.4	16.2	18.9	25.8
Portugal	5.9	8.6	5.6	13.9
Germany[c]	12.1	17.9	24.8	29.4
UK	11.1	16.9	17.7	28.8

[a]Economic Intelligence Unit, 1993.
[b]Extrapolation based on growth in period 1983–88.
[c]Based on W. Germany only.

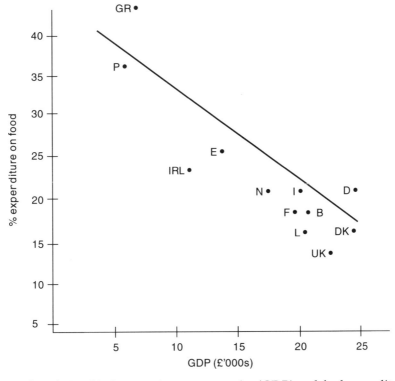

Figure 4.2 *The relationship between income per capita (GDP) and food expenditure. (For abbreviations see Table 4.1.) (Updated, after Tangermann, 1986)*

(see Table 4.2). This should also mean the proportion of income spent on food will continue to decline for all members of the EU.

Obviously the relationship between income and expenditure is not a perfect one because there are many other factors influencing consumption, such as taste, availability, national preferences and so on. However, at the level of analysis usually employed in economics the relationship broadly holds.

It is also the case that these global relationships hide more detailed relationships. Within a food commodity, such as meat, the prices of individual meat types such as chicken, beef and pork will vary. As incomes grow consumers switch to more luxurious and expensive items such as more expensive cuts of beef or in fact into meat and away from more basic foodstuffs such as bread and vegetables.

Similarly, another phenomenon occurs in that as incomes grow people switch away from raw foods to those where some extra process has occurred which will involve extra costs of preparation and packaging.

Both these factors combined mean that as incomes grow the expenditure on food may increase in absolute terms, but will fall as a proportion of income. The quantity of food consumed will increase less than expenditure, and may even fall. Hence some foodstuffs, the more luxurious or higher valued ones, are more susceptible to changes in income.

Consumers switch to higher valued, more expensive items as their incomes grow. The perception of what is a higher valued foodstuff will vary over time and from country to country. Fifty years ago, chicken was evaluated as much more of a luxury than it is nowadays and in the UK fresh vegetables may be more highly valued than in Italy. However, in all countries foods such as meat and cheese tend to fall into the category of higher valued commodities. At the other end of the scale are foodstuffs where consumption is negatively correlated with income. As people get more money they eat less of items such as potatoes and bread.

Quantity

The essence of the previous comparison is to analyse income against food expenditure based on monetary values. While the broad shape of Engel's Law holds, cross-country comparisons do not allow for the fact there are differences in price levels and exchange rates from one country to the next.

The OECD makes available data on food consumption based on calories per capita per day. This does at least get nearer to comparisons concerned with the quantity of food consumed although again there are difficulties because some foods, such as fruit, do not generate a lot of calories.

Overall total food consumption increased in the thirty-year period between the early 1960s and early 1990s (see Table 4.3). However, there was a particularly fast increase in calorie consumption in the poorer countries (as measured by GDP) such as Italy, Spain and Portugal. At the same time the variation in calorie consumption is decreasing, with less difference between countries in the early 1990s than the early 1960s.

Blandford (1986) shows that as income rises so too does food consumption measured as calorie intake. However this relationship does not hold forever since a plateau is reached. In poorer countries such as Portugal and Spain, consumption has increased in the past few decades in proportion to the rise in income. In richer countries such as

Table 4.3 *Food consumption in countries of the European Union (cal/day)*

	1960/61	1979/80	1990[a]
Belgium	3142	3282	3850
Denmark	3343	3455	3512
France	3124	3437	3273
Germany[b]	3150	3423	3800
Spain	2617	3073	3365
Greece	N/A	N/A	3688
Ireland	3482	3520	3692
Italy	2726	3435	3494
Luxembourg	3142	3282	N/A
The Netherlands	3270	3480	3258
Portugal	2640	3126	3134
UK	3214	3228	3257

Source: Blandford D. 1986.
[a]Economist Books, 1990.
[b]W. Germany only.

Denmark or the UK, no consistent, strong relationship exists between income level and quantity of food consumed. For all countries of the EU it is therefore likely that food consumption will not continue to rise as incomes improve. In fact, the reverse may be true as there is a switch away from high calorie diets.

At the same time as total consumption is plateauing, a detailed analysis of the consumption of different types of foodstuffs supports the earlier view that there is a switch away from inferior goods (such as grain-based products) to higher value goods (such as meat).

In 1960–1 Blandford (1986) showed the mean percentage of animal derived products such as meat, milk and eggs eaten in European countries was 35 per cent, ranging from 16 per cent in Spain to 46 per cent in Denmark. By 1979–80 the average percentage had risen to 40 per cent with a figure for Spain of 30 per cent and 50 per cent in Denmark.

The pattern is therefore as before. In the relatively poorer countries of the EU, such as Spain and Portugal, the increase in consumption of animal products has been particularly rapid. However, across the EU the rapid growth in consumption of animal products combined with a plateauing of growth in total food consumption has meant animal products have tended to replace vegetable products in the diet. At the same time, as with total consumption, the gap is closing between one country and another in the volume of animal products consumed per capita.

Blandford (1986) is therefore able to summarize the broad characteristics of the diet in EU countries based on OECD data for consumption, economic trends in GDP and extrapolations for the future.

Belgium, Luxembourg, Denmark, France, Germany and The Netherlands have a diet characterized by a low cereals component and high meat, eggs, oils and fats component. Ireland and the UK are broadly similar but with a higher share of calories derived from milk products and a smaller share from meat and eggs. Italy and Spain obtain a higher proportion of calories from cereals and lower proportions from milk and sugar. Portugal alone obtains a substantially large proportion of its calories from cereals and less from meat, eggs and milk.

In the mid 1950s 40 per cent of total calories were obtained from cereals in the EU area. By the 1970s this had been reduced by 10 per cent due to an increase in meat and eggs (5 per cent), oils and fats (3 per cent), sugar and milk (1 per cent), fruit and vegetables (1 per cent).

From this economic analysis Blandford also makes projections about the likely developments in diet in OECD countries, from which those related to the EU have been extracted. These are identified in Table 4.4.

Table 4.4 *Projected developments in diet of members of the European Union*

	Substitute animal for vegetable	Substitute vegetable for animal	Increase animal and vegetable
No change in per capita total food consumption	Denmark	Ireland UK	
Increase in per capita total food consumption	Belgium, Luxembourg, France, Italy, Holland		Germany Portugal Spain

Price

Besides income, the other major factor influencing food purchase is price. The simple relationship is obvious and applies to all commodities. It would be expected that as price rises, the quantity of a foodstuff bought goes down. Put more specifically, it would be expected if there were no other factors at play, then for every 1 per cent increase in price, there would be a corresponding 1 per cent decrease in consumption.

However, things are never this simple. If a person is shopping for meat, if the price of the beef they intended to buy has been put up they might do a number of things. They might still buy the beef even if it is more expensive; they might switch to a cheaper meat such as chicken; they might still buy beef but less than they were going to; or they might substitute something entirely different for meat such as eggs or vegetables. So, in other words, if the price of a foodstuff goes up, a whole variety of things can happen. However, in general the quantity purchased is negatively related to the price.

At the same time as the price of one foodstuff increases, resulting in a decrease in consumption, this may lead to increased consumption of substitutes. In the example of an increase in the price of beef, one result is higher consumption of chicken. However, sometimes a price rise of one foodstuff can also take down consumption of similar or related foodstuffs. An increase in the price of one type of meat might drive sufficient consumers away from the purchase of all meats that consumption is decreased across the board. Rather different is the case where a price rise of one commodity, such as pork, will also take down the consumption of a related or complementary product such as apple sauce.

So, overall, it is not possible to make any clear statements about the relation between price and consumption. When a price rises, generally consumption decreases, although not if there is no ready substitute. So there may be an increase or decrease in the consumption of other foodstuffs.

Elasticity

Engel's Law shows that if income rises then the quantity of food consumed does not increase at the same rate. Put into figures, another way of saying this is that a 10 per cent increase in income is accompanied by a 2 per cent increase in food consumption. This relationship or the ratio of the percentage change in quantity of food consumed to the percentage change in income is a measure of the income elasticity of demand.

Generally for foods this figure is less than one, showing that consumption increases at a lesser rate than rises in income. In the case of inferior goods, such as bread, the figure is negative, indicating that as income rises, consumption of bread decreases. This measure allows more precise definitions of the relationship between income and consumption.

Table 4.5 shows that in each of four EU countries consumption of grain, such as bread, decreases as income rises while, on the other hand, meat consumption is much more directly affected by a rise in income. Coffee consumption is particularly affected by rises in income, although these data are now 15 years old. Nowadays, such a one-to-one relationship might be weaker. On the other hand, consumption of milk is less

Table 4.5 *Income elasticity of demand for selected food items in four EU member states*

	France	UK	Italy	Spain
Wheat	−0.4	−0.2	−0.2	−0.3
Meat	0.4	0.2	0.7	0.7
Eggs	0.2	0.0	0.5	0.6
Milk	0.1	−0.1	0.3	0.5
Coffee	0.5	0.8	1.0	1.0

Source: From Tangermann, 1986.

susceptible to increased income and, in the UK, actually decreased with increased income.

A similar relationship also holds for price. Hence, if a price increase of 10 per cent results in a decline in consumption of 2 per cent, we would say the price elasticity of demand is −0.2.

As consumption does not follow income changes in a direct way, so too consumption is not affected by a price change in a totally proportionate way. When the price of a foodstuff is raised due to crop failure or cartels operating, then consumption does not decrease at the same rate. However, as a generalization, it is true it will tend to decrease, so price elasticities for demand fall between 0 and −1.

Economic environment in the EU

Consumer incomes and hence spending patterns have been affected by the economic climate in Europe. Since the Second World War the economies of most West European countries have grown. Most national governments have been in favour of more market and less state influenced economies with the exception of Spain and Portugal, which until recently had dictatorships and very centralized economies. For most members of the EU, income and productivity increased rapidly in the past decade with an average real growth in GDP of 5 per cent per annum and growth rates of the economy averaging 2.9 per cent per annum (Somers, 1991).

The highest growth rates in the past 30 years (1960–90) have been in Spain, mainly due to a catching up of the economy following the end of the Franco regime. Spain averaged 4.6 per cent per annum growth in the past 30 years but the per capita income is still only three-quarters of others in the EU.

Growth in Italy was 3.9 per cent over the same 30 years but with a big differential between the north and the much poorer south of the country.

France showed a strong growth pattern in the 1980s to achieve an average 3.7 per cent per annum growth. This was ahead of growth in Germany which averaged only 3.1 per cent in the period 1960–90, slowed down recently by the reunification between East and West Germany. The lowest growth rate in this period was in the UK (2.4 per cent), although this has picked up recently.

During the period between 1980 and 1990 inflation varied considerably throughout Europe. Taking 1985 as a base year, Italy and Spain had their lowest consumer prices at the beginning of the decade but amongst the highest by the end of the decade. On the other hand, prices were high in West Germany at the beginning of the decade, but in comparison with other countries inflation remained low, so by the end of the decade the increase had not been great (Table 4.6).

A similar trend is revealed from data on consumer expenditure where Italy and Spain demonstrate growth of over 300 per cent in the period between 1977 and 1990. However, this is a comparatively small rise compared with growth in expenditure in the same period of over 1000 per cent in Greece and Portugal (Table 4.7).

West Germany has the highest food expenditure of any of the EU members, with Greece at the other end of the scale (Table 4.8). The data in that table also demonstrate that food expenditure takes up a higher proportion of total household expenditure in poorer countries, as already indicated in Figure 4.2.

Table 4.6 *UK and European trends in consumer prices (index 1985 = 100)*

	1980	1982	1985	1988	1990
France	63	80	100	109	116
W. Germany	83	93	100	101	107
Italy	52	72	100	117	132
Spain	56	74	100	120	137
UK	71	86	100	113	133

Source: IMF/ILO/Statistical offices; *Euromonitor,* 1992.

Table 4.7 *European growth in total consumer expenditure, 1977–1990 (per cent rise)*

France	153
Germany[a]	61
Greece	1285
Italy	325
Portugal	1031
Spain	311
UK	139

Source: National Accounts; *Euromonitor,* 1992.
[a]W. Germany only.

Table 4.8 *UK and European food expenditure and percentage of total expenditure, 1989*

	Food expend. (US$) (m)	Food as % of expend.	Population (m)	Per capita food expend. (US$)
France	106 947	15.1	56.4	1896
W. Germany	138 371	17.3	63.1	2193
Italy	124 989	18.8	57.7	2166
Spain	77 913	24.4	39.0	1998
UK	68 462	11.1	57.4	1192
Greece	19 198	41.8	10.1	1900

Source: Eurostat Basic Statistics of the Community, 1990.

Conclusion

Economic variables impact on consumer purchase behaviour. One of the few laws in consumer behaviour, first elaborated by Engel, shows that the poorer people are the higher the proportion of their income which is spent on food. The same is true of whole nations. Analysis of the GDP, the average income per capita of each member state, shows that as income increases the percentage of income spent on food decreases. This trend is likely to develop further as GDP rises across the EU, but the gap between nations will close as the poorer nations catch up with richer ones.

Within this broad relationship more subtle variations occur. As peoples' incomes grow they switch to the purchase of more luxurious food items, such as meat and cheese, and away from staple items such as bread and potatoes. A similar relationship holds with respect to the quantity of food consumed, in that calorie intake in the EU increased in the period between 1960 and 1980, again with a more rapid rise in what were poorer countries such as Italy, Spain and Portugal.

The relationship between price and purchase is not a simple one, although generally as price rises the quantity of a foodstuff purchased decreases. However, purchase of foodstuffs generally increases at a lesser rate than rises in income which, put another way, is an income elasticity of demand of less than one. However, this varies with the product; as before, consumption of bread decreases as income rises resulting in a negative income elasticity of demand while for meat there is a positive figure across the EU which is more pronounced in poorer countries.

General economic data support the trends already identified. Since its establishment, members of the EU have experienced economic growth. The most rapid has been in countries which joined later but started membership with weak economies, often after periods of dictatorship (Spain and Portugal). This is reflected in very rapid increases in consumer expenditure of over 1000 per cent in countries such as Portugal and Greece in the thirteen-year period before 1990.

The implications for consumer expenditure revealed by this analysis are to suggest continued decline in the proportion of income spent on food as incomes continue to rise. The tendency to switch to higher calorie intakes and more luxurious items may be offset by increasing concerns with health and diet in countries such as the UK and Denmark. On the other hand, this is unlikely to have much impact in countries such as Spain, Greece or Portugal which are still in the 'catching up' phase of economic growth.

Questions

1 What is Engel's Law?
   What evidence is there from European data to support the concept?
2 Using the data produced by Blythe (1993), graph the past and predicted changes in GDP of European countries and suggest the effects on food consumption patterns.
3 Give examples of how consumption of one food product is affected by changes in consumption of another.

4 Explain why the relationship between price and consumption is not always one to one.
5 Choose one member of the EU and find information on the change in the economy of that country in the past thirty years. Explain how these changes may have affected patterns of food consumption.

References

Blandford, D. (1986) 'The food people eat' In *The Food Consumer* (eds C. Ritson, L. Gofton and J. McKenzie, Wiley, New York

Blythe, R. (1993) Twenty years on in Europe after 2012. *Journal of Marketing Management*, **91**, 79

Cathro, J. (1992) Trends in the consumer perception of foods, *Food Technology International Europe – Review for the European Food and Drink Processing Industry*, 29–32

Chesher, A. (1991) 'Household composition and household food purchases' In *National Food Survey; the Last 50 Years*. (ed. J. M. Slater), HMSO, London

Economist Books (1990) *Vital World Statistics*, Economist Books, London

Economist Intelligence Unit (1994) European Marketing Book, NTC publications, Henley-on-Thames

Euromonitor (1992) *Marketing Data and Statistics*, 27th edn, Euromonitor, London.

Eurostat Basic Statistics of the Community (1990) 27th edn, Brussels

Somers, F. (ed.) (1991) *European Economics*, Pelican, London

Tangermann, S. (1986) 'Economic factors influencing food choice' In *The Food Consumer* (eds C. Ritson, L. Gofton and J. McKenzie), Wiley, New York

5 *Technological influences*

Introduction

At each stage in the production, distribution, retailing and home storage of food, technology has had an impact on the ultimate choice of food consumed.   This chapter includes a consideration of how technological innovations have aided the development of new food products. Part of what influences consumer choice is how long and in what way the food product, whether originally fresh or processed, can be stored, be it in the warehouse, retail outlet or at home. Preservation techniques and the technical developments behind the growth of convenience products are explained. This is followed by speculation about future developments in food product design.

Besides food manufacture there has been rapid technological progress in systems of distribution. Technology is also becoming increasingly important within the food store both to record consumer purchases and hence to influence stocking and reordering, but also to shape the consumer's behaviour by tracking it and rewarding certain purchase patterns.

The products consumers eat and drink are also a consequence of technology in the home, to both store and prepare food. This is briefly considered together with possible future developments in shopping behaviour.

Overall, therefore, the aim of the chapter is to consider the ramifications of technological developments as they affect consumer choice in the purchase and preparation of food.

Food preservation

The purpose of food preservation is to make foods available all year round and to build up supplies so that the manufacturer can react to fluctuations in demand. After harvesting of fruit and vegetable crops, or killing of animals, deterioration occurs quite quickly due either to the natural chemical processes, under the influence of enzymes, or because of microbiological decay. The processes are explained in greater depth by Bralsford (1986). Chemical deterioration is difficult to stop completely but it can be slowed down by removing oxygen or water, or chilling, freezing or blanching the food. Microbiological deterioration is most simply stopped by removing water from the food so the micro-organisms cannot grow. Sun-dried meat, fish and fruit are examples of this. Simple dehydration suffers from the fact the product is then usually inedible, meaning rehydration is necessary. In turn this can be a long process which never achieves the taste and texture of the original product.

A variation of this is used in the case of processed peas which, once picked, are first dried, then rehydrated and sterilized in cans. There is a small but relatively stable market for such products. A later development, first used in the 1960s, is freeze-drying, effectively the drying out of water from the product once the water has been frozen in a vacuum chamber. The process is now mainly used for products which are in granular form such as coffee, or of very high value such as prawns.

An alternative to the removal of water from a product is to 'dilute' it by dissolving other materials in it. At a certain point a solution with, for instance, sugar or salt in it will stop the growth of all the most serious food poisoning bacteria and moulds. The same effect can also be achieved by making the foodstuff more acid since again micro-organisms will not grow in a low pH.

Food preservation therefore depends first on reduction of the microbe level by pasteurization followed by a combination of reduced water level, 'diluting' the water, increased acidity and finally the use of preservatives. Chilling slows down the microbial decay even further and is used for products such as fromage frais, desserts and yoghurts.

However, without doubt the most common and successful method of food preservation is deep-freezing. Again the principle is to reduce the water available to micro-organisms by freezing it. Very few foodstuffs cannot be frozen and there is also the advantage that when defrosted products are generally not affected in terms of taste or texture when compared with the original.

The impact of technological innovations such as freezing, chilling and processing of chicken meat is described in Illustration 5.1.

An alternative process of preservation is to exclude the micro-organisms entirely by killing them, usually by heat. Heating in a sealed container only became possible with the invention of the tin can. Two similar approaches to food preservation are the sterilized plastic pouch and semi-rigid, plastic lined aluminium containers pressed to a variety of shapes to preserve products such as meat pies. To a great extent canned products have been superseded by frozen ones, particularly in the UK. However, in France consumption of canned foods at 3.1 million tonnes was the highest in the EU in 1991 and has risen by 8 per cent per annum since 1986. Similarly consumption in Germany has risen by 3.7 per cent per year. Sales of canned fruit and vegetables are particularly high, boosted by the growth of discount food chains such as Aldi.

Consumption in the UK is about half that in France, although with a rise in sales of canned fish of 5 per cent since 1986. Italy and Spain represent lower levels of sales, most probably because of the availability of fresh fruit and vegetables (Eurofood, 1992).

Convenience foods

Consumers seek food products with a short preparation time and also do not necessarily eat a complete meal at one time but graze on snacks. The development of many snack foods and breakfast cereals has depended on technological innovations in extrusion, a process originally developed by the plastics industry. The idea is relatively simple; material is fed into one end of a barrel, mixed, compressed, and by the turn of

Illustration 5.1 Technology and chicken

Chicken used to be an expensive and luxury meat which in the period immediately after the Second World War was eaten only at Christmas. In 1956 Sainsbury in the UK combined with Poultry Packers to make frozen broilers available in their self-service stores.

At the time there was limited storage at processing plants. Refrigerated transport was non-existent so the frozen birds were transported in insulated containers using dry ice. At the retail end the birds were thawed and not sold as frozen because there was inadequate cold storage in the stores.

In 1960 Buxted set up a state of the art processing plant capable of handling 300 000 birds a week sent from 150 large-scale chicken farmers. The methods of plucking, chilling the birds to prevent cross contamination, freezing at −40°F, and packing the birds in wrappings which could withstand deep-freezing and carry an advertising message were all major technological innovations.

As a consequence of these technological improvements the price of chicken fell, but it was still mainly bought for the weekend and roasted or boiled.

The growth of supermarkets with larger freezer display capacity and the home ownership of freezers both stimulated sales of frozen chicken. Portioning stimulated sales for mid-week consumption. The development of chilled chicken presented a greater technological problem than frozen. Developments in this area were pioneered by Marks & Spencer who believed the fresh, chilled birds were of better quality than the frozen. The birds were air chilled, distributed to the stores in refrigerated vehicles and immediately transferred to chilled display cabinets.

Chilled chicken created a demand because the product was similar in quality to fresh and more convenient than frozen chicken because thawing was not necessary before cooking.

Innovations in processed chicken began to appear from around 1960 onwards when breaded chicken portions were introduced. Birds Eye launched tray meals but the quality was not good. Sainsbury tried to introduce cooked chicken around this date but it was unsuccessful as was Chicken Kiev, first produced by Marks & Spencer in 1967. Both products were re-introduced later on. Perhaps the demand for cooked chicken had to wait until chains such as Kentucky Fried Chicken had become established.

Until the early 1970s the retail market for processed chicken was dominated by Birds Eye and Findus. The products included frozen breaded chicken, frozen southern fried chicken, and tandoori chicken. The prepared meat market began to take off in the early 1980s with the increase in ownership of microwaves and the introduction by Marks & Spencer of chilled recipe meals.

The development of the chicken meat market therefore demonstrates the effect on consumer demand of technological innovations and the influence of major retailers in affecting what producers provide.

Technological innovations in chicken meat processing

Year	Product
1956	Frozen chicken
1959	Chilled chicken
1960	Frozen chicken portions in see-through wrap
1964	Chilled chicken portions
1968	Gourmet frozen meals for caterers
1970	Cold cooked chicken
1980	Chilled recipe meals

Percentage household ownership of domestic appliances

	Refrigerator	Fridge/freezer	Freezer	Microwave
1960	18	–	–	–
1965	39	–	–	–
1970	58	1	2	–
1975	75	6	13	–
1980	72	19	29	–
1985	61	36	36	20
1990*	48	53	34	48

Food Pocket Book, NTC publications, 1992

Based on Senker (1988)

a screw is pushed to the other end of the barrel where it comes out through a shaping die. Under high temperature and pressure raw materials such as maize can be converted to products such as breakfast cereals or savoury snacks.

Hot snacks such as pot-noodles or soups are reconstituted by adding hot water to dehydrated ingredients. Instant beverages, such as coffee, are obtained by drying coffee liquor either by freeze-drying or spray-drying. In the latter case the liquid is first concentrated by partial evaporation of the water then sprayed into the top of a large tower where it meets a current of hot air. It quickly loses moisture and the dried droplets fall as powder to the base of the tower. The fine powder is then clumped into larger, loosely adhering aggregates which can readily disperse when water is added.

Instant tea has been technically a more difficult problem to solve, although products have recently reached the market. They have not yet, however, replaced the alternative solution of packaging dried leaves in tea bags.

Foods of the future

There is likely to be increased pressure throughout the 1990s to produce food products which are virtually fat-free. At present manufacturers are looking for an acceptable reduced fat cheese. A new milk introduced in 1993 is 98 per cent fat free and the fat it does have is monosaturated which is believed to have a beneficial effect on cholesterol levels.

The same trend is likely to continue with meat products, where the attempt will be to 'hide' the fat by marbling it into the meat rather than leaving a trim around the product. In Holland research has shown this is more effective than removing all the fat which affects the taste adversely.

In the beverage market a recent technological innovation has been the ability to produce an authentic Italian style froth leading to mass produced cappuccinos and espressos in instant form. In the soft drinks market the search is to find healthy sugar-free products (Illustration 5.2).

Illustration 5.2 Clash of the cans

PepsiMax is a new sugar-free cola designed to taste like the original product.

Market research amongst consumers that had tried but rejected diet colas revealed two problems. One was the distinctive, slightly bitter, aftertaste left by artificial sweeteners. The other was image. Many consumers thought diet products were effeminate or associated them with disorders such as diabetes or obesity. After a lot of work with consumer panels the manufacturers were able to pin down more exactly what consumers meant by 'mouthfeel' or 'aftertaste'.

The chemists from Pepsi used a new blend of basic ingredients, adding ASK, a new sweetener, to the standard aspartame to devise a sugar-free formula with a muted aftertaste which got a good response in consumer trials.

Based on G. de Jonquieres 'Clash of the cans', *Financial Times*, 4 March 1993

Tea manufacturers have joined forces to fund a major world-wide study lasting three years which is expected to prompt claims about the role of tea in the fight against heart disease. This together with some increased consumer acceptance of instant tea may revive the long-term decline in tea sales.

In snacks a recent technological innovation which has just been achieved is printing a cartoon character onto a crisp in edible caramel. Novelties like this are likely to increase still further the growing children's snacks sector, expanding at 18 per cent per year (Hyam, 1993).

In the alcoholic drinks sector one of the major technological innovations in recent years has been in the 'widget', an in-can draught system which enables canned beers to recreate the 'head' of draught beer. This is likely to spread to become the norm throughout the industry (Harrison, K., 1993a).

A possible long-term change in the type of foods which are available is in so-called functional foods, which are suggested to have a physiological or medicinal benefit. At present Western governments impose restrictions on claims that foods have medicinal properties. For now the same restrictions apply in Japan, even though more products are appearing which may breach this constraint. A yoghurt called Yakult is drunk en route to work by the Japanese to prevent ulcers 'enabling sustained levels of work pressure to beat the world'. However, even in the UK it is predicted by analysts that sales of bio-yoghurts will increase dramatically and there is evidence they improve digestive functioning. (Harrison, K., 1993b). In the US recent legislation has allowed health claims to be made for some foods; 'this fruit and fibre cereal may help to reduce cancer'. This may increase pressure to allow such developments in Europe. It may also mean major drugs companies move into the functional foods business.

Several attempts have been made to find new sources of protein. The best known is soya which can be converted by an extrusion process into textured vegetable protein which is intended to mimic meat. However, as a meat substitute it has not had much acceptance from consumers and is increasingly used as a minor ingredient in recipes where it has a specific technical function such as imparting texture.

Biotechnological techniques are concerned with growing micro-organisms on a substrate derived either from oil or from waste food products. Protein can be extracted from the micro-organisms, then converted to a meat substitute. At present these processes are very expensive and given the surpluses of conventional foodstuffs in most of the developed world it seems unlikely these substitutes will replace existing foods.

Distribution and choice

As consumers have become more demanding and want more choice, retailers have responded by building larger and larger supermarkets. These not only offer greater choice but better layout, service, access and economies of scale on price.

The growth in power of retailers has meant they have come increasingly to dominate the relationship with manufacturers and suppliers. As they have built larger supermarkets, retailers have had to maximize their selling space and cut down storage space. They have set up their own warehouses and told suppliers to deliver to them instead of direct to the stores.

In the late 1970s and early 1980s many of these small warehouses were consolidated into a set of much larger warehouses. Technology advanced rapidly so that computer systems linked to scanning devices in the store gave retailers much more information on customer purchases and hence more control over the supply chain.

The centralization of distribution has now reached over 90 per cent with about 50 per cent of this contracted out by the retailers to others. The net effect is distribution costs have been cut from 12.3 per cent of total costs in 1983 to 4.7 per cent in 1992. This makes distribution costs in the UK much cheaper than in the rest of Europe, and is one reason why retailers in the UK achieve higher margins than on the continent. It has resulted in higher investment in new store openings which in turn has provided greater quality and choice to consumers (see Illustration 5.3).

The benefit of electronic point of sale (EPOS) information is that data on customer purchase behaviour can be transmitted direct to the manufacturer to affect their production schedules. Asda are already doing this in the UK (Buckley, 1993). As far as the consumer is concerned, it means food reaches the retail outlet directly as a result of

---

Illustration 5.3   Distribution systems

Sainsbury processes products from more than 1000 suppliers through twenty depot locations. Some 1000 lorries distribute 11 million cases a week to 335 stores. Within this network are 17 000 commodities and more than 65 000 individual stocking points. Over 80 per cent of the volume is delivered within 24 hours of it being ordered. The supply chain operates 24 hours a day for 364 days of the year.

Argyll have contracted out their distribution of temperature sensitive food to Wincanton Distribution.

The agreement covers 300–400 chilled foods such as butter, cheese, meat and dairy food. A large warehouse at Solihull near Birmingham is the main centre with three out-bases in the south-west, south-east and north-west of England with sixteen lorries and 100 people. The distributors have to get food to 300 stores throughout the UK every day.

Based on P. Hastings 'Retail chain management', *Financial Times*, 15 June 1993

---

changing demand with less delay. Costs of distribution and storage are also kept to a minimum.

Tracking the customer

Information technology is increasingly being used to record consumer purchases. Electronic point of sale (EPOS) devices mean it is possible for the checkout assistant to pick up a record of the product sale from the bar code. Not only does this trigger information which is printed on the bill given to the customer but it also provides a record of customer purchase behaviour and is linked to the stocking record as indicated in the previous section.

Credit card transactions at the checkout can also provide the retailer with information to track purchases and relate them to particular consumer types. It can provide information to target direct mail to the cardholder's home address. Linked with this are loyalty schemes intended to encourage repeat use of the same store by offering airmiles (Sainsbury), computers in schools (Tesco) or discounts (Tesco). In a recent survey published in *Supermarketing* (1993) by far the most attractive promotion was the offer of vouchers to give a discount on future shopping bills, despite the supposed popularity of holidays and air travel incentives. A variation of this technique is for purchases recorded at the checkout to prompt the offer of money off vouchers which therefore encourage repeat purchase of the same item on a future occasion.

Further technological innovations coming on stream in retailing are devices which record customer movements. The idea is basically very simple; to know at any moment how many people are in a shop, where they are, and where they are going. Datatec, launched in 1992, uses infra-red beams, projected down from a ceiling mounted bar which bounce back when they encounter a person-sized object. This allows the height of the object to be calculated and eliminates from its count anyone or anything under 4 ft tall – such as children, prams and trolleys.

ShopperTrak's software can calculate the number of 'buying units' entering a store, such as a family rather than individuals, and combine its data with the EPOS information to calculate the ratio between people in the store and those who actually buy something. The information can also be used to detect the impact of staffing levels on sales. Used in this way decisions could be made on what number of checkout staff to have, which in turn will affect customer satisfaction and the likelihood of repeat purchase.

The effect of changes in store layout or promotional activity can be measured. For instance, the impact of window advertising could be checked in terms of whether it simply brought in more people or did in turn lead to greater sales (Bradshaw, 1993).

Shopping in future

A US study has shown that 64 per cent of people dislike going to the supermarket for their basic shopping which is as many as hate going to the dentist (Fisher, 1993). Already in the USA shopping by television has become a reality for larger or expensive items. The growth of video links to the home and multimedia may make the scenario in Illustration 5.4 a reality in future.

Shopping for replenishment rather than enjoyment and social reasons may be done from an armchair, browsing through items on a screen and ordering by scanner. Shopping trolleys will have video information about goods on offer and where they can be found. Already in France Telecom's Minitel has been a success (Harrison, B., 1993). The Minitel approach is to attach a small screen to a phone for database display of retail offerings including groceries.

Illustration 5.4 Cooking tonight?

On a summer evening in a few years' time you want to put on an outdoor barbecue. You call up the American barbecue page on your computer screen and the system linking your home with the local supermarket asks whether the meal will be for two, or a party. You give your answer. It asks what sort of appetisers, main courses, and desserts you want and even how much you want to do yourself with a food processor. All the screen options are illustrated, some with video. You tap in your preferences and recipes with ingredients, brand names and prices appear which can be called up and printed.

You order the shopping electronically with a bar code scanning device and direct from the screen. The goods are delivered through a secure entry point to your home or can be picked up from a suitable collection point nearby.

Technology at home

The choice of foods bought by consumers is affected by the opportunity for storage and different ways of preparing food in the home. An obvious example of this is frozen food, where sales in the UK have been increasing by 3–4 per cent per annum in the past decade. Equipment to freeze food is available in most homes throughout Europe, with a lower penetration in poorer countries such as Spain and Ireland (Table 5.1).

Table 5.1   *European households owning deep-freezing and microwave cooking equipment, 1990*

	Any deep-freezing equipment	Microwave (%)
Belgium	86	21
Denmark	92	14
France	77	25
W. Germany	73	36
Ireland	58	20
Italy	89	6
The Netherlands	82	19
Spain	55	9
UK	81	48

Source: Food Pocket Book, 1992.

A related piece of equipment, now in half the households in the UK, but much less common elsewhere in Europe (Table 5.1), is the microwave oven. In the UK this device has a broad appeal across different classes, ages and regions of the country but predominates in family homes, especially those with older children and homes with working women.

These trends are reflected in the methods of preparation used in the home, with an increase between 1985 and 1991 in cooking food by microwave and baking, but a decrease in frying (Table 5.2).

Table 5.2   *Home cooking habits in the UK (percentage occasions)*

	1985	1991
Uncooked/cold	87	83
Grilled/toasted	29	30
Boiled/steamed	26	24
Heated	22	20
Fried	15	12
Roasted/baked	14	16
Microwaved	4	8
Stewed	3	2
Other	0	2

Columns add up to more than 100% as more than one method can be used in a meal.
Source: Taylor Nelson Family Food Panel, 1991.

The frozen foods sector was one of the most dynamic in the 1980s, fuelled by greater numbers of working women, the trend away from formal set meals and the growth of freezer and microwave ownership.

In 1989 the sales of frozen or chilled ready meals took over from green vegetables as the product category with highest sales figures, reflecting the swing from purchase of commodities to high quality, convenience products which can be prepared quickly in a microwave (*The Grocer*, 1991). Amongst this type of meal, the sales of healthy meals such as 'Lean Cuisine' and 'Healthy Options' have grown to take 20 per cent of the market. The increase in the sales of snacks is also a reflection of the move away from formal meals (see Tables 5.3–5.5).

One of the interesting issues is whether in Europe there will be a backlash against frozen food as there has been in the USA. Americans are demanding more convenience products but want better quality. This can be provided from chilled, refrigerated rather than frozen products. The net effect is better quality compared with frozen products many of which come out of the microwave soggy, hard or overcooked. Longer life, microwaveable products can now be produced which do not need to be frozen.

Table 5.3 *Frozen food consumption in the UK, 1974–89 (oz per person per week)*

	1974	*1979*	*1984*	*1989*
Convenience meats	0.73	1.31	1.85	2.26
Convenience fish products	0.68	0.81	1.02	1.02
Peas	1.29	1.75	1.70	1.63
Beans	0.44	0.56	0.47	0.49
Chips/potato products	0.48	0.80	1.87	2.82
Other vegetables	0.45	1.01	1.15	1.76
Fruit/fruit products	0.05	0.08	0.03	0.03
Convenience cereal products	0.19	0.44	0.78	1.19

Source: Ministry of Agriculture Fisheries and Food, National Food Survey, 1989.

Table 5.4 *Frozen food buying habits in the UK (percentage of households)*

Vegetables	90
Ice cream	89
Fish/fish products	73
Potato products	72
Meat products	60
Dessert and cakes	53
Poultry/poultry products	51
Ready meals	37

Source: The Grocer, 1991.

Table 5.5   *Sales of prepared meals and snacks in the UK 1985–1993 (£m)*

	Prepared meals		Snacks		
	Frozen	*Chilled*	*Crisps*	*Savouries*	*Nuts*
1985	234	99	541	231	103
1989	350	209	687	374	134
1993[a]	481	297	664	563	188

[a]Estimate.
Source: Mintel, *Market Intelligence*, November 1989; February, 1990.

Conclusions

Foods can be preserved by slowing down the rate of chemical deterioration and preventing microbial growth. The most successful technique for doing both is by freezing, although in some markets, particularly France and Germany, canned goods are popular. Modern innovations in product development have been possible because of techniques such as freeze-drying, spray-drying, vacuum packaging and extrusion. Future innovations are likely in products such as functional foods and the use of novel forms of protein.

The stocking and distribution of food is increasingly sophisticated and linked to in-store computer systems which register sales. EPOS systems also enable analysis of consumer purchases and can trigger the award of vouchers and other incentives to encourage repeat purchases. It may be speculated that in future home shopping might replace the need to visit a food store.

The availability of home technology has affected the type of products bought. The growth in ownership of fridge-freezers and microwaves, in particular, has enabled the purchase of convenience products especially frozen or chilled ready meals and snacks. However there are variations throughout Europe in the ownership of these devices and a growing backlash against frozen food and growing interest in chilled products with a taste and texture nearer to that of the fresh product.

Questions

1   Consider how changes in farming practice have affected the availability of food to the consumer.
2   Why is it necessary to preserve food?
    What technological innovations have appeared in the past twenty years which have increased the storage time of food products?
3   What is meant by convenience food?
4   What is EPOS?
    How is the information produced by EPOS helpful to the consumer, retailer and manufacturer of food?

5 In what way could customer tracking help to improve the service available to the consumer?
6 Consider whether in your view 'home shopping' is likely to catch on with respect to food purchase.
7 What is the effect on the consumer of centralized distribution systems as established by major food retailers?
8 Gather information on the growth and change in sales of frozen food in the past decade.
9 What technological innovations already known to you do you consider will lead to increased sales of particular food products in the next five years?
10 Use your imagination to identify new foodstuffs which you think could be available in the next ten years.

References

Bradshaw, D. (1993) 'The science of shopping', *Financial Times*, 8 October
Bralsford, R. (1986) 'Food processing' In *The Food Consumer* (ed. C. Ritson, L. Gofton and J. McKenzie, Wiley, New York
Buckley, N. (1993) 'Changes ahead', *Financial Times*, 5 October
Eurofood (1992) *European Canned Food*, September, Agra Europe, London
Findus (1988) *Frozen Food Report*, Findus, Croydon
Fisher, A. (1993) 'Tapping into convenience', *Financial Times*, 11 November
Food Pocket Book (1992) NTC Publications, Henley-on-Thames.
The Grocer (1991) 'Focus on Frozen Foods', 4 May, 71–98.
Harrison, B. (1993) 'Selling on the sofa', *Financial Times*, 1 April
Harrison, K. (1993a) 'Product management: predictions', *Supermarketing*, 17 December
Harrison, K. (1993b) 'The face of foods to come', *Supermarketing*, 27 August
Hyam, J. (1993) 'Snacks: the food of the future', *Supermarketing*, 10 September
Senker, J. (1988) *A Taste for Innovation: British Supermarkets' Influence on Food Manufacturers*, Horton Publishing, Bradford
Supermarketing (1993) 'What price customer loyalty?' 17 September

Part Two

Cultural and Social Influences

People buy and consume food not only because of its instrumental and physiological benefit but also so as to be able to socialize, to indulge in celebrations or to reflect their own persona.

What food we buy, where we buy it and how we consume it is intimately connected with the culture in which we have been brought up. By this is meant the set of accepted values and ways of behaving which shape the society in which we live. This has a determining effect on the products a consumer buys. These concepts are discussed in general terms in Chapter 6 although the latter half of the chapter is focused on one cultural value, healthiness, which currently appears to have a significant influence in Western society. Here it is related to the consumption of food in order to show how an apparently amorphous concept, such as culture, has a direct impact on purchase behaviour in the supermarket.

Earlier chapters suggested that the demand and consumption of certain foods is heavily influenced by household income and price. This is certainly true but analysis of trends in consumption over the past fifty years shows that since the late 1970s the impact of changing lifestyles and attitudes has become more significant. In Chapter 7 the argument which is supported by trend analysis is that a demand for convenience products and those which either are, or are perceived to be healthy, has replaced demand patterns linked exclusively to income and price.

Some foods are completely taboo in a particular society, sometimes because of deeply held religious beliefs. There may be restrictions imposed not only on what is consumed but when too. A cult has many features in common with a religion. It can also have a restrictive influence on consumption. Vegetarianism is described as an example to illustrate the concept in Chapter 8. Some foods are said to have medicinal or restorative properties. In some cases there is truth in the claim, in others not. In a similar way periodically consumers become concerned about the harmful effects of a particular foodstuff. As in the case of mad cow disease it can lead to disputes between scientists and even countries about whether there is genuine harm. Myths and scares are examined in Chapter 8.

A considerable influence on consumption is the changing size, structure and age of the population throughout Europe. The emphasis in Chapter 9 is on an analysis of birth-rate, population size and age structure in member states of the EU, together with projections for the future.

Although it has been argued that social class structures are disappearing from modern society most individuals still recognize a class structure and their position within it. To market researchers socio-economic grouping is still the most widely used mechanism for market segmentation because there are identifiable links to purchase behaviour which are discussed in Chapter 10.

Groups are of particular significance to consumer researchers because their behaviour is often more predictable than that of individuals. Many purchases are subject to group pressure as consumers buy products they think will make people believe they belong to a particular group. The way in which people are influenced by opinion leaders and by the peer pressure of others in a reference group is discussed in Chapter 11. Perhaps the strongest and most powerful group of all is the family unit, in which different members may have different roles and influences on consumer purchase. The family goes through a series of stages as it develops from just a couple living alone to a group in which there are children and then back to a couple or single person when the children leave home. The impact on consumption during these different stages is significant and is explored in Chapter 12.

This part of the book therefore explores the often intangible cultural and social forces which shape consumer behaviour. The social environment constructs the individual but also serves as the platform on which he or she lives out the particular lifestyle they prefer. In doing so these social forces will have a strong impact on the products an individual demands and consumes.

6 *Culture*

Introduction

People in Western society find it difficult to understand that the Chinese eat dogs, because dogs remind them of people and as such are treated as pets and objects of affection. Cows have a special religious significance to Hindus in India so they cannot understand why Europeans eat them. The French eat horsemeat and frogs which the British disdain. If biological reasons alone were the major explanation of what people eat then diets around the world would be similar. In fact they are not, because what and when we eat, and how it is prepared and served, is a reflection of our cultural upbringing.

This chapter is concerned with defining the meaning and characteristics of culture. Some cultural values are common to all cultures but those which have current prominence in Western Europe are emphasized here. One translation of cultural values is through the products consumers buy and the meaning placed on them. To illustrate this concept in greater detail one cultural value, healthiness, is chosen and related to trends in consumption of healthy foods.

Defining culture

People need food for physiological reasons. Unlike the purchase of many products, consumers literally cannot live without a regular supply of food and liquid. Obviously there are also psychological needs which are satisfied by food consumption. People get enjoyment from eating and from the social interaction that often accompanies eating. However, eating and drinking are also cultural events and as such fall within the remit of anthropology which is the study of knowledge, skills, beliefs, values and activities which are passed on from one generation to another. Culture is about the way of life, the language, behaviour, myths, symbols and signs which are passed on within a particular group. That group can be Western Europeans, the Irish, a regional group of Basques or an ethnic minority of Turks living in Germany.

While the culture of different groups may vary, culture itself is a common characteristic of all human groups. It logically has a strong influence on ways of life and hence on the products people buy to support their way of life. Put another way, the marketing environment is strongly affected by the cultural environment. An effective advertisement or new food product in one culture may not be successful in another.

Characteristics of culture

Human beings are not born with a set of behaviour, they have to learn it. What they learn is dictated by the culture into which they are born or within which they grow up. Formal instruction comes from parents; informal by imitating others or watching the behaviour of others in the media. Technical instruction is acquired via the education system. This process by which people absorb their values, motivations and habits is defined as socialization. It goes on throughout life, causing people to acquire attitudes and behaviour which in turn affect their consumption.

Culture is shared and social. It is to do with passing on of social norms which are particular to a group of people rather than specific individuals. The primary agents for this transmission are parents, school, college, mass media, friends. What these agents transmit is knowledge but also beliefs in the form of accepted perceptions, myths, or religion. Additionally values are transmitted which represent a consensus of what is accepted by the majority as 'good' as a lifestyle or ideal. This results in cultural norms which become regulatory or prescribed ways of behaving reinforced by public pressure.

Customs are acceptable expressions of behaviour in specific situations, such as eating with a knife and fork in Western society but with chopsticks in much of Eastern society. The central values or standards of a society, such as a belief in free enterprise, or the state, or the family, are mores which if formalized become enshrined as laws.

Culturally acceptable behaviour is rewarded by approval and support while unacceptable behaviour is punished or shunned. Because culture is something transmitted both within a group and from generation to generation, it requires a language. It is often the non-verbal elements of that language which carry symbolic meaning. Meaning rather than information can be critical in either establishing or preventing real communication. Advertising campaigns and new product developments have been known to fail because of a lack of appreciation of symbolism which may have adverse meaning in a particular culture.

European values

Much of social anthropology is concerned with the differences between cultures, but there are some values or concerns which are remarkably similar in all cultures (Table 6.1). There are also cultural values of significance to a particular culture or at a particular point in cultural history. The core values of a society provide the framework of what is acceptable in the promotion or properties of a particular product. Some of the cultural norms accepted in European society are identified in Table 6.2.

Forecasters attempt to identify and spot changes in cultural norms because these will shape consumption behaviour. The whole field of lifestyle analysis and changing values is considered in great depth in Chapter 14 but here a simple comparison of the 1980s and 1990s shows the adaptive nature of culture. In Table 8.3 the comparison shows that people are becoming less concerned with getting rich quickly and more with the quality of their lives. Concern with pollution and the environment has made them choose products believed to have less damaging effects. In Europe people have taken up an American trend, with more consumers concerned with an opportunity to

Table 6.1 *Cultural universals*

Age grading	Dream interpretation	Incest taboos
Athletics	Education	Marriage
Body adornment	Ethics	Property rights
Cleanliness	Etiquette	Religion
Courtship	Faith healing	Status differentiation
Cosmology	Funeral rites	Surgery
		Tool making

Source: Foxall, 1980

Table 6.2 *Core values in Western society*

1 A more casual lifestyle with less formality
2 A focus on individuality and personalization – the desire to be different from others
3 Flexibility of sex roles; men and women performing roles in the house or at work traditionally associated with a particular gender
4 Instant gratification; living for today, intolerance of things not available and working right away
5 Pleasure seeking and novelty; a desire for products and services which make life more fun
6 Simplification; a removal of time or energy spent on unnecessary things
7 Changed morality; premarital and extramarital sex is more tolerated
8 Concern with appearance and health; youth, keeping fit, looking good
9 Natural things; the advantages of technology but not synthetics
10 Personal creativity; the desire to make and create what has traditionally been bought
11 Changed work ethic; work to live rather than live to work; work buys fun and leisure
12 Eroding confidence in institutions – government and big business are seen as non-effective and impersonal
13 Consumerism – increased concern over value for money with rising expectations about quality and performance
14 Energy, ecology and environment – concern with conservation of natural resources and energy
15 Eclecticism – anything goes, no one fashion dictates. Peer pressure is significant more than national norms
16 Time conservation – time has to be used effectively
17 Achievement – hard work and getting things done are important
18 Freedom to choose and not be dictated to is important
19 Humanitarianism – caring for others; support for the underdog
20 Improvement – a desire to get better
21 Security – conservatism and low risk taking triggered by recession

Table 6.3 *Cultural values in the 1980s and 1990s*

1980s	1990s
Young	Middle-aged
Singles	Alternative families
Get rich quick	Quality of life
Conspicuous consumption	Socially aware consumer
Outer directed	Inner directed
American influence	European influence
Gloss, brash	Authentic, natural
Busy, stressed	Organized, laid back
Assertion	Democracy
Convenience	Products punctuate time
Women as good as men	Men as good as women
Live to work	Work to live

Source: Henley Centre for Forecasting, 1990.

grow and develop as individuals rather than constantly taking a lead from reference to others. On the other hand, Europe rather than America is becoming more obviously a centre of gravity and reference point in terms of values and fashions for European consumers (see Table 6.3).

Marketing strategies based on changing consumer values therefore have to be adaptive and to capitalize on whatever cultural norms are paramount at that particular point in history.

One of the instant successes in recent product innovation throughout Europe has been premium-priced ice creams. This capitalizes on rising concerns with quality and luxury which have become important cultural concerns. The battle for this market is explained in more detail in Illustration 6.1.

The way in which cultural values change is also illustrated by the growing consumption of ethnic and international foods. As consumers have experimented with travelling further afield on holiday and with eating in restaurants, their home based consumption has changed. Patak Indian Foods saw a 93 per cent increase in sales in 1993, and sales of international foods increased by 12.5 per cent (Halpin, 1994).

Cultural influences on purchase behaviour

It is apparent that if culture determines the norms of a particular group or nation then it will have an effect on what and why people buy particular products. Consumers buy a product because they expect it to have a functional value. Food is necessary to provide calories, vitamins and so on to the consumer. However, the expectation is also that a product will be available in a particular form. Unlike the Japanese, Europeans do not expect to eat raw fish. Foods are expected to be 'soft' or 'tender' or 'easy to cook'.

Illustration 6.1 Europe's cold warriors – the luxury ice cream market

In 1989 Mars launched premium-priced ice cream versions of its chocolate bars. Almost overnight it had created a thriving luxury sector of the market into which other manufacturers, including Unilever, then moved.

In mid 1993 Unilever and Mars got into battles, Unilever defending a commanding 40 per cent of European ice cream sales, valued at about £6 bn annually at retail prices. The dispute centred on Unilever's control of distribution and, in particular, its use of 'cabinet exclusivity'. Most ice creams are bought on impulse at small shops. Unilever has supplied freezer cabinets free of charge to small retailers, who sell the bulk of ice creams, on the condition the freezers do not carry competitors' products. Mars has complained to the EC that Unilever's distribution methods violate EC competition law.

In 1992 the EC gave Mars a partial victory when it outlawed arrangements made by Unilever and Scholler, a German ice cream manufacturer, to keep rivals' products out of German retail outlets.

Making a success of ice cream is especially important to Mars, an American company, which has built a £20 M plant in eastern France to supply the entire European market. This is especially so since Mars' confectionery sales are on the decrease in Britain and Germany. Mars is the second largest producer of confectionery after Nestlé.

Meanwhile, just to confuse matters further, Nestlé has recently acquired Clarke Foods, the UK's second largest ice cream manufacturer. Not only is Nestlé the world's biggest food manufacturer; it also distributes and stocks Mars' ice cream in the 20 000 cabinets it owns. It would seem unlikely to continue with this practice if it is intending to become a third big player in the cabinet ice cream sector.

All this suggests that Mars may be bleating rather too late. Competitors of all sizes are still pouring into the premium ice cream market. Mars may have missed its chance to pin down the market when it had it to itself.

Ice cream sales 1992

	Selling price (Europe, £m)
Unilever	1550
Nestlé	200
Scholler	400
Haagen Dazs	50
Mars	150

Unilever ice cream sales in Europe 1992

	Market volume (litres m)	Unilever market share
Germany	520	40%
Italy	400	40%
UK	420	40%
Spain	180	30%
France	320	20%
Benelux	160	30%

Based on G. de Jonquieres 'Europe's new cold warriors', *Financial Times*, 19 May 1993

Products also provide symbols of meaning which is explored more fully in Chapter 8. Fish is often thought of as a brain food, or spinach, because of associations with Popeye, as a food for strength. Some foods become part of family or religious rituals or celebrations and so take on meaning associated with an event. Turkey is an obvious example which is associated with Christmas. Coffee took the whole of the eighteenth century in central Europe to evolve from a beverage drunk only by upper social groups to one drunk also by members of lower social orders (Mennell *et al.*, 1992).

The particular culture in which we live affects the availability of a product. Although as a generalization, in Western Europe, food is available in abundance, culture determines where it is available and at what cost. The politics of the EU, as described in Chapter 3, shape what food is available from different parts of the world and also at what price. In addition, cultural norms in the form of laws determine what can be used in the manufacture of food and hence its storage life, colouring and how it is promoted and described. Consumption is also about the acquisition of social meaning attached to and communicated by a product. Market research on fish products (Bareham, unpublished) showed that products eaten in either their raw state (sushi) or very nearly (lobster) have a high social status which is reinforcing both for those who consume the product and for those who aspire to consume such products. On the other hand the success of fish fingers is partly because they are completely unrecognizable as natural fish yet are known to contain the nutritionally beneficial characteristics of fish. They avoid the characteristics of raw fish such as 'smelly', 'slippery' and 'stare at you' which consumers find objectionable.

The way in which such cultural values are reflected in the meaning attached to food is explored in the next section on health and food consumption.

Health and food consumption

Healthiness is a concept universally applicable to all cultures. However, the emphasis on it has risen and fallen and taken different directions in different societies, at different times in their history. At present it is a predominant concern in most Western societies. It is used here as the focal point of a discussion as to how a value of importance to a culture translates into purchase behaviour related to food.

In the UK emerging emphasis on health as a cultural value shaping consumption of food first became apparent around 1984/85. Surveys showed (Table 6.4) that people rated the type and amount of food they ate as significant factors affecting their health, although not as critical as stress or smoking.

Products are bought if they are perceived as healthy, whether or not this is true in a nutritional sense. Flora, the UK brand leader in margarine sales, is perceived as healthy because the promotion of it has emphasized the level of polyunsaturated fat it contains which make the blood less viscous and decreases plasma cholesterol. Notwithstanding the fact that the technical basis of this claim has recently been questioned, Flora after its initial introduction rapidly became the best selling margarine in the UK (Whitehorn, 1994) because it was perceived as more healthy than other margarines and butter.

When asked in a survey, 1000 adults said the healthiness of food equates with the amount of vitamins, fibre and protein the food is said to contain. Much less important is the absence of sugar, salt and additives and further down the list are cholesterol and E numbers. Least healthy are perceived to be fried and irradiated foods. Microwaved

Table 6.4 *Evaluation of influences on health*[a]

Stress	4.04
Smoking	4.01
Type of food	3.91
Sleep	3.69
Alcohol	3.66
Exercise	3.64
Amount of food	3.40

[a]1000 interviewees were asked to score the various factors according to their perceived influence on health.
5 = very important; 1 = not at all important.
Source: Bareham, 1990.

foods have gone from being perceived as healthy to unhealthy while Japanese and Chinese foods, on the other hand, are both becoming more popular and are perceived as more healthy than Western foods (Bareham, 1990).

Health as an issue in relation to food consumption has been stimulated by UK government reports such as the National Advisory Committee on Nutrition Education (NACNE, 1983) and the Committee on Medical Aspects of Food Policy (COMA, 1984). These reports argue that dietary intake of fat should be reduced to 30 per cent of total energy, fibre consumption increased by 50 per cent and sugar and salt consumption decreased by 50 and 25 per cent respectively. In fact, since the beginning of the century consumption has fallen of potatoes, bread, sugar, red meat, dairy food, eggs, milk and fat (Table 6.5). On the other hand, there have been increases in consumption of

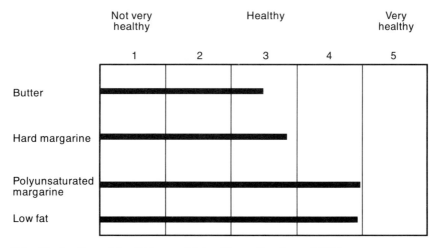

Figure 6.1 *Evaluation of healthiness of fats. (From Bareham, 1990)*

Table 6.5   *Differences in food consumption in the UK, 1905 and 1983*

			1905	1983
UP	↑	Meat	2.3	2.6 lb
		Milk	3.0	3.7 pts
		Margarine	1.3	4.1 oz
		Tea	0.2	2.0 oz
		Coffee	0.5	0.7 oz
		Bread	4.4	1.9 lb
		Potatoes	4.3	2.5 lb
		Fish	8.6	5.0 oz
		Butter	4.1	3.3 oz
DOWN	↓	Sugar	14.4	9.8 oz

Source: National Food Survey.

Table 6.6   *Changes in eating habits in the UK, 1989 versus 1988*

	Up	*Down*
Sugar	1	37
Salt	1	29
Butter	1	35
Eggs	5	23
Red meat	3	24
Coffee	6	14
Fibre	42	1
Fruit and vegetables	41	1
Poultry	20	7
Fish	21	4
Yoghurt	18	5

Percentage of 200 adults.
Source: Euromonitor, 1990.

perceived healthy food; yoghurt, natural cheese, wholemeal bread, poultry, fish and low fat spread (Tables 6.5, 6.6).

In Mediterranean countries the diet with an emphasis on vegetables, fruit, fish and wine has always been more healthy than in the UK and this persists. In Spain, for instance, consumption of fruit and vegetables has doubled in the past 25 years and fish consumption has also risen greatly, accounting for over 12 per cent of spending on food in 1991 (*Actualidad Económica*, 1992).

Health foods as opposed to healthy foods go even further in capitalizing on the virtue Western populations make of health. A UK Ministry of Agriculture survey of 2000 people in 1988 showed that the presence of vitamins in a health food was the single fact most likely to stimulate sales. One in five people buy dietary supplements. Some experts believe all this intake is simply wasted since a balanced diet should already contain more than the recommended daily amount of vitamins. Murcott (1983) has argued the current fashion for health foods is more to do with cultural influences than any nutritional benefit. She argues that health foods have overtones of naturalness, purity and wholesomeness. They provide 'a reconciliation between our urban, industrial and synthetic present, and our rural, pre-industrial and natural past'. In this sense Murcott believes eating health foods allows a person to chew their way back to a lost harmony with nature.

So one of the major appeals of health food is a mythological or symbolic one. It offers the natural, good life, although of course this is not provided simply because the product is bought. If anything, such products offer a substitute for action. Almost like a magical act, consumption of health foods can substitute for changes in everyday life by allowing the consumer to ingest virtue in concrete form.

However, before getting too carried away, it is as well to remember that the switch to healthy eating may be over-estimated. People say they eat more healthily than they actually do. Flora is still the lead brand in the margarine market, with sales greater than the combined sales of all low fat spreads even though the latter are more healthy. Individuals also switch their behaviour. Some believe that if they eat healthily for most of the time then it will be all right to switch occasionally to an unhealthy diet or foodstuff. Interestingly the number of true vegetarians is no longer increasing dramatically as it was a few years ago. In the UK there is a tremendous rise in the number of people giving up eating red meat, currently put at as many as one in ten. However, recent surveys show that these same people are mainly rather than

---

Illustration 6.2 A 3 per cent fat promise

The fat content of spreads has continued to fall over the years, representing a response by manufacturers to consumer demand for healthy foods. Butter and standard margarines still contain 80 per cent, low fat spreads 40 per cent and very low fat lines 20 per cent.

Van den Bergh Foods' Project Apollo represented the company's first UK move into the virtually fat free spreads sector.

This was in response to Tesco, who marketed a 5 per cent fat product in 1992. VdB set itself the task of producing a product with less than 5 per cent fat and a flavour comparable to Delight. They came up with Promise, which has just 3 per cent fat and only 74 calories per 100g (less per portion than is found in one peanut). It is being manufactured in Denmark. Test marketing in the Central and Granada TV regions of the UK in 1993 has proved positive: 84 per cent of consumers said they would definitely or probably buy the product even though it is priced at the top end of the spectrum for similar products.

Based on 'Only 3% fat, and that's definitely a promise', *The Grocer*, 30 October 1993

completely vegetarian, that is to say they find it expedient to use battery produced eggs in recipes to keep the price down and still eat digestive biscuits which contain animal fat (Drummond, 1993).

Conclusion

People do not consume food simply and only for physiological reasons. Food, like any other product or commodity carries symbolic meaning besides its instrumental value. The meaning attached to it derives crucially from the cultural background of the consumer. Culture encompasses the knowledge, beliefs, attitudes and behaviour of a particular group of people. These are acquired but may go on changing throughout a person's lifetime.

Some cultural values are common to all societies, others only to particular nations or groups. One particular cultural value – and a focus of this chapter – is healthiness. Healthiness has risen in pre-eminence in the past decade in Western Europe as a cultural value shaping behaviour and hence food purchase in particular. Products which either are, or are perceived to be, healthy are sought after. This has been encouraged in the UK by government commissioned reports which make recommendations about change to encourage healthy eating. This appears to have had some effect amongst some groups in society although the British diet is still not as healthy as the typical Mediterranean one with its emphasis on fruit, vegetables and fish.

However, the concept of healthiness, and hence which foods are healthy, can vary, just as any other cultural norm can be changed as society reinforces the value of one concept and denounces another.

Questions

1   In what way is culture passed from individual to individual?
    Give examples of cultural learning.
2   What is the difference between belief, value, custom, mores, law?
3   As the media planner for a large advertising agency you have been asked by top management to identify recent cultural changes that affect selection of media in which to place advertising of your client's pre-portioned frozen dinners.
    What product features would you emphasize in the advertising?
4   What cultural sub-groups do you identify in the UK?
    Indicate not only national but religious, lifestyle, race, age and sex sub-groups.
5   The population of elderly people will increase up to the year 2000. What effect would this have on product plans for a major food company?
6   In what way has the changing culture of women affected the types of food product available and the way in which such products are advertised?
7   Why should a product which is successful in one culture fail in another?
8   Using the core values identified in Table 6.2, indicate what food products you think could be developed to capitalize on these values.
9   Do you agree that Table 6.3 gives a fair reflection of cultural values in the 1990s? Change or add to this list, giving reasons.

10   What evidence is there that interest in healthy food in the UK is simply a reflection of changing cultural values?
     Is there any evidence of similar trends in other countries?

References

Actualidad Economica (1992) 'El coste de comer bien', 5 April

Bareham (1990) Consuming interests. Inaugural lecture, University of Brighton (unpublished)

COMA (1984) 'Diet and cardiovascular disease', *Report on Health and Social Subjects No. 28*, DHSS, London

Drummond, G. (1993) 'The whole hog', *Supermarketing*, 15 Oct

Euromonitor (1990) *Change in eating habits 1989 versus 1988*, Euromonitor, London

Foxall, G. (1980) *Consumer Behaviour*, Croom Helm, London

Halpin, T. (1994) 'The take away', *Daily Mail*, 16 June

Henley Centre for Forecasting (1990) *Planning for Social Change: Origins and Prospects*. Henley Centre for Forecasting, Henley-on-Thames

Mennell, S., Murcott, A., van Otterloo, A. H. (1992) *The Sociology of Food*, Sage, London

Murcott, A. (1983) *The Sociology of Food and Eating*, Gower, Aldershot.

NACNE (1983) *Proposals for nutritional guidelines for health education in Britain*, Health Education Council, London

Whitehorn, M. (1994) 'Food experts are out to lunch', *Observer*, 17 April

7 Historical trends in consumption

Introduction

In Chapter 6 the definition and characteristics of culture were explored in a general sense. There was a focus on the consumption of healthy food as an example of how a cultural value can influence food purchase behaviour.

The purpose of this chapter is to examine trends in food consumption in the United Kingdom. In itself such data do not offer any explanation of what causes changes in consumption and so do not add to the discussion about what influences consumer behaviour. However, analysis conducted by researchers in the field suggests that although food consumption prior to 1980 was strongly influenced by income and price, since then the dominant influences have been fundamental changes in attitudes and social behaviour (Ritson and Hutchins, 1991). Hence it is logical to include discussion of this information in a section of the text which is concerned primarily with cultural and social influences on behaviour. Changes in food consumption in UK households are relatively easy to track because data have been collected annually for over 50 years as part of the National Food Survey. This information, and analysis of it by a variety of authors, is used as a basis of much of the chapter and compared with data for other European countries.

Historical trends

Overall, in the period between 1940 and 1990 UK household expenditure on food fell from 30 per cent of income to 12 per cent. There were major decreases in the consumption of bread, fish and sugar, but rises in the consumption of fruit and vegetables (Maclean, 1991). It has been argued that changed food consumption in the UK is mainly the result of rising personal incomes in the period between 1940 and 1980. (Ritson and Hutchins, 1991). Certain foods would be expected to be purchased in greater amounts, and other 'inferior' goods purchased less. The examples in Table 7.1 illustrate the point and link back to the earlier analysis in Chapter 4, which explained the decreased consumption of items such as bread but increases of those such as cheese as related to income.

There is certainly evidence that following the austere period during and after the Second World War and with the rise in incomes until the early 1970s, consumption of food did change in the direction predicted. At that point prices became a much more significant factor in food consumption. Volatility of prices was caused by a variety of

Table 7.1 *Influences of income on food purchase in the UK*

Purchases increase as income rises	*Purchases decrease as income rises*
Cheese	Sausages
Beef	Margarine
Pork	Lard
Chicken	Potatoes
Salad vegetables	Canned vegetables
Chocolate biscuits	White bread
Wholemeal bread	Tea
Ice cream	
Coffee	

factors such as the onset of the Common Agricultural Policy in Europe, drought and shortages. Thereafter in the 1980s price volatility decreased and the relationship between income and consumption lessened.

Once price and incomes are taken out as influences on purchase behaviour, the underlying trend in demand, which is what is left, can be identified. Demand analysis shows that purchase of meat in the 1970s fluctuated mainly as a result of price fluctuations, but the underlying demand for meat remained relatively stable. However, a critical point was reached both for meat and many other products between 1975 and 1980, when underlying demand for meat decreased quite rapidly even though prices fell. For other products the opposite was true.

The turning point seems to have been the ascendancy in demand for products associated either with convenience food or healthy eating. Ritson and Hutchin's (1991) analysis of demand for different products in the UK confirms this point (Table 7.2). For example, there is increased demand for convenience products such as frozen foods and foods perceived as healthy, such as fresh green vegetables. This is obviously related to the fact that technologically it became possible in the past two decades for food manufacturers to produce new products which both met consumer demand and to some extent fuelled it.

An obvious example of how consumption has changed dramatically, independently of price, is seen in the case of eggs. Wheelock (1991) has shown that the consumption

Table 7.2 *Annual percentage change in demand for foods in the UK (1975–1980)*

Fresh green vegetables	+29	Fresh white fish	−22
Wholewheat/meal bread	+18	Fresh peas	−16
Frozen chips	+13	Processed fat fish	−15
Low fat spreads	+12	Soft fresh fruit	−15
Frozen convenience foods	+11	Instant potato	−10

Source: Ritson and Hutchins, 1991.

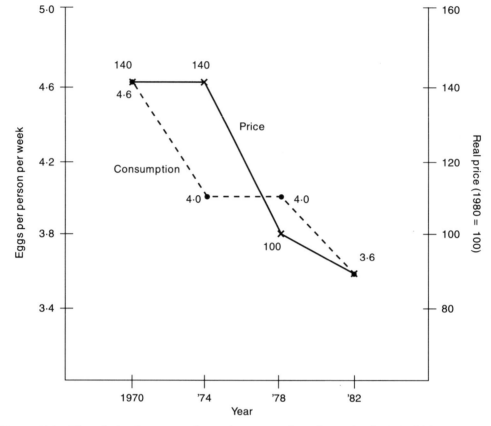

Figure 7.1   *The relation between price and consumption of eggs in the UK. (After Wheelock, 1991)*

of eggs declined in the 1970s and early 1980s, even though the real price fell (see Figure 7.1). On the other hand, there has been a growth in demand for cheese even though the price has risen.

The important point derived from this analysis is that current changes in demands for different foods and then actual measures of consumption show, first, that quite dramatic changes are taking place, and secondly, that these have a lot to do with changing values and lifestyle. These changes are analysed next in greater detail with respect to different constituents of the British diet.

UK trends

Introduction

The broad pattern of the British diet in the past fifty years has remained remarkably consistent and recognizably different from the French, German, or Italian diet. It is still based to a large extent on bread, milk, meat and potatoes; is relatively low on fruits and vegetables, even though these have increased, and beer is drunk rather than wine. However, there have been changes within each of these food categories. As an example, traditional vegetables such as swedes, parsnips and Brussels sprouts have been replaced by mushrooms and salad vegetables.

A major change has been in the number of meals eaten out a week, which rose by 15 per cent from 3.2 to 3.69 of all meals between 1979 and 1988. The proportion of adults who had ever been to a restaurant in the evening more than doubled in the 1980s, largely through an increase in participation by the over 55s. Although pubs still constitute the largest proportion of all catering outlets in the UK, the biggest growth in the 1980s was in fast food outlets (*Lifestyle Trends*, 1990).

There has been a major drop in energy consumption by the British population since the 1950s. The average British person now lives a sedentary life and, within limits, dietary energy does match needs. There is a greater desire to avoid obesity, but still no improvement in the percentage of the population who are overweight. Perhaps the rise which might have been expected to accompany a sedentary lifestyle has been avoided.

Fats

During the 1940s people were encouraged to eat fat, which was in short supply such that a *minimum* requirement was specified in school meals until as recently as 1975. Fat consumption therefore rose steadily from the mid 1950s to the early 1970s. In 1984 there was a government recommendation that energy derived from fat should not exceed 35 per cent, although it had reached 42 per cent at the time. However, during this period the source of fat in the diet had changed dramatically. Over a thirty-year period the fortunes of butter and margarine went up and down due to price fluctuations related to availability of raw materials such as vegetable oils. The concern in more recent times about saturated fat, fostered by the margarine companies, has led to a drop in butter consumption to only a quarter of 1970 levels with a correspondingly marked increase in consumption of vegetable oils and, most recently, in low fat and very low fat spreads.

In the past twenty years, diet in the UK has been changing in line with the advice to avoid saturated fats. The polyunsaturated/saturated fatty acid ratio (P/S ratio) has risen steadily from 1975 to a current value of approximately 0.4, although this is still significantly lower than many other countries.

At present there is a lot of interest in the potential importance of monosaturated fatty acid in the diet because of the relatively low incidence of cardiovascular disease in Southern Europe where olive oil, which is rich in this component, is used a lot.

Fruit and vegetables

Among vegetables, declining consumption of cabbage, cauliflower and Brussels sprouts has been only partly offset by the increased purchase of salad vegetables. Consumption of traditional root vegetables and canned vegetables has declined, while

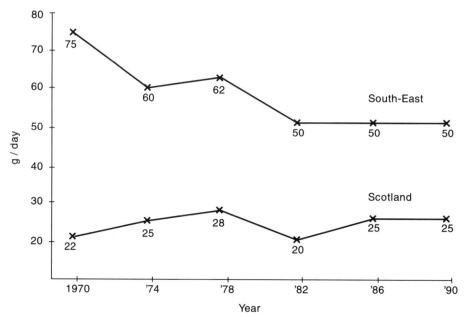

Figure 7.2   *Consumption (g/day) of green vegetables in different regions of the UK. (After Whitehead and Paul, 1990)*

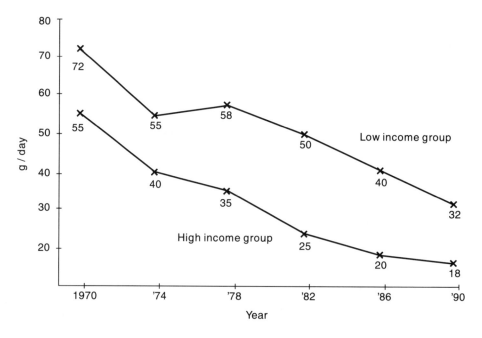

Figure 7.3   *Consumption (g/day) of sugar in the UK in relation to income group. (After Whitehead and Paul, 1990)*

frozen vegetable purchase has increased. Since the mid 1970s the increase in consumption of fruit is partly accounted for by the increase in purchase of fruit juice and greater availability of fruit from other parts of the world. Apples, oranges, pears and bananas continue to account for the majority of fruit purchased while consumption of soft fruits, with the exception of grapes, has gone down.

The consumption of fruit and vegetables varies widely between different regions of the UK and in different social classes. Compared with south-east England and East Anglia, fruit consumption is about one-half in Scotland and there are similar differences in relation to vegetables (Figure 7.2).

Likewise there are consistent differences in relation to social class, with the top 10 per cent of wage-earners consuming around twice the quantity of fruit and vegetables compared with those on a low wage.

This social class difference is also apparent in relation to sugar. Overall consumption has dropped by one-half, but it is the less well off who are the greatest users of the product (Figure 7.3).

Milk

Milk consumption was heavily encouraged during the Second World War and immediately afterwards, particularly amongst children. Since the 1970s the consumption of whole milk has fallen, although this has been largely replaced by increases in skimmed and semi-skimmed varieties as people have become more concerned to avoid fat (see Figure 7.4). At the same time the popularity of soft drinks has risen.

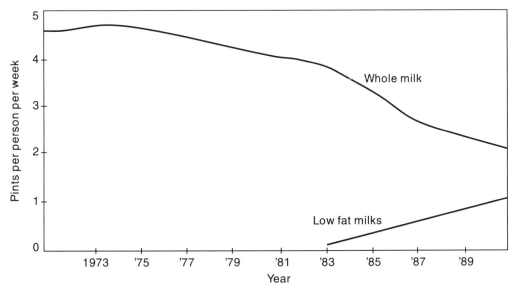

Figure 7.4 *Consumption of milks in the UK. (After Ritson and Hutchins, 1991)*

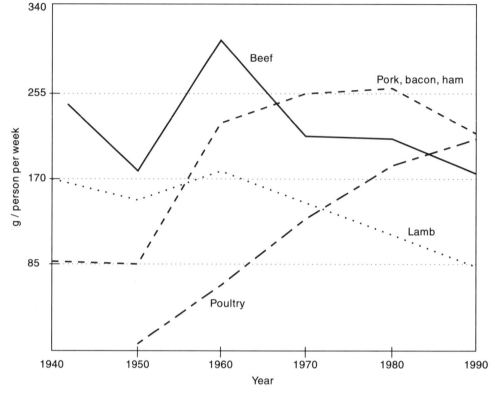

Figure 7.5   *Consumption of meats in the UK. (After Buss, 1991)*

Meats

Consumption of beef, lamb and pork all rose in the early 1950s but since then there has been a major decline in consumption of lamb and a dramatic rise in poultry consumption (Figure 7.5).

Although 75 per cent of the population ate beef in 1987, the scare over bovine spongiform encephalitis (BSE) boosted the numbers who avoided red meat altogether to between 10 per cent and 20 per cent of the population in 1990.

Bread and cakes

One of the most dramatic changes in food consumption has been the rapid decline in consumption of bread, with an approximate halving in the period 1940 to 1990. The rise in wholemeal and wholewheat consumption because of interest in fibre and texture has not reversed this trend.

The decline in the consumption of cakes, which was very rapid between 1968 and 1978, appears to have stopped and the purchase of biscuits has been relatively stable in recent years. On the other hand, the consumption of breakfast cereals has doubled in the past 30 years.

Drinks

The overall per capita consumption of alcoholic drink has been in decline since 1979. However, between 1979 and 1989 consumption of wine rose 51 per cent, with a clear preference for white wine. Consumption of vermouth and fortified wines such as sherry are in serious long-term decline. Although the spirits market was virtually static in the 1980s, consumption of whisky and gin have fallen while the reverse is true of vodka and brandy.

Coffee consumption was static in the 1980s, while tea consumption continued to decline, by 24 per cent in the decade.

The soft drinks market continued to expand, with volume shares of bottled water (800%), fruit juice (147%) and carbonates (83%) all continuing to rise (*Lifestyle Trends*, 1990).

Convenience foods

There has been a significant shift in demand from basic commodities which require a lot of preparation to foods such as burgers, pizzas and frozen vegetables which can be quickly cooked.

Senker (1988) has argued, for instance, that although people are consuming fewer calories, they are buying a greater percentage of food which has already been subjected to some form of processing. As an example, while purchase of raw potatoes has declined this has been partially offset by an increased purchase of frozen chips, which has doubled since 1978.

Speciality foods

At the same time there is a trend towards speciality foods. Examples, quoted by Wheelock (1991), in British supermarkets include:

- In-store bakeries offering croissants and freshly cooked breads.
- In-store butchers offering quail, partridge and pheasant as well as prime meats.
- Cheese counters with many continental European varieties.
- Produce sections with kiwi fruit, passion fruit, endives.
- Delicatessen counters with fresh caviar, quiches and extensive lines of pre-mixed carry-out salads.

European trends

The typical UK diet is changing, as identified in the previous section, but it is still essentially dependent on bread, meat, potatoes and beer. It is very different from diets eaten elsewhere in mainland Europe. Data in Table 7.3 show that in France, West Germany, Spain and Italy consumption of meat, fruit and vegetables is much higher than in the UK. In comparison, the UK diet is high on cereals and dairy products. The intake of fats is also higher compared with Mediterranean countries, which have a higher consumption of oils containing the more healthy monosaturated fatty acids.

Table 7.3   *Food consumption in Europe in 1990 (kg/year per capita)*

	Meat	*Cereals*	*Vegetables*	*Fruit*	*Butter*
France	110	102	117	77	8.6
W. Germany	105	100	78	118	8.5
Italy	88	160	174	103	2.4
Spain	95	98	162	91	0.4
UK	77	120	68	63	4.2

Source: OECD/GATT/*Euromonitor,* 1992.

In West Germany the main trend in consumption between 1981 and 1990 has included a steady rise in consumption of meat from 99 to 105 kg/year per capita, in cereals (including bread) from 88 to 100 kg/year per capita and in vegetables from 65 to 78 kg/year per capita. Consumption of eggs, butter and margarine are fairly stable.

More consumers in unified Germany are turning to lighter and healthier foods instead of the traditional heavy foods like dumplings, roast pork and potato salad. As a result, 1991 data showed that consumption of fruit and vegetables continued to rise but meat consumption fell for the first time in decades (*New York Times*, 1992).

In Italy cereal consumption is high because of the heavy use of pasta but this has declined from 178 kg/year per capita in 1981 to 160 in 1990. Meat consumption, as in Germany, has steadily risen from 77 to 88 kg whereas vegetable consumption first decreased then rose between 1983 and 1985 and is now back to 174 kg, still the highest level in Europe. Consumption of eggs, oil, butter and fats rose between 1981 and 1987 but has dropped back recently.

Similarly to Italy, vegetable consumption in Spain is high and as in Italy and Germany meat consumption has risen; from 82 kg/year per capita in 1983 to 95 kg in 1990, with a slight fall in cereal consumption in the same period.

In France again meat consumption rose slightly in the 1980s to give the highest per capita consumption in Europe. Vegetable consumption has oscillated but is still midway between that in northern Europe (UK and Germany) and southern Europe (Spain and Italy).

Ranked simply in terms of weight the proportions of foodstuffs in the diet show distinct differences between these five European nations:

France	Germany	Italy	Spain	UK
Vegetables	Fruit	Vegetables	Vegetables	Cereals
Meat	Meat	Cereals	Cereals	Meat
Cereals	Cereals	Fruit	Meat	Vegetables
Fruit	Vegetables	Meat	Fruit	Fruit

Three lesser trends are apparent in continental Europe. First, there is an increased appeal of luxury items, for example, high value processed bakery products such as biscuits and chocolate items. Second, there is a growing demand, as in the UK for processed or pre-prepared foods. In Spain the market is expected to grow by 10 per cent in the next few years as a result of changing lifestyle, although consumption at 1.3 kg per person per annum is still lower than France at 6 kg (*Pais*, 1992). Finally, eating out in cafes and restaurants is already at a high level. In Spain it represents 24 per cent of all food and drink consumed and is expected to grow even further (*Actualidad Economica*, 1992).

Conclusion

Analysis of data on food consumption over the past fifty years shows considerable change in the average British diet. Up until the late 1970s this can be shown to be closely related to changes in income and price. However, from this point onwards both demand and actual consumption of food seem to be linked more closely to changes in the cultural and social environment. In particular, since that time demand has increased for products which offer convenience in terms of preparation time or ease of storage, and for products which either are, or are perceived to be, healthy.

More detailed analysis shows some of the major changes in British eating habits include a decrease in energy intakes as a consequence of more sedentary lifestyles, the rapid increase in consumption of poultry meat but decline in red meat, a shift to lower fat margarines, high in polyunsaturates and away from butter, a reduction in bread consumption, an increase in consumption of skimmed and semi-skimmed milk only partially offsetting a fall in whole milk consumption, a rapid rise in drinking of fruit juices, soft drinks and wine and finally an increase in eating out.

However, the British diet is still essentially based on bread, milk, meat, potatoes and beer. Although the changes have moved the average diet nearer to those of other European countries the differences are still large. In comparison the typical mainland European diet contains a higher component of fruit, vegetables, meat and wine whereas the UK diet has a stronger emphasis on cereals and dairy foods.

Questions

1 Use national statistical data (e.g. from the UK National Food Survey, *Social Trends*, NTC publications) to plot the consumption of a particular foodstuff over a ten-year period.

2   What has led to the increased demand for frozen foods and low fat spreads?
3   How does the British diet differ from the Italian diet? To what extent is this related to cultural factors or to climate?
4   Track the rise and fall in consumption of butter and margarine in the UK from 1940 until 1990.
    Identify the major factors which have influenced purchase patterns.
5   What, in your view, has led to the growth of speciality food sales from British supermarkets?

References

Actualidad Economica (1992) 'El coste de comer bien'. 5 April

Buss, D. (1991) The changing household diet. In *Fifty Years of the National Food Survey 1940–1990* (ed. J. M. Slater), HMSO, London

Chesher, A. (1991) Household composition and household food purchases. In *Fifty Years of the National Food Survey 1940–1990* (ed. J. M. Slater), HMSO, London

Euromonitor (1992) 'European marketing data and statistics'. In *European Marketing Pocket Book*, NTC Publications, Henley-on-Thames

Lifestyle Trends (1990) *Food and Drink*. NTC Publications in association with the Advertising Association, Henley-on-Thames.

MacLean, D. (1991) Food policy and the National Food Survey. In *Fifty Years of the National Food Survey 1940–1990* (ed. J. M. Slater), HMSO, London

New York Times (1992) 'Forget the Sauerbraten', 20 July

Pais (1992). 'Hoy cocino yo', 12 September

Ritson, C. and Hutchins, R. (1991) The consumption revolution. In *Fifty Years of the National Food Survey 1940–1990* (ed. J. M. Slater), HMSO, London

Senker, J. (1988) *A Taste for Innovation: British Supermarkets' Influence on Food Manufacturers*, Horton Publishing, Bradford

Wheelock, J. V. (1991) Coping with change in the food business. *Food Marketing*, **2**, 3

Whitehead, R. G. and Paul, A. A. (1990) Secular trends in food intake in Britain during the past 50 years

8 *Religion, cults and scares*

Introduction

People do not consume all those foods which potentially they could do. This may be because of deep-seated beliefs about certain foods which are enshrined in religious doctrines. Devout Jews will, for instance, avoid all pig meat, or any food such as some jellies, which in manufacture may have involved an extract of pork.

A cult is in some senses similar to a religion, in that it can cause restrictions on behaviour. In this chapter particular attention is paid to the growth of vegetarianism as an example of a cult which has had a significant impact on consumer purchase.

Another factor which can have a restrictive or enhancing effect on purchase is if a myth or fad becomes associated with a particular food. Consumers may come to believe a food has medicinal or enhancing properties, such as slimming products, when there is no evidence to support this. Or alternatively foods may be avoided as they are suspected of having adverse effects. In some cases there is a justification for the latter. Food scares are often based on scientific fact, although not always.

As well as being accepted or rejected, foods also fall within a hierarchy and hence have associated status. Meats, particularly in a raw uncooked state, are seen as high status, while vegetables are at the opposite end of the spectrum. Consumers can be affected in their purchase behaviour and in their acceptance within a meal structure of foods because of hierarchical status. Such status is also reflected in the cuisines of different nationalities throughout Europe.

This chapter therefore takes further a discussion of cultural influences on consumer behaviour with a particular focus on the effect of religion, cults, myths, hierarchies and scares related to food. These can have quite profound effects on consumption.

Meaning, symbolism and status

Different cultures communicate what they are and what they do through their use of food. Food therefore is an important medium to predict and understand people's behaviour. Obviously at the basic level food is necessary for nutritional reasons; no person can survive without an adequate amount and variety of nutrients.

However, food also serves other purposes. Eating food with others provides a mechanism to maintain interpersonal relationships. Drinking coffee, tea or wine has become the symbolic means by which people get to know each other and take the chance to gossip, show off, explore personal problems or deal with work issues.

The whole process by which food is given, received and eaten varies with the status of the people involved and with the occasion. There are subtle rules which determine what is eaten in what order. At the first level many foods are avoided. For instance, the dietary rules governing the Jewish meal originally forbad the Israelites to eat pig, camel, hare and hyrax. According to Mary Douglas (Douglas and Nicod, 1974) these rules are in turn part of a set of rules about worship and ritual cleanliness. Therefore the behaviour shown towards food is simply the outcome of a deeper set of religious beliefs.

Each culture, of which this is only one brief example, has its own criteria of what is acceptable to eat and its own rules about permitted sequences and combinations of food. A more elaborate example, but of the same basic kind, is illustrated in Nicod's analysis (Douglas and Nicod, 1974) of the structure of British meals, which separates between very structured meals eaten on particular occasions (e.g. Sunday dinner) and unstructured meals such as snacks or light meals. New products can be introduced as alternative unstructured meals but the Sunday meal has great symbolic value as an event to which family members gather and which cannot easily be altered in format.

This latter example also illustrates that food is used to communicate ceremony, ritual and the importance of an occasion. The quantity, quality and type of food eaten indicates what type of event it is. Roasted turkey or goose, special puddings or cakes indicate Christmas or Easter. The foods are usually expensive, exotic, scarce, highly preferred and require special cooking and serving.

Food is used for social status and social prestige and so particular foods such as caviar come to acquire high status. Lobster is a high status seafood served in virtually its natural state. On the other hand, pies and sausages are highly processed foods, far removed from their original state and generally perceived for this reason to have low status.

Food is also used to cope with psychological tensions and stresses. Compulsive eating helps to allay tensions for some people. Milk or alcoholic liquor may be used to make a person less 'tense' and to increase social interactions with others so as to reduce

---

Illustration 8.1 Ginger it up!

In the past three years imports of ginger into the UK have gone up by more than 60 per cent. The fashion for Thai food has sparked the trend but what seems to have sustained it is the realization ginger is a health food. Ten years ago students at an American college were given a capsule of powdered ginger, or a placebo, then spun in a rotating chair. Those with no ginger were sick in two and a half minutes. Those who had taken ginger lasted six minutes without feeling ill. Ginger has been found to contain an antibiotic, borneal, which combats fevers, high blood pressure and stimulates the circulation. Research in Denmark has shown it lessens the pain of inflammatory joint disease and cuts swelling. The dose prescribed was 12.5 g a day, mixed with jam or yoghurt.

Based on D. Hutchinson, 'Ginger joins garlic as the great cure all', *Daily Mail*, 21 December 1993, 31

tension. Sweets and drinks are commonly used to relieve boredom and to reward and comfort oneself. They can also be used to reward others. Many foods are also used to help prevent or cure illness. Garlic, for instance, is well known to contain antibiotic and so prevent illness.

However, similar almost magical properties can be assigned to other foods, such as ginger, as indicated in Illustration 8.1.

Religion

Many of the factors which shape food habits are derived from religious laws. These may take the form of restrictions or prohibitions, some of which are arbitrarily created merely to put a distance between that religious group and other people.

Roman Catholics and most Protestants believe that individual choice is the correct approach to eating. Given these are the dominant religions in most of Europe it means there are few religiously invoked restrictions on eating. On the other hand, Jews, Hindus and Muslims insist on strict dietary observance even when it means refusing food offered in friendship.

Briefly, the restrictions imposed by these religious groups is outlined in Table 8.1. Further detail and an extensive consideration of the impact of other religious restrictions on diet is given by Fieldhouse (1986).

Besides completely prohibiting some foods, religious groups also have time periods when consumption is restricted. Until recently Roman Catholics did not eat meat on Fridays, but in 1966 this law was changed to apply only to Fridays in Lent. In the Greek Orthodox church every Wednesday and Friday are fast days. Usually time restrictions apply to orthodox Jews and Greeks during fasting such that eating is restricted in the period between sunrise and sunset. Muslims fast during the month of Ramadan.

Judaism requires that ritual slaughter of animals ensures the maximum drainage of blood. Meat must be koshered before cooking by a complex process of soaking in water, salting and draining. Separate utensils then have to be used for meat and dairy products. Muslims also require ritual slaughter proceedings.

Food symbolism is paramount in the festivals of the Greek Orthodox Church. A great lent fast of 40 days precedes Easter and during this period animal foods cannot be

Table 8.1 *Major restrictions in the eating habits of religious groups*

	Jew	*Muslim*	*Sikh*	*Hindu*
Any animal	–	–	–	No
Beef	–	–	No	–
Pork	No	No	–	–
Blood	No	No	–	–
Fish with no scales or fins	No	–	–	–
Mixed meat and dairy food	No	–	–	–
Intoxicating liquor	No	No	–	–

eaten. On Maundy Thursday lambs are killed and prepared for the resurrection feast. Hard boiled eggs are cooked and dyed red to symbolize Christ's blood and broken up on Easter day to represent opening Christ's tomb.

For Jews the major feast is at Passover, commemorating the flight of the Israelites from Egypt, and the beginning of the spring harvest. Unleavened bread, called matzah, is used in the Passover and represents the fact the Jews did not have time to allow the bread to rise on the night they fled from Egypt. Many of the other foods have symbolic meaning, for example, horseradish represents the bitterness of slavery in Egypt, celery the poor diet of slavery. Matzah is broken to symbolize the parting of the Red Sea.

Amongst Hindus the caste system means there are many rules about who can eat with whom. Devout Hindus are vegetarians because of their belief in the sanctity of life. There are eighteen festivals at which special foods are eaten and in which food is spread to a wider population. Naturally these various religious taboos will have varying degrees of influence on the diet of the population throughout Europe.

Vegetarianism

A related phenomenon to religion, which can also cause restrictions on eating, is a cult. Here vegetarianism is explored as an example of a cult.

Vegetarianism takes on many of the dimensions of a religion. It is not just about food and eating but a statement about beliefs an individual has about their world, humanity and the relationship between man and animals.

The vegetarian ideal first emerged in ancient Greece. Pythagoras made a powerful statement on the virtues of vegetarianism: 'the earth affords a lavish supply of riches, of innocent foods, and offers you banquets which involve no bloodshed or slaughter'. The birth of modern vegetarianism was in the eighteenth century. Medical practitioners began to ascribe it with positive qualities. In 1809, for example, a Dr Lambe reported that a vegetarian diet, together with large quantities of distilled water, was good for tumours and ulcers. By 1847 the Vegetarian Society was founded in England and still exists today with a membership of 16 500 (Silverstone, 1993a)

Vegetarians perceive vegetarian food as alive and meat as dead and rotting and hence reverse the terminology usually applied to these foods. Vegetarianism reverses also the value traditionally given to cooking as evidence of our civilized, non-animal state. Rawness is seen as the desirable and natural organic state.

The most restrictive category of vegetarians are fructarians who only eat fruit, nuts and certain vegetables where harvesting allows the parent plant to survive. Vegans eat neither eggs nor dairy produce and to varying degrees avoid all animal by-products. Lacto-ovo-vegetarians eat both eggs and dairy products while lacto-vegetarians will eat dairy products but do not eat eggs. The most recent group to emerge is demi-vegetarians who eat a predominantly vegetarian diet but will occasionally eat fish and poultry. A variation of this seems to be people who switch between vegetarian and normal diets depending on who they are with and their mood.

Vegetarianism seems to evoke two contrasting perceptions. The first is that such a diet is nutritionally deficient and leads to weak, pallid people incapable of work. This view is reinforced by the Victorian image of red meat as synonymous with virility and strength. The alternative view, supported by much modern research, is that the vegetarian diet is healthy with high fibre and low fat content leading to an incidence

Table 8.2 *The population of vegetarians in the UK*

% population	1984	1993
Vegetarian	2.1	4.3
Eat less meat	30.0	40.0
Male vegetarians	1.6	3.2
Female vegetarians	2.6	5.4

Source: Vegetarian Society, 1993; Silverstone, 1993b

Table 8.3 *Age distribution of the UK vegetarian population*

Age group	% vegetarian
15 – 17	14
18 – 34	7
35 plus	5

Source: NOP, November 1992; Silverstone, 1993b.

of coronorary heart disease which is 30–50 per cent lower than that experienced by omnivores (Silverstone, 1993a).

The most authoritative analysis of vegetarianism in the UK by the Gallup Realeat poll, covering 4,000 adults, shows a doubling in number of vegetarians over the past decade, with a substantial proportion of the population moving towards a demi-vegetarian status. This trend is likely to increase given the highest percentage of vegetarians are young people (see Tables 8.2, 8.3). These trends are reflected in growing retail sales, with specialist vegetarian foods valued at £308 million in 1992. Sales in the UK of meat alternatives such as tofu, quorn and TVP trebled between 1988 and 1992.

Food myths and fads

Myths are simply repetitions of a story which may or may not have a factual base. Some myths about food seem to have their origin in malicious rumour. When machinery first replaced labour in the canning industry unemployed workers spread rumours that the acid used in cans produced with a soldering machine poisoned the contents. It helped to build a strong prejudice against cans (Fieldhouse, 1986).

Other myths derive from a group wishing to see itself as separate from others. Horseflesh is readily eaten in France and in several other cultures, and there appears to be no nutritional reason why not. Antagonism to it may have arisen from the fact that in the eighth century the then Pope ordered his emissary to the Germans to forbid the consumption of horseflesh because the pagans ate it. In the eighteenth century widespread starvation conditions in France caused people to eat horse flesh and it is estimated that now one-third of French people eat horseflesh, although the practice is mainly urban-centred and working-class orientated.

Some myths appear to have a quasi-scientific basis. Fish is thought to be a brain food and indeed it is a good source of dietary potassium which is found in large quantitites in brain cells. However, the link between fish eating and braininess has not been established scientifically.

Modern food faddism has revived the notion that food can be a medicine. Fieldhouse (1986) identifies three reasons why such fads arise; a particular food has a virtue which is exaggerated and said to cure disease (e.g. garlic); a food should be avoided because of so-called harmful properties (e.g. white bread, sugar); a food has natural properties (e.g. organic vegetables). Dr Kellogg's cornflakes were known as 'Elijah's manna' when first produced and admired for their technological and hence spiritual purity. Two most recent examples of faddism are the interest in health foods (considered in Chapter 6) and in slimming products.

Food scares

Related to myths about food which can persist are scares which may suddenly blow up and then die down again. Some are related to genuine, proved problems of food safety. In 1992 there were 65 000 cases of food poisoning in the UK, 11 000 more than in 1991. In the case of a number of scares, however, although there may be an element of a public health problem, the story may become exaggerated and have a disproportionate effect on buyer behaviour.

One of the most significant recent scares was that triggered in 1988 by a UK government minister, Edwina Currie, who virtually admitted that eggs could be contaminated with salmonella and thus cause food poisoning. Sales fell dramatically and took two years to recover. In a similar way the UK government was shaken by concerns over patulin levels in apple juice (Illustration 8.2).

Another problem was caused by listeria found in some pâtés and soft cheeses, particularly those imported to the UK from France. In elderly people it can cause meningitis and in pregnant women miscarriages or stillbirths. BSE, bovine spongiform encephalopathy, is caused by an infection that attacks the brain of cattle. It is believed cows are infected by eating animal feed containing the remains of brain-diseased sheep. An estimated 100 000 cows have contracted the disease, which has only a very slight chance of being passed to humans.

However, while the problems of BSE have been played down by authorities in the UK, in 1994 the German govenment attempted to ban the import of beef from the UK because of the risk of BSE, as outlined in Illustration 8.3.

In England and Wales 400 cases of *Escherichia coli*, many from contaminated beefburgers, were reported in 1992, compared with 77 in 1987 (*Which?* 1993).

Scares such as those have caused people to avoid the purchase of several foodstuffs leading to a slump in sales from which the product has not recovered in some cases. One analysis is carried out for a women's magazine shows that a comparatively high percentage of foodstuffs are avoided by women in the UK (Table 8.4).

Illustration 8.2 Apple juice

The first 'food scare' of 1993 hit the headlines in a big way in February:

> 'Juice scare shakes Tories to the core'
> 'Apple juice is safe from cancer risk, says Food Minister'

On the face of it, the scare concerned a mycotoxin, patulin, which is produced by a mould growing on apples. Routine surveillance by the Ministry of Agriculture Fisheries and Food (MAFF) had shown that patulin levels were higher in apple juice of the 1990s than they had been in the 1980s. 'Extreme' consumers of cloudy short-life juices could possibly exceed the Provisional Tolerable Weekly Intake which had been set by JECFA (FAO/WHO's advisory committee). The results were drawn to the attention of the Department of Health's Committee on Toxicity (COT) and MAFF's Food Advisory Committee (FAC), who both recommended that Ministers should seek industry cooperation in reducing levels of patulin to the lowest level technologically achievable (50 g/kg). They also advised Ministers to give advice to the public to avoid eating mouldy apples, but it was decided that this was best done in a Food Sense leaflet about a range of natural toxicants in foods and that the apple juice issue did not require a special publicity initiative.

The 'core' of the problem was that the patulin results gave a wonderful opportunity for consumerists and pressure groups to question why the government was working 'hand in glove' with the industry 'behind closed doors', rather than taking immediate action to safeguard consumers. The perceived impact of any food-related issue is the sum of the severity of the hazard and the outrage attached to it.[1] Enormous outrage was attached to this minimal hazard probably because of its potential effect on a vulnerable sector of the population, i.e. children.

It is pertinent to contrast the government handling of the apple juice scare, i.e. to crush it completely and immediately, with the way it handled the vitamin A in liver hazard.[2] In the latter case, the severity of the hazard to pregnant women consuming too much liver and therefore risking birth defects was considered quite high and so the government actively encouraged media coverage of the issue. The correct message was then more likely to be taken on board by the appropriate vulnerable group.

In the case of apple juice, the government sensibly concluded that the risks to the general public of drinking apple juice were *not* sufficient to outweigh the benefits of encouraging people to eat more fruits and vegetables and to drink their juices, as a consistent nutritional message.

Perhaps some important lessons can be learned from this scare. The effect of other food scares, e.g. salmonella in eggs in 1988 and BSE in beef in 1990, made MAFF crucially aware of its public image. Among other initiatives, the Consumer Panel was set up. Some government attempt to involve and reassure this Panel about the proposed action on patulin and apple juice might have prevented this 'storm in an apple juice carton'. Perhaps the 'publicly available' summaries of decisions reached by the FAC could also be made more consumer-friendly to allay, rather than increase, the suspicions of the pressure groups?

[1] Ashwell, M. (1991) Consumer perception of food-related issues. *BNF Nutr. Bull.*, **61**, 230–35
[2] Conning, D. M. (1991) Vitamin A in pregnancy. *BNF Nutr. Bull.*, **61**, 3–4

Based on M. Ashwell (1993) Apple juice scare, *BNF Nutr. Bull.*, **18**, 90–1

Illustration 8.3 BSE in Europe

BSE was discovered with the first case confirmed in 1985. Yet it took nearly three years for the Ministry of Agriculture, Fisheries and Food (MAFF) to declare the disease notifiable and to ban the use of animal proteins in cattle food, and a further year before some beef offal including brains, stomach and spleen, was banned from human food.

Consumer confidence fell sharply, with a dramatic drop in beef sales and some local education authorities withdrawing beef from school menus.

But now beef sales have bounced back and anxiety has receded. The government insists that matters are rapidly improving, the trend of BSE is on the decline and it is business as usual.

Such comfort coming from the UK government is, however, at odds with the European view. Earlier in 1993 the European Parliament in Strasbourg examined, and supported, a highly respected report on BSE from a Portuguese MEP, Vasco Garcia. As a result the Parliament demanded a series of new measures – more research, better controls on animal feed, stricter checks at abattoirs – as part of a Community-wide campaign to combat the disease.

Garcia's report identified the problem as being very much a 'British' disease, with over 60 000 cases reported to date, but that other countries had started to show significant numbers of cases too: Northern Ireland (337 cases), Ireland (46), Switzerland (10), France (5) plus several cases outside Europe.

The European Parliament backs the view that the abrupt outbreak of BSE can be traced back to a specific matter. It believes that the disease was catalysed by changes in the manufacturing of cattle feed. In the late 1970s the main rendering plant in the south of England which processes abattoir 'waste' into food to be fed back to cattle changed its system from a solvent-based, high temperature method to the less costly continuous sterilization method. This change may have mattered little were it not for a second potential hazard. It is thought that many of the sheep carcasses being rendered were infected with a disease, scrapie, which is similar to BSE. To make matters worse, before the government's 1988 ban came into effect, the remains of cows which had died from BSE were being recycled back into cattle feed.

The British government, too, believes that the cause of BSE was contaminated feed, and because all such feed was banned in 1988 the disease can be expected to tail off by the year 2000, once the maximum 8–9 year incubation period is passed.

But, as Garcia points out, the ban did not apply to exports. 'Between 1987 and 1989 the UK had already disposed of between 30 000 and 40 000 tonnes of possibly contaminated feed in France,' he reveals. So France (given the incubation period) may now face the prospect of more cases of BSE from now until at least the end of 1995.

While Garcia accepts the British government's belief that BSE will peter out by 2000 and not affect humans, he stresses it is far too early to be complacent. There is still a possibility of the transmissibility of BSE to other animal species, from which humans cannot be totally excluded.

Garcia also considers two more possibilities. The first is that there could be vertical transmission from cow to calf. This would prolong the disease for a few years and it may have to be controlled through slaughtering. The second is that

BSE could be transmitted horizontally by contact. In this case the disease could become endemic.

Despite the UK government's repeated assurances that it has BSE under control, the responses of other European governments is far from confident. Several appear to have no faith in the UK's ability to control BSE: Germany, for example, continues its ban on certain UK beef imports and demands BSE-free certification for others. World-wide, British beef continues to be banned in nearly 30 countries.

British farmers themselves have not helped the situation. The government's figures for BSE now show over 400 cattle developing the disease even though they were born after the ban on infectious cattle feed was in place. The ministry believes this is due to farmers continuing to use old stocks of cattle feed, a suggestion that does not inspire confidence.

Based on J. Blythman 'A myth rammed down our throats', *Independent*, 6 February 1993

Table 8.4 *Types of food avoided by women, 1990).*

Food avoided	(% of adults)
Beef	38
Eggs	37
Pâté	35
Chilled-cooked food	31
Tapwater	19
Chicken	18

Source: Today, 11 June 1990

Eating disorders

There appears to have been a real increase in eating disorders in the past 100 years. Up until the eighteenth century the upper classes often distinguished themselves from the lower classes by the sheer quantity of food consumed. From this time onwards social distinction came to be expressed through quality and refinement of cooking rather than simple quantity of food consumed.

In the nineteenth century the value of moderation was beginning to be expressed although the lower class were still being encouraged to the view that a plump figure was an ideal. The problem and fear of fatness did not really get a grip until the twentieth century. The increase in expected self-control with respect to appetite appears to have created social pressures which, in turn, have led to the growth of eating disorders such as anorexia and bulimia. Such disorders appear to be most prevalent in modern industrial countries amongst young, white, affluent women.

Studies of women's magazines and *Playboy* magazine centrefolds show that the mean weights of the 'ideal' women portrayed are less than the average weight of women in the population. These ideal weights also dropped in the period between 1959 and 1979. At the same time, however, the average body weight of women in 1979 was heavier than in 1958. In other words, the average weight of the population is increasing at the same time that pressures to be slim are getting greater and the size of the 'ideal woman' is getting smaller (Mennel *et al.*, 1992).

In the past 100 years the majority of people in Western Europe have acquired the means to be plump which has resulted in social status being acquired by being thin! Thinness was adopted as an ideal first by upper social groups and has spread to lower groups. Research has established that the majority of women in Western culture, probably as many as 80–90 per cent, constantly monitor their daily calorie intake. What is interesting is that what is considered socially accepted and normal eating behaviour has many of the characteristics of the abnormal. One survey showed 11.6 per cent of women often engaged in fattening food binges. Bulimic behaviour may therefore only be an extreme version of normal behaviour as women switch in and out of extreme concern with 'thinness'. Some writers have argued that the modern phenomenon of food disorders is a direct result of an emerging conflict for women caught between emancipation and caring for others (Mennell, Murcott, van Otterloo, 1992).

Food hierarchies

Food exists as part of a hierarchy which may relate to particular food items, to whole cuisines and to the elements which make up a meal. At one extreme some sorts of eating are considered revolting even though there may be no obvious nutritional reason for avoidance. Cannibalism is despised, but we also have a more subtle hierarchy of things we will eat. People live with pets which could be eaten and on the other hand have very little contact with wild animals such as lions. Our degree of closeness seems to affect what animals are considered as food. Cows and sheep are domesticated but do not live with humans and so fit the bill. The family pet dog on the other hand is sufficiently humanized that eating it would be equivalent to an act of cannibalism. Of those meats we do eat Western society demonstrates a hierarchy of foods of which raw, red meat has the highest status. However, meat is rarely ever eaten in that state. This illustrates a familiar anthropological concept which is that the object of highest status is also taboo; the highest prized can simultaneously be the most defiling (Mennell *et al.*, 1992).

Usually meat is eaten in a cooked state although sometimes only just cooked. After raw meat the highest status foods are 'red' meats such as steak and roast beef, which are often only lightly cooked and in what Lévi-Strauss called a semi-raw state. Lower down are bloodless or white meats such as chicken and fish. Below them are 'abnormal' products such as eggs or cheese. High status items figure as the centrepiece of meals although eggs and cheese can be the centrepiece of lighter meals or snacks. On the lowest level are vegetables, which to most except vegetarians are not sufficient to form a meal alone and are simply additions to a main item.

The highest items in the hierarchy are those associated with blood and nearness to the raw state of the animal. Blood is associated with strength, virility, aggression and power. Meat is for many the most highly regarded food because of the strength and passion it represents. Victorian training diets for boxers had an almost exclusive emphasis on meat. Even today astronauts have a pre-flight steak.

Red meat is macho and sexual but therefore overpowering to the sickly. Victorian and Edwardian invalid diets included chicken or white fish. Invalids needed delicate food and red meat was thought too strong. Intertwined with notions of strength, some red meats are simply too powerful for anyone to eat. Usually in this category are meats from carnivores or uncastrated animals such as lions or bulls. Somehow both these categories are too strong or tainted, even though there is no nutritional reason for their avoidance.

This categorization, proposed by Twigg (1983), makes it apparent there is a hierarchy of foods to which all people respond. Not all available meats are eaten by anyone. Vegetarians take this process further and move down the hierarchy to foods which they do feel able to eat. The first items to be given up are red meats followed by poultry then fish. A true vegan cannot eat animal products of any kind.

National cuisine

Cuisines also illustrate elements of a hierarchy, with some being perceived as more superior to others. Mennell (1985) has argued that the emergence of national cuisines broadly mirrored the emergence of national states in most of Western Europe. However, fundamental differences have evolved in the cuisine of France and England in particular. The French tradition of haute cuisine essentially grew out of the emergence of court society. Aristocratic life centred on the royal court and French nobles became more and more like royal slaves in constant attendance. Social display, courtly intrigue, affectation and conspicuous consumption became the primary means of self-expression rather than power and influence achieved in governing the country. On the other hand in England the Civil War shifted the balance of power away from the sovereign and courtiers and towards the class of landed gentry who gained political power. The argument is that these differences were reflected in the French preference for elaborate dishes which took time and money to prepare, in contrast to the simple meals and puddings of the English. The model for the English diet was that of the country gentry living off simple but abundant food from the land. The model for the French style of cuisine became the elaborate sauces and methods of preparation familiar at the royal court.

Dutch domestic cookery shows a thrift and simplicity more reminiscent of England than of France or Belgium. The simple amount of food available to different social groups persisted until the turn of the century since when qualitative differences have been apparent. Over-eating is now a problem in lower social groups, whereas vegetarianism and suspicion of the food industry and its products has grown amongst upper social groups in Holland.

In Germany regional culinary preferences have predominated rather than a particular national cuisine.

Meal structure

The structure of meals also demonstrates the concept of hierarchy, with certain food items attaining particular status in the pattern of a meal.

Murcott (1983) has studied what is meant by a 'proper' meal eaten by men and women living in South Wales over ten years ago. Women easily agreed both what was in the meal and how it should be cooked for it to count as a proper meal. Meat in the form of fresh flesh was the centrepiece. Chicken or turkey were acceptable. Potatoes were essential together with one other vegetable which had to be green. Two or three other vegetables might also be available and gravy poured over all the items on the plate. The meat had to be roasted or grilled and vegetables boiled.

Roasting was considered particularly important for Sundays, holidays or banquets when both meat and vegetables are roasted. What was not 'proper' were meals prepared quickly or not cooked, such as raw salads. A real cooked dinner was associated with a long preparation and regular attention during the cooking process.

Cooking is a particularly human characteristic which, besides softening the food or combining ingredients so it is easier to eat and digest, also explains a paradox according to anthropologists such as Lévi-Strauss. We are human so need to eat, but we consume food in the very way animals cannot, so as to differentiate ourselves, because we cook it.

Conclusion

The foods people buy and consume are strongly affected by the beliefs associated with them. Some foods are avoided altogether because of taboos. Religious doctrine can also lead to avoidance, and hence the growth of specialist retail outlets selling, for instance, only kosher food. A related phenonomenon of the cult, illustrated by the growing interest in vegetarianism, demonstrates the strong impact this can have on food consumption, with the development of restaurants and foodshops specializing in vegetarian foods.

Food is often assigned characteristics and qualities which may or may not be valid. The many slimming products on the market illustrate the point, although few have been shown to have a consistent effect on weight loss. On the other hand, some food such as garlic does have proved medicinal powers. The reverse is also true. Occasionally there are food scares triggered by the supposed harmful effects of food. Sometimes this is proved, in other cases not. The British government, for instance, believe that there is no risk of BSE-infected cattle causing illness to people. The Germans think otherwise and have tried to block imports of British beef to Germany.

Cuisines, foods within a meal, and the foods themselves all illustrate the concept of hierarchy. The French cuisine with its aristocratic origins is generally considered higher status than English cuisine. Some form of meat is usually the centrepiece of a meal while other elements such as vegetables have a lower status. Raw, uncooked meat is of higher status than other foods.

Taboos, religious doctrines, cults, scares and the status of different foods can thus all have a considerable impact on food consumption.

Questions

1   What changes in food supplied by major retailers would you say are due to current food cults or fads?

2   In what way do the cultural norms of college life cause the eating habits of college students to differ from those of middle-aged housewives?

3   In what way has the changing cultural climate *vis-à-vis* women affected the types of food product available and the way in which such products are advertised?

4   Give examples of the effect food has on mood, state of mind, behaviour.

5   Give examples of foods which have a symbolic meaning.

6   What foods would you say are masculine, feminine, or only for children?

7   Give examples of any foods which you believe have medicinal properties.

8   What foods do you eat when stressed?

9   Give examples of foods associated with prestige or status.

10 Think of a particular brand of food with which you are familiar. What type of personality would you say this brand would have if it were to come alive?

11 In what way is food used as a way of communicating with other people?

12 What is the typical structure of British meals? How do these vary during the day and week?

13 How do you account for the rise in vegetarianism in the UK? Is the same true of other European countries?

14 Create your own status hierarchy for different forms of cooking.

15 Identify a recent food scare and research both how it started and public and government reaction to it.

References

Douglas, M. and Nicod, M. (1974) Taking the biscuit: the structure of British meals. *New Society*, **30**, 744–7

Fieldhouse, P. (1986) *Food and Nutrition: Customs and Culture*, Croom Helm, London

Mennell, S. (1985) *All Manners of Food: Eating and Taste in England and France from the Middle Ages to the Present*, Blackwell, Oxford

Mennell, S., Murcott, A., Otterloo, A. H. van (1992) *The Sociology of Food*, Sage, London

Murcott, A. (ed.) (1983) *The Sociology of Food and Eating*, Gower, Aldershot

Silverstone, R. (1993a) Vegetarianism – food for the future. *Nut. Food Sci.*, **6**, 20–4

Silverstone, R. (1993b) *Healthy Eating*, Macmillan, London

Twigg, J. (1983) 'Vegetarianism and the meaning of meat'. In *The Sociology of Food and Eating* (ed. A. Murcott), Gower, Aldershot

Which? (1993) 'How safe is your food?', June

9 Demography

Introduction

One of the over-riding influences on consumption patterns is the size and make-up of the population. How many people are there now? How many will there be? Where are they living now and where is it likely they will live in future? What is the current and future age distribution? What is the size and make-up of different households? How many people are working or not working?

The study of population or demography makes it possible to divide the total mass of people into groups with relatively similar characteristics. The assumption is that those in each group will have similar purchase behaviour.

A study of population and how it is changing is of key importance in understanding the total market and segments of it. Unlike some aspects of consumer behaviour it is also relatively predictable in the sense that once a person is born it is possible to make predictions of their lifespan. Once the records of millions of individuals are put together it is possible to count the current population size and make-up, and to make predictions of the future population size and make-up.

This chapter considers key attributes of current and future demography in member states of the EU, and from this makes projections about the impact on food consumption.

Birthrate

A key variable affecting population size and structure is the birthrate, which is the number of live births per 1000 population in a given year. In the EU the overall birthrate has dropped in this century. In the early 1980s the birthrate in some members of the EU fell to around 10 per 1000 live births (Denmark and West Germany), whereas in others, particularly Catholic countries, the rate was much higher. For example, in Ireland the birthrate in 1984 was 18.1 per 1000 and in Portugal 14.2. Linked to this are obviously other social and legal dimensions such as a ban on contraception and divorce and the age structure of the population which affects the number of people of childbearing age. However, data in Table 9.1 show that some of these trends have recently been reversed, with a fall in live births in countries such as Ireland, Portugal and Greece but an increase in the UK, Denmark and West Germany.

Table 9.1 *Birthrate: live births per 1000, 1984 and 1989*

	1984	Rising 1989		1984	Falling 1989
Belgium	11.7	12.2	France	13.9	13.7
Denmark	10.1	12.0	Spain	12.3	10.6
Germany	9.5	11.0	Greece	12.7	9.8
Luxembourg	11.5	12.3	Ireland	18.1	14.7
The Netherlands	12.1	12.7	Italy	10.5	9.9
UK	12.9	13.6	Portugal	14.2	11.5

Source : European Marketing, 1992.

Total population

The current population of each EU country is measured by census data. The overall size of the population is 328 million. After 200 years of population growth the size of the EU is more or less static and is expected to stay so. The only factors likely to change these projections are unknown catastrophies, such as war or epidemics, or a sudden and dramatic change in attitudes to childbirth (Table 9.2).

Given the recent political changes in eastern Europe, another unknown is the level of immigration to countries of the EU.

Although the overall population of the EU is expected to remain static, because of differences in economic status, in social attitudes towards childbearing, and the proportion of women of childbearing age in the different members of the EU, the population projections for the next twenty to twenty-five years show considerable differences between different countries.

Forecasts of the population size over the next twenty-five to thirty years vary slightly according to the source and hence the assumptions made about rates of birth and death. Some of the variation in estimates is also a consequence of whether numbers are included for emigration or immigration.

Table 9.2 *Population of countries of the European Union, 1990 (millions)*

Belgium	9.8	Italy	57.7
Denmark	5.2	Luxembourg	0.4
France	56.4	The Netherlands	14.9
W. Germany	63.1	Portugal	10.6
Greece	10.1	Spain	39.0
Ireland	3.5	UK	57.4

Source: OECD

Table 9.3 *Population projections for countries of the European Union – percentage change*

	Eurostat 1995/2015	UN 1990/2020	Euromarketing 1995/2020
Belgium	−5.0	−0.1	−6.0
Denmark	−3.9	−1.9	−3.4
France	+3.1	+6.7	+4.0
W. Germany	−8.6	−10.8	−7.0
Spain	+2.5	+7.7	−4.0
Greece	+4.6	+1.0	+5.0
Ireland	+14.8	+37.7	−4.0
Italy	−5.5	−3.2	−7.0
Luxembourg	0	−4.3	+3.2
The Netherlands	+2.5	+2.2	+10.0
Portugal	+3.0	+5.3	+2.5
UK	+2.6	+0.4	+6.0

Source: Eurostat and government statistical offices; UN world population prospects (1988 base); Euromarketing, 1992.

Future estimates indicate an indigenous population for the European Union as constituted in 1994 of around 325–330 million. This may be inflated slightly by a net inflow of people from eastern Europe and from further afield in the world.

Overall the forecasts agree that the populations of Belgium, Denmark, West Germany and Italy are in decline. Obviously the case of Germany is affected by recent unification. On the other hand, the populations of France, The Netherlands, Portugal, Greece and the UK are on the increase. Less clear is the case of Ireland. Some estimates show Ireland has the highest level of growth of any member state, others a marginal decline. Similarly the population of Spain is on the increase in most estimates but in decline in one. In Luxembourg the population appears to be more or less static.

Overall the scenario developed from Eurostat information is most likely to apply. The consequences in different countries are identified in Table 9.3 and show slight falls in population in Belgium, Denmark and Italy but slight rises in France, Spain, Greece, The Netherlands, Portugal and the UK. In what was West Germany the population is projected to fall more dramatically and in Ireland to rise dramatically.

Age structure

At the same time as there are significant variations in population growth between one country and another, in some ways the more significant change in terms of the impact on consumer behaviour is the change in age structure of the population in different member states. Overall the population of the EU is getting older. In the UK the population in 1985 contained four times as many people over 60 as in 1911. Between

Table 9.4 *Age structure of countries of the European Union, percentages in 1990*

	0–14 %	15–34 %	35–49 %	50–64 %	65 + %
Belgium	18	30	20	17	15
Denmark	17	30	22	15	16
France	20	30	20	16	14
Germany	15	31	20	19	15
Spain	20	32	18	16	13
Greece	21	29	19	18	13
Ireland	28	31	18	12	11
Italy	17	31	20	18	15
Luxembourg	17	30	21	18	13
The Netherlands	18	33	22	15	13
Portugal	21	32	18	16	13
UK	19	30	20	16	16

Source: Eurostat

1961 and 1985 the number increased by 2.5 million and is expected to increase by a further 2 million by 2015.

A major reason why the population of countries like Ireland will continue to grow is because there is a higher percentage of younger people under 14 (28 per cent) compared with say West Germany (15 per cent). On the other hand, the percentage of people over 65 in Denmark and the UK is 16 per cent compared with 11 per cent in

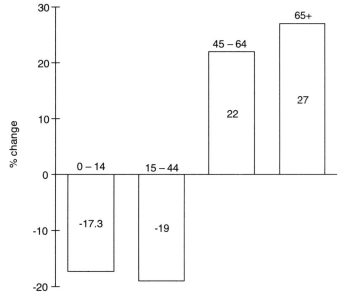

Figure 9.1 *Changes in population structure within the European Union, 1995–2020. (Based on data from European Marketing, 1992)*

Table 9.5   *Percentage shift in age structure of the population between 1990 and 2020*

Age	15–44	65 +
Belgium	−24	+24
Denmark	−18	+21
France	−13	+36
W. Germany	−26	+26
Spain	−23	+18
Greece	−8	+22
Ireland	−17	+40
Italy	−30	+32
Luxembourg	−14	+37
The Netherlands	−13	+50
Portugal	−21	+30
UK	−7	+18

Source: Euromarketing, 1992.

Ireland. However, in both cases these effects may not persist. Emigration from Ireland has traditionally been high and the reunification of Germany will have a significant influence on population structure.

The shift in the population structure within the European Union in the next twenty-five years is quite dramatic. Overall there is a sharp decline in the number of younger people under 45 and a corresponding increase in the number of people over this age (Figure 9.1).

By 2020 there will be more people over 65 than under 14; an extra 15 million over 65 compared with now.

In some countries the increase in the older population compared with the current base will be particularly significant. In The Netherlands there will be a 50 per cent rise in the number of people over 65 by the year 2020 compared with 1990. For Ireland the comparable figure will be 40 per cent. The changes will be less dramatic in countries such as Spain and the UK, with an 18 per cent increase (see Table 9.5). On the other hand, the decline in the number of young people, aged between 15 and 44, will be more significant in Italy (30 per cent) than Greece (8 per cent).

Household size

The number of households in the EU increased from 114 million in 1977 to 128 million in 1990. However, this is not due to any significant increase in population size but mainly because average household size has decreased in the same period, from 2.77 to 2.56. This is due to a variety of reasons; the higher number of older and younger people who live alone; the breakdown of the traditional nuclear family and hence more single parents, and increased affluence so that people may choose not to live with others.

Table 9.6 *Average household size in countries of the European Union*

Belgium	2.6
Denmark	2.3
Germany	2.2
Greece	3.0
Spain	3.7
France	2.7
Ireland	3.4
Italy	2.8
Luxembourg	2.7
The Netherlands	2.5
Portugal	3.2
UK	2.6

Source: Government statistical offices, 1990

The average household size is also linked to the age structure of the population and to the effects of cultural and religious differences. Particularly in countries in southern Europe people traditionally live in larger social groupings (e.g. Spain, Portugal, Greece), whereas in northern Europe the average household size is smaller (e.g. Denmark, Germany). Household size is also high in Ireland, perhaps due to traditional cultural and religious reasons or to economic factors (see Table 9.6).

The proportion of people living in single households is highest in those same countries (Denmark, Germany) and correspondingly low in southern European

Table 9.7 *Single households as percentage of total households in countries of the European Union, 1989*

Belgium	25.6
Denmark	34.0
Germany	35.3
Spain	10.5
Greece	17.4
France	24.7
Ireland	20.6
Italy	22.5
Luxembourg	23.1
The Netherlands	28.5
Portugal	13.8
UK	26.0

Source: European Marketing, 1992.

Table 9.8   *Changing trends in household type in the UK*

Household type	1971 (%)	1990 (%)
1 adult aged 16–59	5	10
2 adults aged 16–59	14	15
2 adults, youngest child aged 0–4	18	13
2 adults, youngest child aged 5–15	21	16
3 adults	13	12
2 adults, both over 60	17	17
1 adult 60 +	12	16

Source: OPCS.

countries (Spain and Portugal). In the former countries over one-third of households consist of one person (Table 9.7). In every country except Greece and Ireland the largest group of single households consists of females over 65.

More detailed analysis of the changing trends in household size in the UK (Table 9.8) indicates that as well as an increase in the number of old people living alone there is also a trend amongst younger adults to live alone, with a corresponding decrease in the number of households made up of the traditional nuclear family of two adults with children.

There are differences in household size within a country related to ethnic background. For instance, over half the households in the UK with a Bangladeshi or Pakistani as head contain five or more people compared with only 10 per cent amongst white ethnic groups. Similarly a much lower percentage of West Indians or Asians who live in the UK live in one-person households (*Social Trends*, 1992).

Working and non-working population

The proportion of the civilian population available for work varies from 56 per cent in Denmark to 37 per cent in Ireland (Somers, 1991) (Table 9.9). Obviously this is partially related to the age structure of the population.

Table 9.9   *Percentage of civilian population available for work within the European Union*

Belgium	42	Ireland	37
Denmark	56	Italy	41
Germany	47	Luxembourg	43
Greece	N/A	The Netherlands	44
Spain	38	Portugal	45
France	42	UK	50

Source: Somers, 1991.

One of the major social and economic trends in the past quarter of a century is the increased participation of women in the workforce. This is a trend expected to increase but again varies from country to country. Currently it is highest in the UK, at around 50 per cent (Somers, 1991).

Another factor which obviously has an influence on employment is the economic situation. Unemployment figures fluctuate, but across the EU the figure in 1990 was 9.8 per cent, with a high level in Spain (18.6 per cent) and low in West Germany (6.3 per cent) (Somers, 1991).

Demographic profiles

Briefly the overall characteristics of five of the largest EU member states are considered here.

Germany

The population of the former West Germany decreased after 1975 and only recently got back up to the 1975 level of 62 million. A further 16.7 million live in East Germany making the reunified country the biggest by far in the EU (78.7 million). Of these, 4.6 million are foreigners, many unemployed and including one million emigrants from eastern Europe who have been integrated since the dissolution of communism.

By 2040 the population aged over 65 will increase from 25 per cent of the active population (15–64 years old) to 40 per cent.

A relatively high proportion of the population (47 per cent) are in the labour force.

Spain

The population of 39.2 million has a relatively young profile at present but is changing to an older one in common with other EU countries. The large proportion of young people in the population looking for jobs, and the desire by women to find jobs, has created high levels of unemployment (22 per cent in 1985). However, the integration of women into the workforce is still relatively low (30 per cent in 1990) compared with, say, the UK (51 per cent).

The GDP per capita was only 76 per cent of the EU average in 1990, indicating that the Spanish economy creates a standard of living which is below the average for the remainder of Europe.

France

The French population of 56 million is growing only slowly, at 0.5 per cent per annum. This is due to the fact that despite government incentives the number of children born in each family is 1.8.

The population is ageing, so that by 2000 20 per cent will be over 60 and 26 per cent by 2040.

There is a relatively high participation rate by women, who represent 46 per cent of the labour force, many involved with part-time work.

Italy

The Italian population and economy moved rapidly from an agricultural base in the 1950s to an industrial one by the 1980s. The population is similar to that of the UK and France, at 58 million. Development is uneven between the prosperous north–central area and the poverty-stricken and crime-ridden southern half of the country where unemployment is high.

Overall 41 per cent of the population is engaged in the labour force with particularly low representation by women in the south (25 per cent) where per capita income was 55 per cent of that in the north in 1987.

UK

With the exception of Denmark, the UK has the highest proportion (50 per cent) of the total population (57 million) in work and the highest participation by women (51 per cent).

Conclusion

Demography is concerned with an examination of changes in population size and structure over a period of time. It enables fairly accurate forecasts to be made for the future which are important in order to predict likely purchase and consumption patterns.

In the European Union the overall birthrate has dropped over the past century. Currently there is some increase from a relatively low base in countries such as the UK, Denmark and Germany but a decline from a higher base in countries such as Ireland, and Portugal. The net effect is that the population of the current European Union (1994) is static and will remain at between 325 and 330 million for the next twenty to twenty-five years. However, within a fairly static overall population there is a relatively slow increase in population in some countries (e.g. UK and France) but continued decline in others (Denmark and Italy).

The one factor which may cause an unknown effect on population size is immigration, particularly from eastern Europe and from north Africa. Within Europe there may also continue to be population movement, for instance, out of Ireland to mainland Britain.

A somewhat more significant trend is the increasing average age of the population throughout Europe. In future there will be a sharp decline in the number of people aged less than 45 and an increase in those over this age. By 2020 there will be more people aged over 65 than aged under 14. In total the number of people in Europe over 65 will increase by 15 million by 2020. The number of households in Europe has increased to 128 million due mainly to a decrease in the average household size to 2.6. It is higher in the poorer countries of Europe, such as Portugal and Ireland. On the other hand in countries such as Germany and Denmark more than 30 per cent of households contain a single person only. Many are older women but there is a growing trend for young people to live alone.

The population available for work varies from 37 per cent in Ireland to 56 per cent in Denmark. An increasing trend is for more women to join the labour force, often to undertake part-time work. However, this is still most common in the UK. By comparison, participation by women in the workforce is still very low in countries such as Spain or the poorer, southern part of Italy.

The overall trends are therefore a static population; a sharp decline in the teenage market; growth in the middle aged market of people aged 45–64 and the older market of the 65+; a continued decrease in household size; increased participation by women in the workforce; growth in ethnic populations.

These trends have implications for patterns of food consumption. The static population but increased affluence is likely to mean a continuation of the decline in the proportion of expenditure committed to food. People in the 45–64-year-old age bracket attain their highest level of income, and since this age group is to increase in numbers, it will lead to increased demand for high quality, luxury and speciality items. Since this group is also likely to take more holidays, often at exotic destinations, it is likely to increase demand for foreign foods and eating out.

The continued decrease in household size, due to changes in the population age profile together with increased divorce rates and changing preferences amongst younger people, is likely to lead to further demand for individual packaging and products aimed at the single person.

The increased participation of women in the workforce is particularly likely in countries such as Spain, Greece, Portugal and Italy where rates are currently low. The consequence will be further demand for convenience products with a short preparation time.

The younger age profile of ethnic populations within countries such as the UK, Holland, Germany and France is likely to increase demand for products from countries such as India, Indonesia, Turkey and North Africa.

Questions

1   Consider what factors have led to the changed pattern of live births in EU member states in the past decade.
2   Why are there differences between different population forecasts for the next twenty-five years?
3   Take one member country of the European Union. Look in detail at total population and age profile projections for the next twenty-five years and evaluate the potential impact on food manufacturers.
4   What is household size? Why is it a significant grouping for market researchers? What factors are causing changes in household size?

5 Research the demographic characteristics and food consumption behaviour of an ethnic group in a European country of your choosing.

6 Consider how the population projections for one of the countries in list A is expected to differ from one of the countries in list B and explain why you think this is.

A	B
Greece	Italy
Ireland	UK
Portugal	The Netherlands

7 Compare the participation by women as members of the workforce in different member states of the EU. Explain the differences and the likely impact on food purchase behaviour.

8 Research the impact of the dissolution of communism in Eastern Europe in terms of immigration to the current European Union.

References

European Marketing (1992) *European Marketing Pocket Book* NTC Publications, Henley-on-Thames

Social Trends Governmental Statistical Service, HMSO, London

Somers, F. (1991) *European Economics*, Pelican, London

10 *Social class*

Introduction

Although it is fashionable to talk of a classless society, nearly everyone has some impression of a class system and their own position within it. Most people would readily agree that people with certain incomes or occupations fall into categories which may be the same as or different from their own. There is statistical evidence that many of the social, economic and physical characteristics of people vary significantly from one class to another. Patterns of fertility, education, religion, divorce, income, expenditure and occupation are all different between different social classes. The influence of class extends also to consumer behaviour and is manifested in differences in shopping behaviour, susceptibility to advertising and patterns of consumption. Social class therefore forms a meaningful way of segmenting consumers.

In this chapter there is a consideration of the concepts of social class and status, how class is usually measured, whether the concept is still applicable in modern society and what impact class has on consumer behaviour.

Class and status

Class can be defined as a relatively permanent grouping of people who are similar in their values and behaviour based on their economic position in society. What consumers are able to buy is based on their income or wealth which is related to their social class.

Systems of grading people into different social classes have invariably been based on occupation. Once this has happened, it is then common for additional information, either subjective or objective, to become attached to those groupings. Hence one of the strata in a study of Victorian London was 'loafers, drunkards and semi-criminals'. It would seem that occupations were first used because in the period of more rigid social order, earlier this century, the occupation of the head of household was a simple and efficient method of deriving income categories. Since that time other economically related variables, for which data are available, have become used as indirect measures of class. Besides occupation these include income, source of income and dwelling area.

Status does not necessarily equate with class. Status refers to the prestige which society grants to people in certain social positions. A brain surgeon is thought to be of greater status than a doctor or teacher and both are perceived to have higher social status than a supermarket shelf filler. Making a large amount of money may affect the technical classification of a person's class but not necessarily their status. Categorization by status obviously cuts across social class, so there is some overlap between the two concepts.

Many products and brands serve as status symbols so that a person who purchases a particular item may either signal their status to others or acquire status associated with the product. Much of promotional activity is obviously aimed at the communication of status inherent in a product.

Measurement of socio-economic class

Occupation remains the backbone of social classification, even though there are problems with it. There are two major sets of critics; those who argue that an alternative measure, such as income, is better, and those who wish to employ more than one measure at the same time, such as income, education and occupation.

Two of the most common systems used in the UK are the Registrar-General classification, with five groupings, and the National Readership Survey (NRS), with six (Table 10.1).

Table 10.1   *Socio-economic classifications*

	% population
Registrar-General social grading	
Class I Professional	3
II Intermediate	10
III Skilled	52
IV Semi-skilled	16
V Unskilled	11
National Readership Survey	
A Upper middle class, e.g. doctor, pilot	2
B Middle class, e.g. lecturer, pharmacist	14
C1 Lower middle class, e.g. junior manager	27
C2 Skilled working class, e.g. carpenter	25
D Working class, e.g. fisherman	19
E Lowest subsistence, e.g. OAP	12

Source: Monk, 1979; 1991 JICNARS/RSL Marketing Data Book.

European classifications essentially use a condensed version of the NRS categories, with three classes:

Upper   (A, B)
Middle   (C1, C2)
Low   (D, E)

The NRS classification has the advantage of simplicity. It is based on one category, occupation, which is relatively easy to measure. Statistical analysis has shown this measure correlates very highly with social categories and better than any other variable such as income or educational level. As it is relatively easy to collect it makes the NRS categorization much less complicated and cumbersome than American systems which depend on weighted combinations of several measures. Nevertheless there are problems with this method of classification.

The occupation of the head of household is much less appropriate as a measure of social class than it was. This is because there have been changes in household composition, as identified in Chapter 9. It is difficult to classify some jobs, particularly those which have management responsibility. This is because class is crudely related to the size of the organization a person is in charge of. There are also anomalies due to clumping occupations together. As an example, a teacher under 28 is classed as C1 but over this age is in category B. Despite these problems, however, the NRS scheme is the most commonly used.

A related but more concrete system for segmentation is based on the notion that where people live is a good predictor of their class and status. It also has the advantage that houses do not move and their desirability can be easily re-classified. The best known system in the UK is ACORN (A Classification Of Residential Neighbourhoods) (Table 10.2). This system is obviously particularly useful in siting retail operations.

Table 10.2 *Classification of residential areas in ACORN*

	% population
A Agricultural areas	3.3
B Modern family housing	17.6
C Older houses, intermediate status	17.9
D Poor, older terraces	4.2
E Better off council estates	13.2
F Less well off council estates	8.8
G Poorest council estates	7.0
H Multiracial areas, inner city	3.8
I High status non-family areas	4.1
J Affluent suburban housing	15.8
K Better off retirement areas	3.8
U Unclassified	0.5

Source: CACI Ltd (1992) *Lifestyle Pocket Book.*©

Other similar classification systems in use in the UK, such as Mosaic developed by CCN Systems Ltd, use demographic and financial data, the Post Office address codes and statistics from the 1981 Census. Super Profiles is similar again and is based primarily on housing areas.

One of the problems with classification systems of any kind is that the proportion of the population in different categories changes and there is a fundamental shift in the nature of occupations. There is a continual evolution from blue collar to white collar occupations and to professional and away from semi-skilled and unskilled labour. This has led some researchers to argue that those previously categorized in lower social groups are becoming a rarity as they take on the income, consumption patterns, attitudes and values of the middle class. Others dispute whether fundamental beliefs and values have changed even though incomes and occupations may have done.

Table 10.3   *Comparison of living standards in social groups*

Indicator		AB ('000)	% increase	C1C2 ('000)	% increase
Drink brandy	1972	1040		1927	
	1979	2961	184	7516	290
Have credit cards	1972	879		1181	
	1979	3130	256	4751	303

Source: Target Index Group, 1972, 1979.

As one small example to illustrate the former point, Table 10.3 shows that the proportion of consumers acquiring credit cards since they were first introduced is just as great amongst C1 and C2 consumers as amongst the AB group. It has traditionally been assumed that lower social groups would use cash not credit and would not take up new ideas as fast as upper social groups.

Psychological differences

More than thirty years ago Martineau (1958) pointed out that there are distinct psychological differences between different social classes and this is reflected in consumption patterns.

The typical lower class person is suggested to be interested in the here-and-now with short time horizons, a lack of planning and thinking ahead. They are therefore inclined to spend rather than save and make cash purchases spontaneously without too much deliberation. On the other hand the typical middle class person has longer time horizons, is more deliberate about their purchase choices but happy to use credit knowing that future income is secure (Table 10.4).

Table 10.4 *Psychological differences between classses*

Middle class	Lower class
● Abstract	● Concrete
● Long time span and future-orientated	● Live and think with short time scales
● Extended horizons	● Limited horizons
● Make choices	● Limited choice making
● Take risks	● Wants security
● Save	● Spend not save
● Liberated	● Chauvinistic
● Interest in education	● Interest in money
● Credit cards	● Cash

Source: Martineau, 1958.

Market segmentation and purchase behaviour

Analysis of markets by socio-economic profile is still the most common method of segmentation. The assumption in segmentation strategies is that different groups in the population with a similar demographic profile in terms of occupation or housing will exhibit similar purchase behaviour. Hence a marketing strategy would emphasize different attributes of a product or be sold through different outlets at a particular price if targeted at a particular social group.

As far as food consumption is concerned people in higher socio-economic groups are reported to consume a greater variety and range of foodstuffs which are more likely to accord with whatever is thought to be nutritionally good (Mennell *et al.*, 1992). These same authors cite research which shows that following the dietary guidelines of the 1980s which recommended a reduction in intakes of salt, sugar and fat but an increase in dietary fibre, the uptake was class-related. Hence the consumption of skimmed milk, vegetables, brown bread and fruit is greater in higher income and professional groups in Denmark and the UK. On the other hand, diets higher in animal fat are more likely to be recorded among lower social groups and among farmers in countries such as Switzerland and France.

In the UK and The Netherlands, and probably most other industrialized countries, it is the middle classes that are more likely to be vegetarian. Cooking methods also show a class gradient with frying rather than baking or grilling more common in lower social groups. Working class households in UK are more likely to purchase tinned and frozen rather than fresh vegetables. Consumers in this same social group D spend a higher proportion of their food budget on meat, beer, soft drinks, ice cream and confectionery. On the other hand, those in groups AB spend more than double the average on wine and spirits (*Supermarketing*, 1993). This group also has a higher frequency of purchase of products perceived as healthy such as brown versus white bread (Table 10.5).

Data collected from Nielsen's Homescan, an electronic consumer panel, shows that purchase of milk and teabags is broadly similar across all social groups. On the other

Table 10.5   *Percentage of consumers in the UK buying a particular product each week*

	Social class				
	AB	C1	C2	D	E
White wrapped bread	37	49	66	67	58
Brown wrapped bread	54	54	40	46	41

Source: Mintel, 1983.

Table 10.6   *Buyer index of selected grocery items in the UK*

	AB	C1	C2	D	E
Canned meatballs	50	86	124	151	87
Fromage frais	140	112	96	80	67
Frozen burgers	85	96	112	121	85
Ground coffee	149	117	87	69	74
Milk	102	102	99	101	96
Low fat yoghurt	114	109	103	91	74
Tea bags	101	98	102	102	96

Source: Nielsen Homescan, 1992.

hand, items such as ground coffee, fromage frais and low fat yoghurt are bought more frequently by those in higher social groups whereas the reverse is true of products such as canned meatballs and frozen beefburgers (Table 10.6).

Shopping behaviour is also affected by social class. The demographic profile of shoppers in the main UK food outlets shows that Sainsbury and to a lesser extent Tesco have a typically higher class profile. Asda has an appeal primarily to those in social groups C2 and D, although this may have changed as the store has more recently tried to reposition itself. The traditional grocery market for the Co-operative stores persists and comprises consumers from social groups C2, D and E (Table 10.7).

The factors that influence store choice in the UK also vary with social class. Whereas convenience is the most important criterion across all classes, those in social groups DE are particularly affected by prices whereas the quality of the store is of more significance to AB consumers than to other social groups (Table 10.8).

A number of studies have shown that shopping frequency varies with social class. In the UK lower class women shopping for food in Newcastle upon Tyne were more likely to be accompanied by other people and to discuss purchases than were middle class women (Foxall, 1975). This is possibly related to the fact working class communities are more closely knit than middle class communities.

The source and amount of information sought by individuals varies by social class. The lower social classes often have limited information but compensate by relying on

Table 10.7 *Analysis of the social class of users of four main UK supermarkets – Index: mean = 100*

	AB	C1	C2	D	E
Tesco	120	110	98	86	82
Sainsbury	144	127	83	76	66
Asda	89	102	111	114	78
Co-op	57	91	117	112	117

Source: Nielsen Homescan, 1992.

Table 10.8 *Importance of store attributes in choice*

Attribute	AB (%)	C1 (%)	C2 (%)	DE (%)
Convenience	58	56	53	52
Good selection	14	14	15	12
Low price	7	10	14	17
Good quality	11	9	8	7
Other	10	11	10	12

Source: Nielsen Homescan, 1992.

friends and relatives. Middle class consumers rely more on media-acquired information and engage in active search of information from the media (Foxall, 1975).

Conclusion

Although there are continual changes in society, the concept of social class is still readily understood and a frequently used method of segmenting consumers. The principle of segmentation is that it is possible to categorize people and that similar groups will exhibit similar purchase behaviour. Most European methods of classifying people into different social classes depend on occupation, although more recent systems also take account of where people live. This is less complicated than American methods which depend on several criteria which are weighted before being combined.

However, the concept of class has been criticized as there is evidence of a basic shift in occupations with the creation of more professional and managerial jobs and less semi-skilled or labouring jobs. The psychological differences between different classes identified over thirty years ago may also be lessening.

Despite these cautions, socio-economic segmentation is still the most often used method in market research. Analysis of consumer purchases shows distinct class differences. Upper class consumers appear to consume a greater variety and range of foodstuffs, they are more concerned with quality than price in where they shop, they react more readily to nutritional guidance and greening issues, and more actively seek information before making purchase decisions.

Questions

1   What is social class? How is it usually assessed?
2   What drawbacks are there in the NRS classification of social class?
3   For all its drawbacks, why is social class the most usual method of segmentation used by consumer researchers?
4   What effect has the redistribution of income and occupations had on social class structure in Great Britain during this century?
5   What differences are there in the shopping habits of different social classes?
6   In what way does income relate to social class? Why is it so little used as an indicator of social class?
7   A market researcher is speculating on the influence of the upper classes on consumption decisions of the lower classes for food products. What conclusions would you expect?
8   In what way is the consumption of particular food products associated with social class?
9   What differences are there between social classes with regard to what information they use and where they look for it before buying goods?
10   Examine the class structure in any member state of the European Union. What is the impact of social class on food consumption in the country you have chosen?

References

Foxall, G. (1975) Social factors in consumer choice; replication and extension *J. Consumer Res.*, **2**, 1

Lifestyle Pocket Book (1992). NTC Publications, Henley-on-Thames

Martineau, P. (1958) Social class and spending behaviour. *J. Marketing*, **23**, 121

Mennell, S., Murcott, A. and Otterloo, A. van (1992) *The Sociology of Food*, Sage, London

Monk, J. (1979) *The Philosophy of Social Grading*, Joint Industry Committee for National Audience Research Survey, London

Nielsen Homescan (1992) In *The British Shopper 1993*, NTC Publications, Henley-on-Thames

Supermarketing (1993) 'A new slant on statistics', 15 October

11 *Reference groups and opinion leadership*

Introduction

People do not live in isolation, but are surrounded by other people who have various degrees of influence on their attitudes and behaviour and hence what products they buy. A strong influence is likely to be exerted by family and friends and rather less influence by people known only vaguely or not at all, but seen on TV or read about in magazines. These influences can create fashions or trends. Products become 'in' or 'out' because they are seen by a particular group as reflecting the identity of the group and are seen by others as desirable if they wish to emulate that group.

This chapter is concerned with group behaviour and the influence of particular members of a group on the opinions and behaviour of others. In a later chapter the focus is on a particular group, the family.

Defining a group

In everyday conversation it could be said that someone standing in the queue at a supermarket checkout was in a group. For the social scientist the term 'group' has a more precise meaning and would not include people randomly lined up in a queue. A group involves two or more people who share some common goals or objectives and interact to achieve these. Each member of the group sees themselves as being in the group and sees the other members as being in the group. The group evolves beliefs, attitudes and ways of behaving which are similar. These group norms serve to bond the members of the group together.

The greatest impact and influence on individual behaviour is exerted by a primary group. Like attracts like, so that members of the group not only start with many similarities but the pressure to conform within the group reaffirms those similarities. The most obvious example is the family but a primary group includes any tight knit circle – neighbours, friends or a social club.

Secondary groups are less influential, more distant and often more formal. Examples are trade unions, professional associations or a student union. Informal groups are likely to be based on friendship or as a consequence of some factor which brings a set of people together, such as work or similar leisure interests.

Groups create pressure on individual members to conform. Norms are the accepted ways of behaving or accepted values and beliefs of a group. Norms which shape behaviour are often powerful but seldom written down. The pressure to conform is reinforced by frequent face-to-face contact during which expectations of what is acceptable to the group are expressed.

On the other hand formal groups are less obviously influential on individual behaviour even though rules may be written down and codified. The rules of official clubs or societies may appear to formalize expected behaviour but are seen as impersonal and therefore not every member of the group feels motivated to adhere strictly to them.

Reference groups

Much has been written in sociology and social psychology about the formation and influence of different types of groups. The concept which is of particular significance in the area of consumer behaviour is that of the reference group. This can include a group to which a person actually belongs, one to which that person aspires to belong or one to which they aspire not to belong. Most social psychologists view the reference group as a person's major source of values, norms and perspectives.

Reference groups can influence behaviour in several major ways. First, they influence aspiration levels and thus play a part in producing satisfaction or frustration. If the other members of a particular reference group, for example neighbours or close friends, are wealthier, more famous or stay healthier, a person may be dissatisfied with their own achievements and strive to do as well as the others. Second, reference groups influence kinds of behaviour. They establish approved patterns of what to eat, where to shop, how to demonstrate one's wealth. So they produce conformity as well as satisfaction or dissatisfaction.

Both sets of influence imply certain perceptions on the part of the individual. What is significant is not the *actual* norms or aspirations of the reference group but what the individual *thinks* they are. Reference behaviour is therefore a cognitive process in which an individual evaluates their own status, behaviour and norms against the perceived standards or practices of the group.

Reference group influence

Someone going out to buy a kilo of carrots would probably make very little conscious reference to anyone else. However, there might be unconscious pressures on them. Will they go to the local market or to their favourite supermarket? How much is either behaviour influenced by what their friends or relatives do? This is probably an example where it is a struggle to find any obvious reference group influence. On the other hand, if a person was becoming disenchanted with store A, where they usually bought most of their household needs, they might well cast around for others' opinions before switching to another store. The degree of influence of the reference group or groups is higher the more complex, risky, or expensive the purchase is.

Several pieces of research (e.g. Bourne, 1965, Beardon and Etzel, 1982) have shown that the degree of reference group influence will vary between products. There is often a more obvious effect on which brand rather than which product is chosen. Reference groups have a strong influence on whether or not people buy beer and on the brand chosen. Perhaps the most modern example of this is the decrease in consumption of beer versus lager in the UK, but an increase in the sale of speciality, foreign, branded beers. A lot of this switch in behaviour is suggested to be due to peer group pressure. Expensive foreign beers have become trendy and therefore desirable. A related example is the influence of women on where drinking occurs. During the recession it has become more the norm for people to drink at home, often consuming imported beers as outlined in Illustration 11.1.

Whereas peer group pressure can have a strong influence on which brands of beer are bought, there seems to be little reference group influence on whether people buy a refrigerator. It is accepted as more or less a necessity of life which everyone has to have. Similarly there is not much influence on which brand is bought.

A lot of advertising is aimed at trying to position a product so as to appeal to a particular reference group. The product is placed in particular magazines or alongside particular programmes on TV known to appeal to the target audience. However the impact of 'conspicuous consumption' as a motive for people to buy products, pressurized by peer group influence, is in decline as outlined in a later chapter on values and lifestyles.

An example of how products could be better promoted to the growing numbers of consumers over 50 shows how reference group pressure could be more effectively

---

Illustration 11.1 Women put the froth in home beer sales

More people are switching to drinking at home rather than the pub – thanks to the influence of women. The sales of supermarket and off licence sales of beer and lager are soaring and many experts believe this revolution is being led by women shoppers. They are cost conscious and find drinking at home more pleasurable than sitting in a cheerless pub.

A major part in the rise of take-home beer and lager is due to an increase in consumption of canned bitters including the new widget generation of draught beers in cans. Another threat to the traditional pub is the influx of cheap beer being imported from France by trippers. Since January 1993 UK visitors to France have been able to buy virtually unlimited amounts of beer for personal use at prices around six times cheaper than at home. Together with duty free purchases the imports account for 15 per cent of all beer drunk in British homes. The Brewers and Licensed Retailers Association insist however that the pub will still be the number one choice for most UK drinkers. However a spokesperson admitted that 'drinking at home is increasing. There has been a recession and when people are worried about jobs and money they do not go out as much. But the pub has proved resilient and adaptable in the past against changing habits.'

Based on 'Women put the froth in home beer sales', *Daily Mail*, 15 February 1994, 10

Illustration 11.2 Selfish oldies

Recent studies by Crucible Research reveal a huge discrepancy between marketers' views of older people and the self-image of many of the UK's healthier and wealthier recent retirers. Older people in the qualitative study talked of developing a safe rebellion. They could justify a spend rather than save mentality, a shorter rather than long term outlook and a less conformist mentality.

The last thing this group see themselves as is old. They feel younger than they have done for years and dislike any direct reminder of ageing. Specialist products for old people fulfil their worst nightmares. Images they respond to tend to be the generation younger than them. Images which turn them off are of Grannies and Grandads and old frumps.

The Carnegie Inquiry into the Third Age found the over-50s represented 'a growing proportion of the active, independent population' and concluded 'the media should reflect their healthy, active and participatory lifestyles and stop feeding outmoded stereotypes of older people'.

Contrary to popular marketing belief, older consumers are not set in their ways but open to new products and new experiences. In one survey 84 per cent said they would switch brands if a new product or service seemed to be 'for people like me'.

People turning 50 grew up in an era of marketing hype so are worldly wise to marketing ploys. Successful advertising to this group should show older consumers as they really are and how they want to be seen by putting them in contemporary situations where they can show off their vitality. Part of the current problem of how older people are portrayed in advertising is because the average age of brand managers is 29, and marketing managers 31.

Based on D. Smith 'Exorcising those little grey cells', *Marketing Week*, 2 July 1993

---

utilized rather than depending on techniques more appropriate to younger audiences (Illustration 11.2).

Opinion influence

As we have seen, consumers frequently turn to others, friends or family, for opinions about products or retail outlets. This word-of-mouth influence happens in many circumstances. We chat with friends in a bar or cafe about what we have just bought or are about to buy. We ask their opinion or they may offer it in unsolicited form. We may deliberately seek out information from a friend by phone because we do not know enough about the product we intend to buy or what we do know we do not have much faith in because it has come from a salesman or TV advertisement.

The concept of opinion leadership was first identified by Lazarsfeld in the 1940 US presidential election when it was shown that virtually no-one was influenced in their voting by media campaigns but depended on the views of others in their group

Illustration 11.3 Which bread do women buy?

Ten women in Texas were each asked to nominate four friends or relatives with whom they each like to, or would be willing to, go shopping.

Sliced, white bread from a local bakery was packed in clear, unmarked cellophane bags. Large labels (2" × 2") with the letters H, L, M, P were designated as brands to be put on the bread. Each of the 40 women in the study was called on at home twice a week for eight weeks and given her choice of the four previously unknown brands of bread. The women did not know all the bread was from the same bakery. They were told the purpose of the study was to look at how women choose a brand of bread, not that it was really about group influences on purchase behaviour. At the end of the study each woman was given a questionnaire about brand preferences for bread and asked for information to help identify group cohesion and leadership. Leadership within each group of women was based on the perceived attractiveness, expertness and communication effectiveness of each individual.

Rank order of cohesion	Leader's best liked brand	Group's best liked brand
1	H	H
2	M	M
3	H	H
4	P	P
5	H	H
6.5	M	P
6.5	L	H
8	P	H
9	M	M
10	P	M

In the five highest ranked groups in terms of measures of cohesion the informal group leader and members not only preferred the same best liked brand but also did so on an exceptionally high percentage of occasions compared with the rest of the groups. In only one of the five remaining groups did leaders and other members prefer the same brand and then only at a level expected by chance. In more cohesive groups it was more likely the members preferred the same brand as the group leader. The higher the degree of brand loyalty shown by the group leader the more likely were the other members of the group to prefer the same brand.

Based on J. E. Stafford (1966) Effects of group influences on consumer brand preferences. *J. Marketing Res.*, **3**, 68–75

(Lazarsfeld, Berelson and Gaudet, 1948). Further than this, people relied greatly on the social groups to which they relate to help them interpret any message received from the media. Within the social group 'some people in every level of society are most concerned and most influential in relation to a particular topic'.

The concept of opinion leadership is demonstrated in Illustration 11.3, which is based on an experiment first undertaken by Stafford (1966). It shows that in a strongly knit, cohesive group the leader will have a dominating influence on the opinions and hence the behaviour of others in the group.

Recognition of significant opinion leaders led to the formulation of a two-step hypothesis of communication (Arndt, 1968) (Figure 11.1). This argues that the effects of the mass media do not directly influence individuals. Messages are instead picked up by a relatively small number of opinion leaders who in turn disseminate information to others in their social group. There is considerable evidence (Foxall, 1980) that informal or word-of-mouth communication is much more influential than formal advertising or promotional channels as a source of influence. However, the neat two-step hierarchical process has been questioned. The mass media do have an influence on all people not just on certain people. Those people, opinion leaders, assumed in the theory to be the driving force in influencing others, are not always. Word-of-mouth communication is often initiated by someone who is not a strong influence on others, but is simply seeking information from a credible friend or relative.

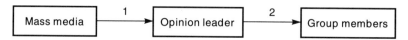

Figure 11.1   *Two-step information flow in communication*

Evidence suggests that opinion leaders communicate with other opinion leaders and obtain information from other sources, not just the media. Many non-leaders transmit information as well as receive it (Figure 11.2).

Consumers use a variety of sources of information, as elaborated further in the chapter on persuasive communication. These include manufacturer or retailer-dominated sources (elements of the marketing mix); consumer-dominated channels (word of mouth) and neutral channels (editorial, consumer reports). Each has its pros and cons. The first is cheap but biased, the second objective but not always available, and the third trustworthy but expensive (Foxall, 1980). What it does mean though is that communication flow is not simply explained as a two-step process; there are many phases to it.

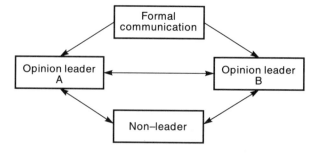

Figure 11.2   *Multiphase communication*

Illustration 11.4 Adoption of a new food product

Four hundred and forty-nine housewives living in an apartment complex were informed of the availability of a new food product together with a coupon which reduced the price to one-third of its normal cost.

Sales information on the product was gathered for a sixteen-day period from the food store which was part of the apartment complex. Subjects were categorized into different adopter groups. The subject's adopter category was based on the time it took for them to redeem their coupon at the store. Opinion leadership was worked out from answers to the question: 'When you want information about new food products you have not tried yet, are there any people you would be particularly likely to discuss the new product with?' Word of mouth behaviour was determined by asking respondents to say if there were any comments they had received about the product.

The results showed that:

1 Opinion leaders were more influenced by formal communication than non-leaders.
2 Opinion leaders were more active communicators both at sending and receiving information.
3 A lot of information flowed from non-leaders to opinion leaders by word of mouth.
4 Favourable word of mouth comment resulted in three times as many sales as unfavourable comments.

The product was adopted by people at different times after it was first available:

Pioneers   12% – adopted within 2 days
Early adopters   18% – adopted between 3rd and 9th day
Late adopters   12% – adopted between 10th and 16th day
Non-adopters   58%

This schedule of adoption is similar to the pattern of adoption shown in much other research which is usually related to the degree of penetration of a new product in the consumer market. It suggests that there is a category of consumer which is first to try a new product and these tend to be more active communicators. This is not to say that these then become the most loyal or heaviest buyers of a product. Their enthusiasm may wane faster than consumers who take up a new product later.

Based on G. Foxall (1980) *Consumer Behaviour*, Croom Helm, London; and personal communication

The example given in Illustration 11.4 shows that people vary in the rate at which they adopt new products but there is a category of consumer which is the first to try a new product. They tend to be active communicators who both receive and give out information about a product which, if favourable, will strongly influence the buying behaviour of others.

Opinion leaders

Extensive research has taken place to try to identify the characteristics of opinion leaders. The assumption of many advertisers, based on a two-step model, is that these were the people to get at, who would then influence others, although the previous discussion shows this to be an oversimplistic assumption. Table 11.1 identifies the characteristics derived from a variety of sources on the profile of opinion leaders. In essence they tend to be people who are gregarious and socially active, try out new things and assert their views.

Table 11.1   *Characteristics of opinion leaders*

Demographic	Usually show low correlation and not a good predictor
Social	Gregarious and sociable
Innovativeness	Try things out, positive to new products
Lifestyle	More fashion conscious and socially active More inclined to expose themselves to mass media and other consumers
Psychographics	No clear correlation although some evidence opinion leaders are more confident and assertive
Conformity	Tend to stick to norms of the group which in itself enhances their status in the group

Source: Foxall, 1980; Engel *et al.*, 1993.

One of the more interesting aspects of opinion leadership research is concerned with where information exchange occurs. Belk (1975) questioned 134 randomly selected housewives to identify their awareness of a new coffee product, Maxim freeze-dried coffee. The results show most information exchange was in food related situations; drinking coffee, talking about food or shopping for it. King and Summers (1971) showed that for a new snack food most discussions occur at a private home, most often in the evening and most commonly between no more than two people. Clearly this sort of study has important implications for how to target promotion in terms of what channel of communication is used at what time of day.

Conclusion

A group is defined by the social scientist as involving two or more people who share common goals or objectives. Groups create pressures on individuals to conform and to adopt norms which are accepted ways of thinking or behaving. Reference groups are both groups to which a person actually belongs and to which they aspire to belong. The effect is that an individual will adopt whatever beliefs, values or behaviour they perceive the reference group has adopted.

In terms of consumer behaviour, reference group influence often has a more significant impact on brand choice rather than product choice. Certain brands are 'in' and others 'out'. As an example, foreign, imported beers are in fashion currently.

The concept of opinion leadership suggests that certain individuals react to new products sooner than others and pass on their evaluations which then influence others. Opinion leaders are more sociable and gregarious than others and assert their views. However, it seems they both give and receive information from others so messages about new products do not simply travel in two steps from opinion leaders to others but in many directions at once.

The impact of opinion leadership is most significant in tightly knit, cohesive groups. In these cases the opinion of one person who is perceived as significant within the group is likely strongly to influence the other members.

The particular significance of these concepts is in an explanation of how new products are first adopted by a minority of consumers who pass on the information to others. Early adopters may not necessarily end up as the heaviest users of the product. They are often inclined to try a new product but quickly move on to something else. Promotional activity is frequently concerned at portraying an image for a product which is consistent with the lifestyle and aspirations of the target consumers.

Questions

1   What is meant by a reference group and how is this a significant concept in the promotion of food products?
2   What groups have an influence on what you eat and where you eat?
3   Consider your own life in the last ten years. Identify points at which your diet has changed as a result of the influence of primary groups to which you belong.
4   Identify a food product or eating out facility and describe how it has risen and fallen in popularity as a result of changes in fashion.
5   Describe the two-step and multiphase theories of communication and critically apply them to decisions you and your friends have made about whether to try a new food product or restaurant.
6   Examine the sales record of a new food product or the spread of discount food retailing and consider whether the concept of adoption identified in Illustration 11.3 gives an appropriate explanation.

References

Arndt, J. (1968) A test of the two step flow in diffusion of a new product. *Journalism Q,* **45**

Beardon, W. O. and Etzel, M. J. (1982) Reference group influence on product and brand purchase decisions. *J Consumer Res.,* **9**, 183–94

Belk, R. (1975) Situational variables and consumer behaviour. *J. Consumer Res.,* **2**, 2

Bourne, F. S. (1965) Group influence in marketing and public relations. In *Dimensions of Consumer Behaviour* (ed. J. U. McNeal), Appleton Century Crofts, New York, pp. 137–146

Engel, J., Blackwell, R. and Miniard, P. (1993) *Consumer Behaviour,* 7th edn, Dryden, Fort Worth, Texas

Foxall, G. (1980) *Consumer Behaviour,* Croom Helm, London

King, C. W. and Summers, J. O. (1970) 'Overlap of opinion leadership across consumer product categories', *Journal of Marketing Research,* **7**, 43–50

Lazarsfeld, P. F., Berelson, B. R. and Gaudet, H. (1944) *The People's Choice,* Columbia University Press, New York

Stafford, J. (1966) Effects of group influences on consumer brand preferences. *J. Market Res.,* **3**, 68–75

12 *The family*

Introduction

Although there has been a rise in the number of people who live alone, most live as part of a family. Although the family as a unit is often suggested to be in an imminent state of collapse, it is still important in the analysis of consumer behaviour. The family unit is an important social institution and an important reference group. It is characterized by frequent face-to-face interaction and plays a vital part in the socialization function which transmits values, self-concepts and norms from one generation to the next. As far as many marketing people are concerned it is the single most important social group. The reasons for this are various. When people buy products they often do so as a family unit. Although women do often shop alone for food, increasingly they do so with their partner, a relative or children. This family group often buys products which are for the family rather than any individual in it. Second, even when one member of the family shops alone, they may be heavily influenced by the preferences of particular individuals in the family. The person responsible for buying and preparing food, usually a woman, is heavily influenced in her choices by other family members even if they are not physically present at the time a purchase is made.

The traditional family, consisting of one parent of each sex and one or more children has also given rise to an important concept used in segmentation – the family life cycle (FLC). This is based on the idea that the family as a consuming unit progresses through a series of stages with different consumption needs at different points.

This chapter examines the family as an example of a group in which all the dynamics of group behaviour are played out and have their influence on consumer behaviour.

Defining the family

The most familiar form of the family is the nuclear family, consisting of mother, father and their children living together and related by blood, marriage or adoption. The extended family is now becoming rarer. It includes the nuclear unit and other relatives such as grandparents, uncles and in-laws. Although an extended family is now less common than it once was, it is apparent that relatives still have an influence on consumption.

J. Walter Thompson (1968) identified that at the time of his study one in two married women under 35 started life in one of the parental homes and one in three lived within walking distance of their parents. The family, whether nuclear or extended, is still a major social grouping for most people. It has a strong influence on the behaviour adopted by individuals within it, including consumer preference. It is also the major group within which an individual learns a particular role.

In respect of food consumption the influence of the family is becoming less powerful than it once was. Changing social trends have eroded the tradition of family mealtimes. Instead, people are increasingly 'grazing' – catching the occasional bite to eat at any time of the day or night – and consuming convenience products that are quick and easy to prepare. The decline of the nuclear family as the model social group has been an important factor in this development. Twenty-five per cent of households now contain a single person (*Social Trends*, 1992) and people living alone tend to be less motivated to cook a formal meal. Even in families there is evidence of meals being eaten alone rather than collectively (Green, 1991). The faster pace of modern life, the shedding of the female housewife role and the increased number of single parent families are all factors that militate against the practicality of a conventionally cooked meal (Equal Opportunities Commission, 1992).

The impact of these changes upon consumption has been quite considerable.

- Frozen food sales doubled between 1979 and 1989 to a value of £3.5bn.
- The chilled ready meal market grew 10 per cent in 1990 to a value of £715m.
- The fast food segment of the catering industry expanded from a value of £1.87bn in 1984 to £4.54bn in 1990.
- The snack food market reached a value of £1355m by 1990.
- Confectionery sales of £2332m in 1984 were greater than the combined sum spent on bread and cereals.

The household

A household differs from a family in that it groups as one all persons, both related and unrelated, who live in a particular unit. This is becoming a more important unit of analysis in market research than the family because of the increase in non-family households and non-traditional families. In Chapter 9 the evidence is explored which shows that household size is decreasing with a corresponding increase in the number of households.

In studies which have controlled for household income it is possible to examine the effect of household composition on food consumption. As household size increases but income is held fixed, there is a tendency for expenditure on food to rise, as would be expected. However, at the same time there is an offsetting effect with extra demand building up to spend the fixed household budget on other items. In most cases as a household member is added it does lead to an increase in food expenditure. The effect of extra hungry mouths is greater than the demand of alternative ways to spend the household budget. However, this effect is not so great in a household which is already large. Partly this is an economy of scale effect, but also because the pressure to spend income on things other than food is also greater in a larger household with a fixed income. An extra household member causes expenditure on all food to rise by between

Table 12.1 *Impact of size of household on buyer index*

	Size of household			
	1 person	*2 persons*	*3–4 persons*	*5 persons*
Beer	63	109	116	115
Cheesecake	58	83	144	121
Frozen pizza	50	85	139	164
Ground coffee	88	110	102	85
Milk	94	101	103	106
Snack meals	61	55	161	163

Source: Nielsen Homescan, 1992.

3 and 6 per cent in small households and by slightly more than half of this in large households. The impact of a new household member increases with age. Adolescent boys have more effect than girls but gender-related differences are small amongst adults.

The effect of extra members of a family is different for different foodstuffs. The impact of expenditure on meat is much smaller when a child rather than an adult is added to a household. This difference is even more marked for items like fish, green vegetables and wholemeal bread, which are generally not liked much by children, so an extra child has little effect compared with an extra adult (Chesher, 1991).

The effect of household size on consumption of typical foods is illustrated in Table 12.1. The impact of household size is very little in the case of milk, whereas buying of pizza and snack meals is above average in larger households.

Group roles

In any group it usually emerges that certain members take on a particular role, perhaps as leader, jollying everyone along, or calming the atmosphere when disputes arise. Similarly within a family group it may be that the adult male decides what food to buy but a female actually goes to the supermarket to buy it. More likely the situation is more complex than this. The teenage child campaigns to get a different sort of breakfast cereal, the father suggests avoiding a new type of meat pie which he did not like last time it was bought, and the mother going round the supermarket buys sausages because they are on offer. It is obvious that although one person often makes the final purchase a variety of role players both within and outside the family affect purchase decision making. Kotler (1984) identified five roles which are of significance in family buying behaviour to which a sixth, a preparer, can be added in the case of food.

1 **Initiator/gatekeeper:** the person(s) who gathers or provides information or advice about a product, or who first suggests a particular purchase.
2 **Influencer:** the person(s) who consciously or unconsciously affects the decision in some way, maybe as an opinion leader or apparent expert.

3 **Decider:** the person(s) who unilaterally or jointly decides whether or not to buy a particular product.
4 **Buyer:** the person(s) who actually makes the purchase.
5 **Preparer:** the person(s) who transforms the product, such as raw uncooked materials, into something else.
6 **User:** the person(s) who consumes the product in its original or transformed state.

In households comprising a wife and husband under 65, surveys reported by Allt in 1978 showed it was quite common for husbands to be involved in food shopping. During an average week one husband in two was involved in food shopping, and during a month, seven out of ten.

Illustration 12.1 Who shops for food?

In 1973 the Mirror Group published a study entitled *Husbands and Wives and Shopping for Food*. It showed women housepersons had a very high awareness of their husbands' tastes and brand preferences. A repeat of the study in 1977 showed four husbands out of five get involved in food shopping either alone or in company with their wives, as against three out of five in the 1973 study.

There was a substantial increase in the numbers of husbands who shop alone and are not given precise or detailed instructions as to the products or brands to be bought. Of all households, in 35 per cent the husband does the food shopping without precise instructions.

Husband's frequency of substantial food shopping (per cent):

	Husband shops alone	With wife
Ever	48	78
Once a fortnight	18	51
Once a month	7	10
Less often	20	12
Never	52	22

When out shopping with his wife the husband also has considerable influence on what is chosen.

When out shopping together (per cent):

Wife chooses everything	26
Husband picks out	14
Husband suggests things	23
Husband suggests and picks out	15
Total who shop together	78

Finally one in ten of those responsible for household catering is male.

Based on B. Allt (1978) *Husbands and Wives and Shopping for Food*, Mirror Group Newspapers Ltd, London (commercial market research report)

The decision-makers

A lot of consumer research has been concerned with which members of a family are crucial in the purchase decision. The answer is, it depends on a variety of factors. No single individual in a family group makes a purchase decision entirely without being influenced by other members of the family unit. Different people may be significant at different stages in the decision process. It depends how important and costly the purchase is, and what type of product is referred to. There is some evidence also that the type of work done by the husband and the social class of the family can have an effect on the decision process.

One of the most significant pieces of research was conducted by Davis and Rigaux (1974) who asked husbands and wives in 73 Belgian households to provide information on decision-making relative to twenty-five products and services. Decisions were classified as:

1   Husband dominant.
2   Wife dominant.
3   Syncratic – joint decisions.
4   Autonomic – decision made by either husband or wife but each decision made individually by one or the other.

Figure 12.1 gives an indication of the influence of different family members in the decision process. It also demonstrates that more complex or expensive items such as food preparation equipment involve joint decision-making.

Komarovsky (1961) has shown that joint decision-making is more likely in middle income families versus low or high income and is more common among younger

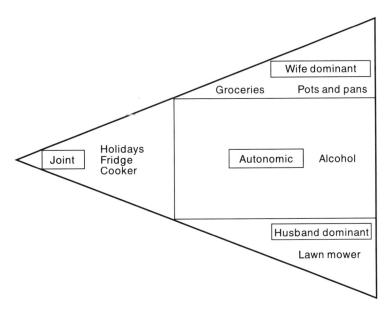

Figure 12.1 *Influence of family members in purchase decisions. (After Engel, Blackwell and Miniard, 1993)*

versus older couples. Edgell (1970) found that if a husband was heavily involved in his work this would lead to a sharp division of roles at home. If the husband was more interested in home than work this would lead to more sharing of decision-making with his wife.

As women assume more of a role in the workforce, decision-making will shift in the family. Wives, especially those who are educated, will become more involved with financial management, insurance and other areas previously dominated by men. As husbands do more grocery shopping they will become more influential in decisions about product choice. The roles of different family members in influencing a purchase is outlined in Illustration 12.2.

Illustration 12.2 Buying decisions in the family

Although the adult female in a family does the majority of food shopping this does not mean she is the only person who decides what to buy. Husband or partner, children, mother, mother-in-law, friends can all have an influence at different stages in the purchase decision.

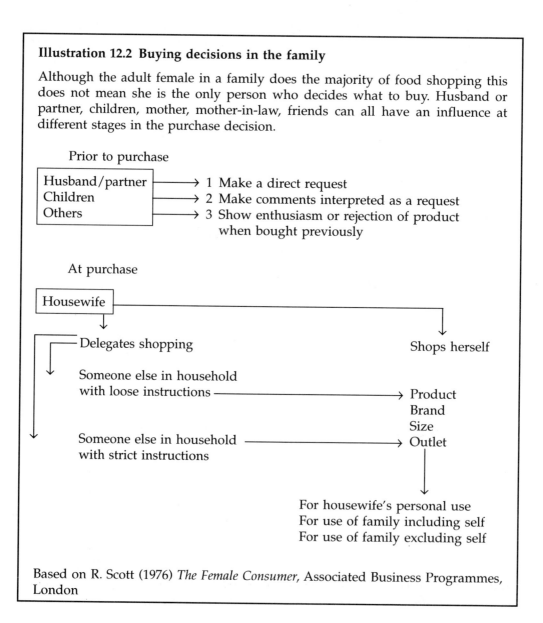

Based on R. Scott (1976) *The Female Consumer*, Associated Business Programmes, London

Foxall and Goldsmith (1994) quoting studies by Pahl, show that in most households (74 per cent) women are responsible for spending on food. Although expenditure on food increased as incomes increased, increases in wives' earnings were followed by proportionately higher increases on food expenditure. Expenditure on food was also higher in families where the wife had control of the family finances.

The young and teenage consumer

There is evidence that children may influence as much as 15 per cent of food purchase decisions. A study by Ward and Wackman (1972) showed mothers were most likely to be influenced by children in the purchase of food rather than any other products. Yielding to the child's demand was more likely the older the child was even though the number of requests was less than the number from younger children (Table 12.2).

Table 12.2 *Influence of children on purchase decision*

	Children suggest (%)	Buy what children suggest (%)
Breakfast cereal	48	68
Tea	4	9
Baked beans	18	70
Ice cream	34	74
Biscuits	30	67

Source: NOP, 1967.

Although the number of teenagers in most of Western Europe has decreased, this is still an important consumer group with considerable discretionary income and a great significance in family purchase behaviour. Food marketers have particularly focused their efforts on this group, which has a strong influence both before and during purchase, particularly in relation to snack foods, soft drinks and fast food (see Table 12.3).

Children in the UK spent more than £220 million on 1993 on sweets and snacks bought on their way to and from school. More young people are grazing, eating snacks periodically during the day. Massey reported a survey in 1994 in which more than one in six give pizza as their favourite meal, followed by what was the overall favourite, hamburgers.

Since one or both parents are in the workforce, or the family is headed by a single parent, teenagers are spending more time grocery shopping for their families. Although guided by lists provided by parents, final choice is often left to them.

Table 12.3   *Personal purchase or purchase influence by 9–15-year-olds in a 2–3 week period*

	%
Personal purchase	
Sweets	71
Snack foods	39
Fast food	37
Purchase influence	
Breakfast cereal	68
Ice cream	62
Soft drinks	60
Bread	29

Source: Hall, 1987.

Family life cycle

Family life cycle (FLC) is a concept borrowed from sociology and applied to the study of family consumption habits. Families change over time and pass through a series of stages. Very briefly, the stages are that people marry, have children, the childen grow up and leave home, one or both of the parents retire, then die (Figure 12.2). In FLC segmentation, these stages are more explicitly defined and associated with typical purchase behaviour. The major groupings are identified in Table 12.4.

At different stages of the FLC families vary in their satisfaction with different products or even their desire to engage in food preparation as indicated in Illustration 12.3.

This idealized model of the FLC has been strongly criticized by Murphy and Staples (1979). The traditional nuclear family is becoming less common. The traditional view of FLC does not account for childless couples; unmarried couples; single parent families; families broken up by separation, divorce or death; people who marry late in life or have children late in their marriage; and people who live in extended families. The demographic analysis which shows decreasing family size, increased divorce, delays in marriage, delays in birth of the first child, increased births outside marriage and a rising number of single person households all indicate that the FLC concept is flawed if applied too rigorously.

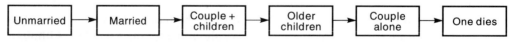

Figure 12.2   *Stages in the family life cycle*

Table 12.4 *Family life cycle*

1 **Bachelor/single**
Low earnings but few rigid demands so can have high discretionary income. Hedonistic, pleasure seeking, fashion conscious, so high spend on clothes, alcohol, eating out, travel, leisure, courtship

2 **Newly married/honeymooners**
With no children but both earning, usually reasonably well off. High expenditure on home, new equipment, e.g. freezer, oven. Substantial spend on car, clothing, leisure, travel

3 **Parenthood: Full nest I**
Arrival of first child causes wife to stop working and drains finances. High spend on home, baby products

4 **Full nest II**
Youngest child 6 or over, husband's income improves, wife returns to work. Buys food in larger packages. Entertainment centres on home. Interest in new products

5 **Full nest III**
Family income continues to grow but so does expense on education and support of children. High spend on bulk food

6 **Postparenthood: Empty nest I**
Income continues to increase but children left home. Couple alone again spend more on luxury items, quality, travel, leisure, recreation. Less interest in new products, more in established favourites

7 **Empty nest II**
Reduction in income as head of household retires. More health orientated expenditure. Move to smaller house

8 **Solitary survivor**
Loss of one spouse. Income may reduce dramatically. Wants single person products

Source: Wells and Gruber, 1966.

Despite this, a Family Policy Studies Centre report (Rice, 1993) claims that in the UK:

● Nine out of ten people will marry at some time in their lives.
● Nine out of ten married couples will have children.
● Two in every three marriages will be ended by death rather than divorce.
● Eight out of ten people live in households headed by a married couple.

However, a major finding was also that not all people will go through all phases of the traditional FLC within one family. The variations on the original concept of FLC therefore reinforce the view that in the future the household may be a more useful unit of analysis than the family.

Illustration 12.3 At what stage are you satisfied?

Four thousand American householders were classified into one of six FLC stages. At the same time these people were scored on their level of satisfaction with food preparation. The score was based on measures such as the time spent on food preparation, the type of food served and the attention given by the food preparer to their own food preferences. The satisfaction score was related to the stage in the FLC.

Stages of FLC

1   Childless young married (married less than 10 years no child)
2   Expanding (youngest child less than 6, none more than 16)
3   Stable (youngest child more than 6, none more than 16)
4   Contracting (one child over 16, none less than 6)
5   Postparental (childless couple, all children left home)
6   Childless older married (childless couple, married more than 10 years)

The most satisfied were the postparental couples, and the least satisfied the expanding families. The childless young married were also more satisfied. It is probable that the satisfied groups have more time for leisure, before or after having children, and more disposable income.

Based on Coughenour (1972) in Engel, Blackwell and Miniard (1993)

Despite the inherent difficulties with the concept of the FLC it still provides one of the best explanations for differences in consumption patterns. The main buying patterns of families at different stages of the FLC briefly are identified next (Micham 1991).

The 18–24-year-old family

This group generally has a positive financial outlook due to their multi-earner status. Convenience is usually considered more highly than price and this has a dominating effect on purchases. Frozen foods, microwave ovens and other convenient cooking appliances are therefore in demand. This group tend to patronize fast food outlets and to shop at convenience stores rather than traditional supermarkets.

The 25–44-year-old family

In this category people are more likely to have children and hence to cut down on expensive items like eating out or entertainment. Bulk food shopping in supermarkets is most likely, and spending on food is highest of all family groups because there are children to feed.

At the same time two other trends are noticeable. First, since more women have joined the labour force the emphasis on convenience products for this group is important, hence the continuing growth in sales of frozen and processed products. Secondly, in some households with no children, i.e. the so-called 'Dinks' (double income no kids), there is high disposable income, which can result in higher levels of purchase of convenience foods and in eating out.

The 45–64-year-old family

Since the children have grown up, the family size is generally smaller and a high proportion of wives may have either continued in the workforce or have re-entered it. Many families in this group have paid off their mortgage and have a higher level of discretionary income. Eating out, travel, hobbies, luxuries and an emphasis on quality become important.

In this group the consumption habits formed in childhood or earlier life are carried through to affect purchase patterns. This is well illustrated by the differences in consumption of mutton and lamb. Older housewives spend above average and younger housewives below average on the product. The reverse pattern emerges for frozen and processed vegetables, where the older housewife spends less on these products than the younger one (Ritson and Hutchins, 1991).

The 65+ family

Although the household size has diminished to only two or even one person, discretionary income is high. In the UK the financial power of pensioners rose by 91 per cent in the 1980s and their spending increased for more than anywhere else in Europe. The increase was fuelled by better pensions and better health. Spending on eating out rose by 85 per cent, but this group also spend heavily on staple foods to be cooked at home (Pryke, 1993; Davis 1994).

Conclusion

Even though the traditional nuclear family of two adults and children is less common than it once was, it is still an important consuming unit which acts as the main reference group for most people. Of growing importance in market research circles is the household unit, which groups together all persons, related or unrelated, who live together. Logically the larger a household the more is spent on food: however, the amount spent per person decreases. Usually this is because in large households there is a switch to the consumption of less expensive food items.

Although one individual may take ultimate responsibility for the purchase of food, other members of the family group will have a strong influence on decisions. It is still the case that in the majority of households women are responsible for spending on food. Where they control the family finances spending is even higher than where they do not. Increasingly children are becoming an important consumer group. Their meal patterns are less structured than adults, with a tendency to graze and hence a particularly high consumption of snack foods, soft drinks and fast food.

The concept of the family life cycle has its critics but identifies that families live through a series of stages, before, during and after the time when children are growing up. At each stage the need for different products varies and therefore leads to a convenient way of segmenting the market.

Questions

1   What is meant by the term family life cycle?
What deficiencies are there in a traditional FLC segmentation strategy?
2   How has family structure changed in the past twenty years and how do you think it might change in the next ten years?
What consequences will there be for the types of food product made available?
3   How does the stage in the FLC influence what food products are purchased?
4   For what food products would you say the influence of children is greatest?
5   Compare the family structure across different countries in the EU? What has led to the decline of the extended family?
How do close relatives of a nuclear family exert their influence on purchase decisions?
6   What changes have you observed in food shopping by male and female members of your family?
7   What roles do you identify in your own family?
What roles were held by which members of your family in respect of the last time you had a meal out as a group?
8   What would you say are the main functions of a family?
How are these fulfilled?
9   Collect examples of adverts to illustrate promotional appeals directed to particular family members.
10   Design your own life stage categories for consumers of snack foods, indicating typical purchase behaviour of the different groups.

References

Allt, B. (1978) *Husbands and Wives and Shopping for Food*, Mirror Group Newspapers Ltd (commercial market research report), London
Chesher, A. (1991) Household composition and household food purchases. In *Fifty Years of the National Food Survey 1940–1990* (ed. J. M. Slater), HMSO, London
Davis, H. and Rigaux, B. (1974) Perception of marital roles in decision processes. *J Consumer Res.*, **1**, 5–14
Davis, J. (1994) 'Richer pickings for the elderly', *Daily Mail*, 23 June
Edgell, S. (1970) Spiralists: their careers and family lives. *Br. J. Sociol.*, **40**
Engel, J. F., Blackwell, R. and Miniard, P. (1993) *Consumer Behaviour*, 7th edn, Dryden, Fort Worth, Texas

Equal Opportunities Commission (1992) *Women and Men in Britain*, EOC. HMSO, London

Foxall, G. R. and Goldsmith, R. E. (1994) *Consumer Psychology for Marketing*, Routledge, London

Green, E. (1991) 'Grazing in the land of fast food fantasies', *Independent*, 16 February

Hall, C. (1987) Youth's middle tier comes of age. *Marketing Media Decisions*, October, p. 58

Komarovsky, M. (1961) Class differences in family decision making. In *Household Decision-Making* (ed. N. Foote), New York Univesity Press, NY

Kotler, P. (1984) *Marketing Management, Analyses, Planning and Control*. Prentice Hall, Englewood Cliffs, NJ

Massey, R. (1994) 'Food junkies', *Daily Mail*, 22 June

Micham, R. (1991) *Lifestyle Market Segmentation*, Praeger, NY

Murphy, P. and Staples, W. (1979) A modernised family life cycle. *J. Cons. Res.*, **6**, 12–22

Nielsen Homescan (1992) In *The British Shopper 1993*, NTC Publications, Henley-on-Thames

Pryke, S. (1993) Generation grain, *Marketing Week*. 2 July, 46

Rice, C. (1993) *Consumer Behaviour: Behavioural Aspects of Marketing*, Butterworth-Heinemann, Oxford

Ritson, C. and Hutchins, R. (1991) The consumption revolution. In *Fifty Years of the National Food Survey 1940–1990* (ed. J. M. Slater), HMSO, London

Social Trends (1992) Household expenditure. In *Social Trends* no. 22, Government Statistical Service, HMSO, London

Walter Thompson, J. (1968) In *The Female Consumer* (ed. R. Scott, 1976), Associated Business Programmes, London

Ward, S. and Wackman, D. (1972) Children's purchase influence attempts and parental yielding. *J. Marketing Res.*, **9**, 12

Wells, W. C. and Gruber, G. (1966) Life cycle concepts in marketing research. *J. Marketing Res.*, **3**, 355–63

Part Three

Psychological Influences

So far the discussion in this text has been concerned with a variety of political, economic, technical, cultural and social influences which can have an impact on consumer behaviour. In a sense these are external and to some extent outside the control of the individual. Consumers can be divided according to class, age, stage in the family life cycle, household size and income level. The opportunity to segment the market in this way is useful and one traditionally used in market research. However, what it does not do is provide an insight into the feelings, attitudes, opinions, values and motives of consumers. These are constructs which are internal to the individual. An exploration of these individual psychological dispositions is what makes up the subject matter of the following three chapters.

Personality is a concept which refers to the unique set of behaviours and traits which differentiate one person from another. Explanations of its source vary from the ideas of Freud with an emphasis on unconscious motives to theories where the attention is more on situational contexts as triggers of behaviour.

There has been a long-running search to identify whether people with particular personality traits buy certain brands or products. Chapter 13 examines this evidence, explains why the relationships are not always as good as hoped, but also refers to more recent research where the links between traits and product choice are more apparent. Personality and motivational theory has also been used as the basis for two other developments. Although past its heyday, qualitative, motivational research has been used as a means to probe the unconscious feelings consumers have towards a product or brand. These ideas also serve as the foundation of lifestyle or psychographic segmentation of markets, which is explained in Chapter 14.

Lifestyle refers to the distinctive ways in which a set of consumers spend their time, what they consider important, what their opinions are about current issues. These activities, interests and opinions can be measured and categorized.

The chapter explores a variety of systems of lifestyle segmentation and also focuses on the changing values in society in order to show how new product developers and those in advertising have constantly to attune their products and messages to a changing environment.

Attitudes are an important part of consumer research since they are assumed to provide an important link with what consumers believe about a product and what they actually buy. Advertisers spend vast sums of money trying to change consumers' attitudes in the hope this will affect purchase. In fact, the relationship between attitude and behaviour is one of the least resolved in social psychology. An attitude may not necessarily predict a behaviour and some researchers believe it only results from a behaviour. However, some recent research shows that if the attitude measured is tightly specified in relation to subsequent behaviour, it can have predictive power. Obviously this whole area, which is explored in Chapter 15, is of significance in market research, which is concerned with the development and testing of new food products and then how best to promote them.

Hence the emphasis in Part Three is on personality, motives, lifestyle and attitude, which represent a variety of internal psychological dispositions which have an influence on consumer behaviour.

13 *Personality and motivation*

Introduction

Most quantitative market research seeks to segment consumers according to their age, how much they earn, what job they do, where they live or which stage of their life they are at. These demographic measures of consumers are relatively easy to determine and are still the basis of much quantitative market research. The assumption is that different categories of consumers will behave in a broadly consistent way and differently from other groups.

Some of the problems with this approach are identified in the chapter concerned with social class (Chapter 10). The changing social structure, and with it the slow dissolution of some traditional class barriers, means that it is not possible to discriminate so easily between consumer groups as was once the case.

Simultaneously, market researchers have become more aware of the obvious point that two people from the same age group or social class background may not behave in the same way nor purchase similar products. The 50-year-old policeman from Turin may have similar purchase behaviour to the 25-year-old female executive from Madrid. The focus of psychographic as opposed to demographic segmentation is on the human characteristics of consumers which may have a bearing on their response to products, packaging and advertising. The purpose of this chapter is briefly to examine some of the theories and concepts derived from personality and motivation research which have developed into psychographic segmentation techniques. In essence the latter idea is to determine the values and beliefs an individual holds dear. The person's attitudes, interests and opinions can be measured to determine their particular lifestyle which is reflected in their purchase behaviour.

In Chapter 14 lifestyle and psychographic segmentation techniques are considered in depth. Before that it is necessary to understand something of the theoretical foundation of this approach, and simultaneously to examine some of the links researchers have tried to make between personality and consumer behaviour.

Personality theories

We are all subject to many of the same influences in our daily lives. Economic recession, war, the changing role of women, simultaneously affect all of us. At the same time each of us has a unique predisposition to behave in a certain way because of our particular social environment, upbringing, schooling and the people we know.

Differences exist between each of us because each of us internalizes these two sets of influences in different ways. The unique set of characteristics which each of us has influences the way in which we behave. These characteristics are relatively stable and are used to identify our particular personality.

Throughout the earlier part of this century researchers tried to identify whether certain personality characteristics are linked to certain buyer behaviour. At the same time the search has been carried out to see whether the unconscious forces which influence personality can explain what motivates the buyer.

Psycho-analytical theory

Freud gave us the idea of subconscious influences which partly make up our personality. He proposed an interaction of three forces, the id, ego and superego. The **id** is the intuitive, subconscious element of our make-up, driving us to seek gratification of our basic needs, i.e. sex and avoidance of death. The **ego** can broadly be described as rationality, the mediator between the hedonistic, pleasure-seeking forces of the id and the perfectionistic, moralistic, restraining superego. The **superego** corresponds roughly with our conscience and is the internalization of the morality of the society in which we live. The continual psychic battle between these forces determines our personal make-up and our behaviour (see Figure 13.1).

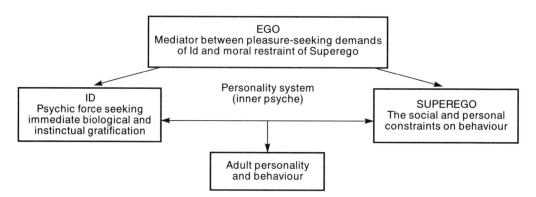

Figure 13.1 *Freudian views of personality*

Applications

Much motivational market research has been based on the assumption that unconscious forces will shape reaction to a product or advert. Depth-interviewing attempts to determine deep-seated motives. Groups of consumers, sometimes called focus groups, are encouraged to talk freely about a product or advert in the hope that unconscious motives may be revealed.

Projective techniques make use of a variety of prompts to stimulate responses which again are intended to indicate deep-seated motives. Consumers may be given a picture, a cartoon or a situation and asked to describe what they see or to visualize themselves in it. The interviewer may provide, for example, a picture of two families, one healthy in appearance, one less so, and the respondent is asked to comment on their relative consumption of milk and snack foods. Other forms of projective technique require consumers to ascribe personalities or characters to brands or to imagine how a product might behave if it were a human being.

As examples, early American motivational researchers suggested women when baking a cake unconsciously go through a process equivalent to the act of birth. Great care is therefore needed with products such as cake mixes which curtail this process. Early versions of the product were rejected as they required the consumer only to add water. Later versions which needed an egg added by the person baking the cake were more acceptable.

Dichter (1964) also showed that products can have personalities linked to consumers' unconscious needs. Rice, he argues, symbolizes health, fertility, strength and femininity which is why it is thrown at women at weddings to symbolize the hope that the couple will have lots of children. Ice cream is associated with gratification of a basic need for love and affection. It is given to a child when they are good and withheld as a punishment.

The view of Dichter and others is therefore that the promotion of such products has to play on these unconscious needs. Ice cream should be associated with love, even giving sexual gratification, which is exactly the pitch in recent Hagen-Daas promotional strategies.

The use of motivational research is now past the peak it achieved before 1970. However, Freudian ideas have had a strong influence in raising the issue that consumers often have unconscious desires which shape their behaviour.

Trait theory

When we describe the personality of someone else we use words such as aggressive, kind, shrewd, nice. Trait theory is a sophisticated version of the same thing. Originally Cattell (1989) identified a long list of adjectives used to describe another person and reduced these down to a list of sixteen factors by the statistical technique of factor analysis. Hence the theory is known as sixteen personality factor (16PF) theory. These traits have been shown to be relatively stable. They are common to many people but the strength of any particular characteristic will vary from one person to another. A list of the dimensions identified by Cattell is given in Table 13.1.

Eysenck has a similar concept for measuring individuals, via questionnaire, on a series of personality scales. The Eysenck Personality Inventory (EPI) indicates personality types on a series of two-dimensional scales (Eysenck and Eysenck, 1964) (Figure 13.2). The extroversion–introversion scale identifies two extremes. Extroverts are sociable, need to talk to others and act impulsively. By contrast introverts are shy and retiring. Extroverts are said to have lower levels of cortical arousal which is why they seek external stimulation. The stability–instability scale gives a high score to worriers. Low scorers are calm, stable, even-tempered and react slowly.

Table 13.1   *Cattell's sixteen principal factors (16PF)*

Cool	A	Warm
Concrete thinking	B	Abstract thinking
Affected by feelings	C	Emotionally stable
Submissive	E	Dominant
Sober	F	Enthusiastic
Expedient	G	Conscientious
Shy	H	Bold
Tough minded	I	Tender minded
Trusting	L	Suspicious
Practical	M	Imaginative
Forthright	N	Shrewd
Self-assured	O	Apprehensive
Conservative	Q1	Experimenting
Group oriented	Q2	Self-sufficient
Undisciplined	Q3	Controlled
Relaxed	Q4	Tense

Source: Cattell, 1989.

All trait or type theories imply that the external evidence of a personality can be measured and that stable underlying personality traits can explain behaviour. Some researchers believe this denies the influence of situational factors in influencing behaviour. However, these ideas have triggered the search for whether consumers with a particular profile of traits demonstrate particular purchase behaviour.

A large body of research has been concerned with the search for a link between personality traits and consumer behaviour. There is a mass of evidence of slight relations between the two but it is not very convincing. This could be for a variety of reasons. It may be that the relationship is indeed only slight; it could be trait theory does not adequately capture personality attributes; or perhaps the measuring devices do not give a reliable or valid measure of personality.

Allsopp (quoted by Foxall and Goldsmith, 1994) used the Eysenck Personality Inventory (EPI) to investigate beer and cider consumption by consumers with different personality types. Respondents were all men aged between 18 and 21 and either apprentice craftsmen or undergraduates. The scales used from the EPI which yielded significant results were extroversion, tough-mindedness, impulsiveness and venturesomeness. The assumptions made before the correlation with drinking habits were

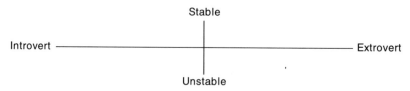

Figure 13.2 *Eysenck's two dimensions of personality*

worked out were as follows. Since extroverts are sociable, talkative, active and impulsive they would be expected to look for stimulation compared with introverts and would get this by drinking in pubs. Those scoring at a medium level on the tough-mindedness scale are self-centred, independent, innovative and risk-taking and so would be expected to consume more alcohol than those low on the scale. Impulsiveness and venturesomeness are aspects of personality involving sensation-seeking so again high scorers would be expected to consume more alcohol than low scorers.

Overall, the correlation of scores on the personality scales with mean weekly consumption of beer or cider showed the results predicted. The craftsmen who scored high on two or three of the personality scales consumed about twice as much per week as those who scored low. Students who scored high on all four scales drank about twice as much beer and cider as those who scored none.

It would be reasonable to expect that consumers with different personality types would not only drink at different rates but would also be attracted to different physical and social environments which would therefore have implications for the design of pubs.

Consumers segmented according to personality traits have been shown to differ in their response to new product innovations. People differ in their perception of the difference between a new brand or product and an existing one. Broad categorizers discriminate less sharply between existing and new products and perceive less risk in buying new products. Narrow categorizers are more cautious. Dogmatic consumers are less willing than flexible ones to choose new products and tend to stick to established or traditional versions. Consumers tolerant of ambiguity are more likely to buy new products than less tolerant ones. The latter are likely to seek more information and to dither before committing themselves. Sensation-seekers are more open to risk-taking, and to try new things partly in order to avoid boredom.

Foxall and Goldsmith (1994) have used the Kirton Adaption-Innovation Inventory (KAI) to relate personality traits and hence cognitive style to purchase of new products. On the KAI scale Innovators tend to be more extrovert, less dogmatic, more tolerant of ambiguity, more flexible and more sensation-seeking than Adaptors. The Innovators on the KAI scale purchased a medium level of new products and brands of healthy food. However Adaptors purchased either a low or a very high volume of new products and brands.

This is consistent with the idea that consumer innovators show little or no brand loyalty. They will try new products but quickly move on to others. Purchasers of just a few new products are sound, steady Adaptors. However, consumers who decide on a new lifestyle of healthy eating may not be the flighty, sensation-seeking Innovators but Adaptors, who patiently seek out as many of the new products as possible.

This finding is at odds with the widely held view in marketing that innovators would have the personality profile of flexibility, sensation-seeking, tolerance of ambiguity and so on. Highly involved Adaptors who have none of these characteristics may end up being the highest level consumers of new products.

This analysis has led Foxall and Goldsmith to argue that those who adopt new products may be one of three different kinds of consumers: Innovators on the KAI scale or one of two kinds of Adaptors, those who are either more or less involved in the set of new products.

This also helps to explain the consistently low level of correlations found in previous research which has attempted to link personality and consumer behaviour. The view that those who are the early adopters of new products have a particular personality type is an oversimplification. This may be because previously used personality measures were not able to discriminate between different types of people who are all early adopters of new products.

Social theory

Some of Freud's followers became dissatisfied with his insistence on a biological explanation for personality and began to develop theories with more emphasis on social influences. Adler, for instance, believed the basic human drive was to overcome feelings of inferiority. Choices of products are made in an effort to make oneself feel better and to feel less inferior to others.

Horney (1958) developed an extension of Adler's concept to argue that childhood insecurities stemming from the parent–child relationship create basic anxieties. The personality is developed as the individual learns to cope with these anxieties.

Three broad personality types emerge:

Compliant	Move towards people
Aggressive	Move against people
Detached	Move away from people

The highly **compliant** individual is anxious to be with others, to receive recognition, help, guidance. They tend to be conformist and easily dominated by others. Later work showed this type of person, because of their compliance to be a good target for advertising as they do not wish to cause offence to others. They drink more wine, socialize and buy products to support their personality.

The **aggressive** type is achievement-orientated, wants status and the admiration of others so buys products which make them look better or feel better. The **detached** person is the opposite. They are not interested in impressing other people. They are detached emotionally and behaviourally from others. They have low social horizons hence they tend to be unaware of new brands, or what is socially acceptable to buy.

Riesman *et al.* (1960) have advocated a related but important conceptualization of consumers as affected by different value bases in society, which again differentiates three categories.

Tradition directed	Values of past
Inner-directed	Values of self
Outer-directed	values of others

The **tradition-directed** person has values based in the past. They are dependent on family and friends, tend to be slow to change with low social mobility. The **inner-directed** person is self-reliant, has developed their own perspective on life, and is not easily influenced by others. The **outer-directed** consumer seeks to determine who they are through the eyes of others. Hence, they are dependent on and influenced by others and attempt to influence them.

Applications

It can be seen that many modern adverts exploit the striving for superiority, the escape from loneliness or the need for love. Riesmann and Horney's work, together within that of Maslow, have had a strong influence on the evolution of lifestyle classifications which will be considered later.

Self-concept theory

The essence of this theory of personality is that people have a concept of either who they are or who they would like to be. The sort of person someone believes they are is based on their traits, abilities, possessions, family and friends. This self-image is very much based also on the reactions of others to them. The theory argues that everyone also has an idealized image of what they would wish to be like. Beer drinkers see themselves as more confident, extrovert and sociable than non-drinkers. The suggestion from this is that products should be promoted on the premise that either they match the image of a particular consumer group, or that they give people the opportunity to be better than they are.

Guinness used to have an old-fashioned image. It was drunk by middle-aged women because it did them good. Most drinkers were over 35 years old. To promote to a younger, more sophisticated, more socially aware and higher social group, the promotion strategy was changed to give more focus to individuality, sophistication, younger women, taste and style.

Motivation theory

Put simply, Maslow's (1954) idea is that a person's behaviour is directed to satisfying needs. He arranged these needs into broad categories and into a hierarchy. The hierarchy is most commonly displayed as a pyramid (see Figure 13.3). In this explanation a stepped pyramid is used to illustrate that a person's behaviour will be dominated by trying to satisfy the lowest unsatisfied need before stepping to the next level. Each successive level in the hierarchy must be sufficiently satisfied before the next level becomes operational. The needs range from low order physiological need, through safety and the need to belong, to higher-order needs for self-esteem and self-actualization. The satisfaction of lower order needs triggers the next level into action and so on to the highest level. Achieving self actualisation means the individual has the opportunity to fulfil their ambitions in the broadest sense.

Applications

Maslow's ideas have been criticized as 'armchair' philosophy without supporting evidence. On the other hand they have been used as an explanatory device in many

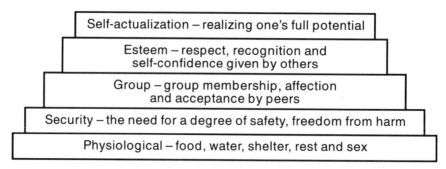

Figure 13.3 *Maslow's hierarchy of needs*

fields ranging from organizational to consumer behaviour. One application which is of interest is explored further in the discussion on lifestyles. The concept also reminds us that a promotional appeal, such as in food advertising, is aimed at satisfying basic needs. However, the message may also have to be concerned with satisfaction of needs to do with group belongingness and relate to higher-level needs as well.

Taken together with Riesman's work, the views of Maslow have developed over time into a dynamic analysis of lifestyles. The broad categorization provided by Riesman can be laid over Maslow's hierarchy as indicated in Figure 13.4. This broad categorization is the basis for the psychographic classification which will be discussed in Chapter 14.

In essence, over this century there has been a shift in the population profile and in consumer needs from an era dominated by the satisfaction of physiological needs. The 1960s and 1970s were characterized by outer-directed behaviour. Conspicuous consumers were motivated by a desire to buy products which showed them off, made them feel good or gave status. From the mid 1980s onwards the proportion of inner-directed consumers has been on the increase. They are concerned with fulfilling their potential, living in an environment of which care is taken and buying products which support their individuality.

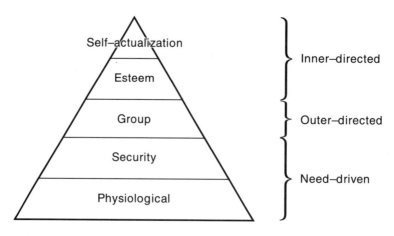

Figure 13.4 *The relation between Maslow's hierarchy and Reisman's needs*

Conclusion

The search for a relationship between personality and purchase behaviour has resulted in a confusing set of results. On the one hand there is a massive set of evidence of correlations of up to 0.3 between different traits and product or brand choice. On the other hand, this level of correlation explains only a small percentage of what influences purchase behaviour. In a way this is not surprising. People would need to have very similar personalities for there to be a clear and consistent link with behaviour.

Personality is only one of a range of variables which influence lifestyle and lifestyle is only one of a range of factors influencing purchase behaviour. There is also the problem that many of the theories on which the applications to market research are based are themselves hotly disputed as explanatory ideas. Further than this, the measuring rods used to measure whatever it is those theories suggest should be measured, are also suspect on grounds of reliability and validity.

All this would be gloomy news were it not for the fact that more recent research has identified a clearer relationship between personality traits and buyer behaviour. Work reported by Foxall and Goldsmith (1994) shows a link between personality traits and beer or cider consumption and a way to identify different personality types who vary in their reaction to new food products.

The personality theories of Riesman and Maslow also provide an important theoretical basis to motivational research and to psychographic profiling which results in consumers being segmented according to lifestyle.

Questions

1 What is meant by the term personality? Why is it not surprising that this concept is less useful for market segmentation than was once thought possible?
2 In what way is a Freudian view useful in analysing consumers' responses to advertisements?
3 How would you explain the paradox that no two people have the same personality and yet personality has been used to segment consumers and there are many of them in each segment?
4 Gather examples of food adverts which appear to be focused on each of Riesman's three value categories.
5 Write advertising copy for a food advert intended to appeal to a particular market segment which tries to build the profile of an 'ideal' consumer.
6 Explain why in early research the corrrelation between personality and product purchase seemed to be no higher than 0.3.
7 Give examples of research that shows a link between personality traits and consumption of food or drink.

References

Cattell, H. B. (1989) *The 16 PF: Personality in Depth*, Institute for Personality and Ability Testing Campaign, Illinois
Dichter, P. R. (1964) *A Handbook of Consumer Motivations*, McGraw-Hill, New York

Eysenck, H. J. and Eysenck, S. B. G. (1964) *Manual of the Eysenck Personality Inventory*, University of London Press, London

Foxall, G. R. and Goldsmith, R. E. (1994) *Consumer Psychology for Marketing*, Routledge, London

Horney, K. (1958) *Neurosis and Human Growth*, Norton, New York

Maslow, A. (1954) *Motivation and Personality*, Harper and Row, New York

Riesman, D., Glazer, N. and Denney, R. (1960) *The Lonely Crowd*, Yale University Press, New Haven, Conn.

14 *Lifestyle and psychographics*

Introduction

The culture and society in which we live has an effect on the values we acquire and also the unique set of traits, or personality, which we demonstrate. Our values are a set of beliefs or expectations about how we or other people should behave. We load these values as good or bad. One person may think it is right that women have become more liberated since the turn of the century, others may have a different view. Our values and our personality modify the effects of the cultural and societal influences to which we are subjected. The way we live, our interests, the things we do and buy, are therefore the result of the interaction of the complex forces of the society in which we live and the mediating effect of the values and personality we have acquired during our lifetime (Figure 14.1). One lifestyle will therefore end up different from another. However, there are groups of people who have very similar ways of life. They tend to do the same things, and to have similar opinions on many issues.

Consumers can be categorized on the basis of their lifestyle. It follows logically that, in order to be able to categorize consumers, it is necessary to determine what sort of lifestyle they have. This is done by measuring their activities, interests and opinions (AIO). The 'A' in AIO sometimes refers to attitudes, but activities are a better measure of lifestyle because they measure what people do.

Psychographics is a related concept. Marketeers and academic researchers dispute whether it is synonymous with lifestyle research as there is an overlap in the meaning and use of the two terms. Psychographics covers measures of AIO but can also include basic personality traits such as aggression, anxiety etc. and the values and beliefs attributed to a particular product (Wells, 1975).

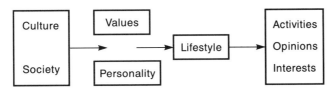

Figure 14.1 *The influences on lifestyle*

Measuring lifestyle

An assessment of lifestyle is made by measuring activities, interests and opinions (AIO). An **activity** is a manifest action, such as watching TV or going to the supermarket. An **interest** is the degree of excitement that is raised by some object, event or topic. An **opinion** is the verbal or written answer given to a question raised; it is a description of beliefs about other people's intentions or of future events.

AIO inventories are developed by first formulating a large number of questions regarding consumer activity, interests and opinions. These may be reduced to a smaller number which seem to clearly cover whichever topic is being asked about. Often this may be in the form of statements attracting answers on a five- or seven-point Likert scale ranging from strongly agree to strongly disagree.

The AIO may also include requests for demographic information as well, covering age, educational background and other variables (Table 14.1). Typical AIO statements are given in Table 14.2.

Consumers can be grouped into different lifestyle segments if the scores in reaction to the statements put to them are similar. For instance, on the basis of the way women

Table 14.1 *Activities, interests and opinions*

Activities	Interests	Opinions	Demographics
Work	Family	Themselves	Age
Hobbies	Home	Social issues	Education
Social events	Job	Politics	Income
Vacation	Community	Business	Occupation
Entertainment	Recreation	Economics	Family size
Club membership	Fashion	Education	Dwelling
Community	Food	Products	Geography
Shopping	Media	Future	City size
Sports	Achievements	Culture	Stage in lifestyle

Source: Plummer, 1974.

Table 14.2 *Statements in AIO*

I prefer meals that can be prepared quickly
I dislike food shopping very much
I buy only the best food for my family
I feel I am very confident at selecting food to buy
A woman should not let children interfere with her career

Source: Roberts and Wortzel, 1979.

Illustration 14.1 Shopping for food

Food on display in a modern supermarket reflects the fact that different people buy different foodstuffs. Even one person may change what they buy from one trip to the next. The traditional, home-based housewife on a low income probably shops mainly with cost in mind, while a 'modern' working woman shopping in her lunch time may be most interested to buy food which does not take long to prepare. Roberts and Wortzel undertook a study in which they gave an AIO questionnaire with 91 items to 169 women in order to find out how lifestyle related to food shopping and preparation. The results were factor analysed to identify groups of women with similar AIOs. There were two sorts of women identified in terms of their role; traditional or modern.

Traditional women tended to be older, married longer, with a larger household, fewer small children and lower income. These women do not cook for pleasure, they cook because they have a sense of responsibility to provide satisfying and nutritious meals for their families. They are also concerned with providing their families with food which is good for them and have a concern with quality. On the other hand they do not agree with anti-cooking statements nor with statements which suggest food preparation should be quick.

'Modern' women can be of any age. They are more likely to be working now or likely to work in future. They are anti-cooking in general but simultaneously agree with statements showing they get a joy out of cooking. This fits with the finding many such women do not like the drudgery of cooking every day but do like to prepare something special for a special occasion. The modern orientation shows a positive correlation with 'concern for time' and 'empirical' shopping behaviour. This reflects the use of point of sale material to help choice by women looking to save time.

The overall results show that differences due to approaches to food preparation explain more of the variation in food shopping behaviour than do simple differences such as whether a woman is working or not. The style of food preparation is in turn related to general lifestyle, namely whether the person is traditional or modern.

Based on M. L. Roberts and L. H. Wortzel (1979) New lifestyle determinants of women's food shopping behaviour. *J. Marketing*, **43**, 28–39.

reacted to the statements in Table 14.2 the researchers classified them as 'modern' or 'traditional', differences which are explained more fully in Illustration 14.1.

A number of lifestyle groupings have been developed which cover the entire population. The groupings are derived from putting together people with similar value sets and lifestyles. In a way value sets are more enduring than lifestyle although over several years or generations there can be shifts in the accepted value norms. Most are based on a combination of ideas derived from Riesman (Riesman, Glazer and Denney, 1950) (inner-, outer-driven) and Maslow (Maslow, 1954) (needs hierarchy) referred to in the chapter on personality (Chapter 13).

Values and lifestyles

One of the most widely popularized studies, the Values and Lifestyles (VALS) study, was developed by Mitchell (1983) at SRI, a management consulting firm in California. Conceptually VALS represents a linkage between the personal orientation of psychology and the activity orientation of the lifestyle approach. The classification assigns people to one of nine VALS segments. These segments are determined by both the values and lifestyles of people in them. In turn the values and lifestyles are based on the basic needs which have to be satisfied and on the drive of humans to improve themselves during their lifetime.

For the classification, a proprietary system of weighting questions was developed. Data were used from a national probability sample of 1635 Americans and their spouses, who responded to an SRI international mail survey in 1980. When the research was first done consumers were categorized in one of three broad groups; inner-, outer- and need- (or substance) driven. The direct comparability with Riesman's categorization is therefore apparent. In turn the three groupings can be broken down to give the nine categories referred to in Figure 14.2.

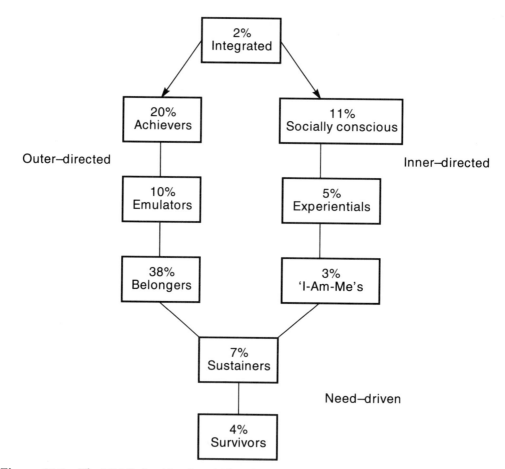

Figure 14.2   *The VALS classification. (After Gunter and Furnham, 1992)*

Need-driven lifestyle

This group represents 11 per cent of the population. Their values and lifestyles are strongly affected by financial restrictions, basic survival needs and security. They are subdivided into Survivors (4%) and Sustainers (7%).

Outer-directed lifestyle

This group covers 68 per cent of the population, representing the mainstream of the population, with two out of every three adults in this lifestyle type. Outer-directed people use others as guides for both values and behaviour. Concern for the social implications and norms of behaviour is quite high. They are subdivided into Belongers (38%), representing the mass, conforming middle market; Emulators (10%), interested in being popular and 'in', and Achievers (20%), who want to show evidence of their success.

Inner-directed lifestyle

This group comprises 18 per cent of the population. They are more concerned with resolving issues in their inner lives than in dealing with the values of the external world. This does not mean that they have rejected the value systems of the outer-directed lifestyle; instead many have been sufficiently successful that they have chosen to pursue additional interests to that of economic success.

They are subdivided into 'I-Am-Mes' (3%), experimental and far out Experientials (5%) and the Societally Conscious (11%), who are into conservation and frugality even if they can afford not to be.

Integrated lifestyle

These are the rare 'self-actualizing' individuals (2%) and represent the highest stage of the hierarchy. Their values and lifestyle combine the power of the outer-directed with the sensitivity of the inner-directed. They are 'one of a kind'; they display self-expression and ecological awareness.

VALS is useful in targeting particular segments of the market on the basis of activity, interests and characteristics. For the different segments it is possible to isolate their choice of media, leisure activities and purchase choice.

As time has gone on there has been a shift first from need- to outer-directed and then from outer- to inner-directed, so that the latter now make up the largest category in Western society. In Europe the highest proportion of inner-directed is in Holland, followed by the UK. This means there is a general shift in values away from conspicuous consumption and keeping up with others and towards doing one's own thing and buying products and services which enable self-fulfilment.

The information in Illustration 14.2 shows how the VALS classification is applicable to different consumer groups throughout Europe.

Illustration 14.2 VALS lifestyle segments in European markets

Survivor

France	Old, poor, fearful, depressed. Out of mainstream, misfit
Italy	Similar to France; live in northern urban slums
UK	Older group is very similar to that in France. The younger, unemployed, are more aggressive – form cliques
W. Germany	Survivors in a psychological sense, not economic or demographic; fearful, envious, and alienated; concerned about social position, physical appearance; antibusiness; many are women

Sustainer

France	Old peasant women and retireds; poor; little education; fearful; live by habit; unable to cope with change
Italy	Ageing; uneducated; uprooted from agrarian society; dependent; concerned with health and appearance; escapist
UK	Working-class values; concerned about economic security; family centred; afraid of government and big business; mainly women; the youngest group is 35 years and over
W. Germany	Sustainers in a psychological sense only; negative feelings toward all aspects of life; resigned and apathetic; avoid risks; high level of hypochondria

Belonger

France	Ageing; need family and community; concerned about financial security, appearance, surroundings, health; able to cope with change, but avoid it
Italy	Ageing; poorly educated; strongly authoritarian; self-sacrificing for family or church; fearful of change; fatalistic; save rather than spend; reject industrial society and its problems
UK	Wanting more satisfying work; traditional but more active, complaining; more concerned about education, creativity, emotions
W. Germany	As in France, although wealthier and better educated; more concerned about prestige and social standing

Emulator

France	Youthful; better educated; entertain at home rather than outside; consider ideologies to be dangerous; concerned about health
Italy	Youthful; mostly male; highly educated; reject family ties; highly materialistic; insensitive to nature; read more than average
UK	Older than others; mostly female; more interested in social status; sacrifice comfort and practicality for fashion
W. Germany	Fairly young; well educated; mostly male; conscious about job status and social standing; concerned about physical safety

Achiever

France	Two groups; older; younger are more intuitive. Achievers; both concerned about ecology, environment, etc
Italy	Middle-aged; predominantly female; links to family and religion; indifferent to self-fulfilment from work; want success and prestige, but otherwise escapist

UK	Too few to be statistically significant; status geared to social position; wealthy become more inner-directed; older people are unwilling to change
W. Germany	As in France, although more are politically active and more concerned about the environment

'I-Am-Me'

France	Aged 20–30; well educated; contemplative; little concern for financial security, social success, or materialism; enjoy their work
Italy	Highly educated; middle- to upper-class; 25–35 age; reject both traditional and consumer/industrial societies; political extremists; live now; bored; take light drugs
UK	Too few to be statistically significant; exhibit self-expressive characteristics, but are more societally conscious
W. Germany	Find work meaningful and self-fulfilling; want to have an impact on society have a high level of anxiety; emotional vacuum, looking for ideologies

Experiential

France	Young; predominantly male; highly educated; not fulfilled by work, but by leisure; enjoy the present; hedonistic
Italy	Too few to be statistically significant, although some 'I-Am-Me''s exhibit Experiential characteristics
UK	Highly educated; want excitement and adventure; risk-takers; creative and self-expressive; want meaningful work; want to demonstrate abilities
W. Germany	Too few to be statistically significant

Societally Conscious

France	Too few to be statistically significant, although most people have strong Societally Conscious tendencies
Italy	Well-educated; generally fairly young; led by protagonists of 1968 protests; satisfied; want more education; socially committed
UK	Family-orientated, young; well educated; creative; want personal growth and meaningful, satisfying work; question authority and technology
W. Germany	Too few to be statistically significant

Integrated

France	Psychologically mature. Tolerant. Understanding. Fit in
Italy	Same as in France
UK	Same as in France
W. Germany	Same as in France.

Based on J. F. Engel, R. Blackwell and P. Miniard (1993) *Consumer Behaviour*, 7th edn. Dryden, Fort Worth, Texas

VALS 2

VALS 2 was developed by SRI in 1990 because VALS 1 had been based on the values of people who had been in their twenties and thirties when the data were first collected ten years previously. Values and lifestyles were dropped as the basis for psychographic segmentation because the link with purchase choice seemed less strong than it had been.

SRI attributed this change to demographic and economic shifts:

- The ageing of the baby boom.
- The increasing diversity of the population.
- The rise of the global economy.
- Decline in consumers' expectations for the future.

The VALS 2 system is based on two nationally representative surveys of 2500 people conducted in 1990. The first survey developed the segmentation system and the second one validated it and linked it to buying and media choices. The questionnaires reveal 'unchanging' psychological stances rather than shifting values and lifestyles.

The psychographic groups in VALS 2 are arranged in a rectangle and variables are stacked horizontally or vertically. Unlike VALS, the segments for VALS 2 are roughly equal in size. The Actualizers at the top account for 8 per cent, while the other segments represent from 11 to 16 per cent of the population.

In the **vertical stack** are **resources**, ranging from minimal to abundant. They include income, education, self-confidence, health, eagerness to buy, intelligence and energy level. Most resources tend to increase from youth through middle age, then diminish with old age.

In the **horizontal stack** are variables denoting **self-orientation**. This dimension captures three ways of buying and each one has two segments.

1   Principle-orientated consumers: guided by their views of how the world is or should be. There are two segments, Fulfilled and Believers.
2   Status-orientated consumers: guided by the actions and opinions of others. The two segments are Achievers and Strivers.
3   Action-orientated consumers: guided by a desire for social and physical activity, variety and risk-taking. The two segments include Experiencers and Makers.

Below the rectangle are located the Strugglers who have the lowest income and too few resources to be included in any consumer self-orientation. The Actualizers are located above the rectangle and have the highest income. They have such high self-esteem and abundant resources that they can indulge in any self-orientations.

List of values (LOV)

This is an alternative approach to VALS, developed by researchers at the University of Michigan Survey Research Center. It is based on values in order to assess adaptation and fulfilment of life's major roles. LOV theory notes the importance of value fulfilment.

The study is based on face-to-face surveys with a probability sample of 2264 conducted by the Survey Research Center. LOV has been related to a number of important measures of mental health, well-being and adaptation to society.

Respondents see a list of nine values, including self-respect, warm relationships with others, sociability, sense of accomplishment, self-fulfilment, sense of belonging, being well respected, fun and enjoyment in life and excitement. Subjects are asked to identify their two most important values or to rank the values. The values could also be evaluated through paired comparison. These values can be used to classify people on Maslow's hierarchy, and to relate more closely to the values of life's major roles (i.e. marriage, parenting etc.).

It has similarities with VALS in that the VALS segments of Achievers and Belongers relate to LOVs 'sense of accomplishment' and 'sense of belonging', respectively. In some instances the overlap seems logically unlikely, such as the LOV classification of 'self-respect', because the groups are semantically quite different.

Novak and MacEvoy (1990) carried out a comparison of VALS and LOV with a national probability sample of US consumers. The predictive capacity was examined with and without demographic variables and compared with VALS. They found that the LOV with demographic items was as predictive as VALS, but LOV without the demographic items was less predictive than VALS.

Social value groups

The Social Value Groups monitor has been developed by Taylor Nelson Ltd, a UK market research agency. The monitor is based on clustering derived from a databank of more than 15 000 interviews conducted in the UK since 1973.

The main purpose behind the Monitor is to help markets to respond to the general changes in social values that are taking place across any given period of time. It comprises of nearly 160 items which measure thirty-seven social trends, from which several social value groups have emerged.

1 **Self-Explorer:** youthful and independent, often female. They are self-aware, confident, imaginative and enjoy a secure, comfortable self-orientated lifestyle.
2 **Social Register:** older and resistant to change, they seek to maintain the status quo. They have a high need for control over the self, family, community and society. There is a tendency to try to preserve traditional ethical and moral codes.
3 **Experimentalist:** these tend to be men in their late twenties or early thirties, who are independent, unconventional, always looking for something new and different. They are energetic, confident, gregarious, intelligent and work-orientated.
4 **Conspicuous Consumer:** this group are predominantly female office workers or housewives with a standard basic education. Conformist, with little need for personal satisfaction, their energy is channelled towards romantic goals and material possessions. They lack self-confidence and mix with similar orientated friends.
5 **Belonger:** generally married and likely to have a young family. Mature, stable and settled, they place great store by the home, family, country, establishment and fair play.

Illustration 14.3 Making ice cream sexy

In the 1980s the European ice cream market was a classic example of a mature market undergoing a radical restructuring due to the emergence of new consumer wants based on changing social values. The mass market for ice creams bought on a hot day to keep the children quiet was being replaced by a variety of niche markets.

The new demands were driven by a variety of emergent values including:

- A new concern for health and nutritional awareness.
- The desire for luxury, hedonsim and the exotic prompted by a reaction against recession and the stimulus of foreign travel.

Maiden Ices was a UK brand experiencing declining market share. Market research had identified the dominant values of its typical consumers, using a values trends mapping technique. These were shown to be declining in terms of market importance. In fact the fall in market share could be closely correlated with the rapid decline in the number of people in the sustenance-driven segment of the market which decreased from 40 per cent of the population in 1973 to 24 per cent in 1992.

The classic response to this situation would have been to reposition Maiden Ices towards a new segment of the market, particularly to capitalize on the growing trend of looking good, being healthy, being nice and generally adopting the value base of the outer-directed.

Unfortunately this position was occupied by Vitalik, a brand produced by the Belgian ice cream manufacturer Blosch to capitalize on the healthy eating trend. Although ice cream is hardly a diet food, Vitalik was stressed to be low calorie and packed with vitamins contributed by the use of real fruit ingredients. 'Vitalik keeps you cool and healthy with less calories than a peanut and more vitamins than your favourite fruit.'

Unable to compete head-on, the decision by Eagle Eye, the owners of Maiden Ices, was to develop an ice cream for a completely new segment of the market, aiming for an international clientele. This meant directing the new brand to the segment of the values map occupied by inner-directeds. At the same time the failing Maiden Ices brand, with its traditional, puritanical image was trimmed back by a reduction in advertising spend and cutting all necessary overheads.

The effect also was to close off the social values trend map to other competitors. The new brand, Eurocreme, was sold by exploiting the sexual undertones normally associated with ice cream. A half-naked male fed it to his girlfriend as she got out of the shower. Ice cream was shown being eaten in unusual places surrounded by a vibrant but placeless, European setting.

The values map below shows how the positioning had capitalized on the values of the inner-directed consumer.

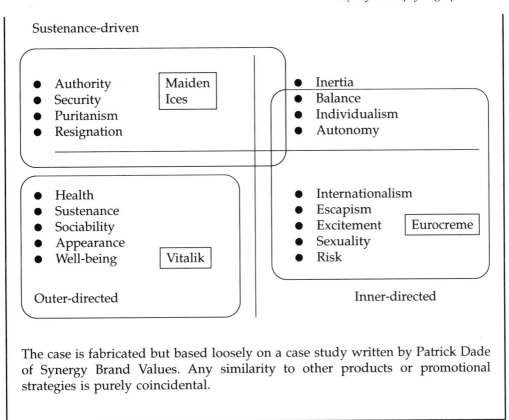

Sustenance-driven

- Authority
- Security
- Puritanism
- Resignation

Maiden Ices

- Inertia
- Balance
- Individualism
- Autonomy

- Health
- Sustenance
- Sociability
- Appearance
- Well-being

Vitalik

- Internationalism
- Escapism
- Excitement
- Sexuality
- Risk

Eurocreme

Outer-directed

Inner-directed

The case is fabricated but based loosely on a case study written by Patrick Dade of Synergy Brand Values. Any similarity to other products or promotional strategies is purely coincidental.

6   **Survivor:** tend to be male, unskilled or skilled manual workers, motivated by basic physical and emotional needs. They are dependent on the protection of authority while also sceptical of its intentions. They identify with the country, family, trade unions or a political party.

7   **Aimless:** lack orientation within society, uninvolved and alienated. Can be aggressive and resentful towards a system's authority. Unhappy and unable to improve their position, they may turn to fantasy and cheap 'kicks' for distraction.

Used in a different way the identification of changing social values can be helped to position new products or reposition existing ones. Although fabricated, the case in Illustration 14.3 shows how the hedonistic, escapist values of the inner-directed consumer are coming to the fore in modern society.

Conclusion

Consumers can be categorized on the basis of their lifestyle. A consumer's lifestyle relates to how they spend their time and money, what they think is important and how they react when asked for their opinions on different subjects. Lifestyle is measured by putting to respondents a series of statements covering (A)ctivities, (O)pinions and (I)nterests which are reacted to in either 5-point of 7-point Likert scales.

Consumers are clumped into lifestyle groups if they react to the series of statements in a similar way. One of the most popular groupings, Values and Lifestyles (VALS) classifies people into one of nine lifestyle segments. The nine groups are subsets of three main categories which relate to the sustenance-(need), inner- and outer-directed profiles first identified by Riesman. Generally there is an increased number of inner-directed consumers amongst the European population. These are characterized as people wanting to do their own thing with less materialistic concerns and who do not wish to keep up with others, as is typical of the outer-directed group. Other segmentation systems based on similar ideas include list of values (LOV) and social values grouping.

The combination of psychographic profiles together with demographic data has allowed market researchers and hence manufacturers to more precisely target market niches, and has enabled their advertising to capitalize on emergent social values.

Questions

Read through the following case then answer the questions at the end.

Flavourfest manufacture and distribute a well-known range of seasonings and sauces. The firm has dominated the market for this and other spices and seasonings.

Consumer research has distinguished three segments which offer the possibility of different marketing strategies. The segments are:

A   Heavy users (39%)
1   Housewives aged 20–45, well educated, higher income; small families, most children under 5, concentration in Northern Europe.
2   Strong motivation not to be old-fashioned with desire to express individuality by using exciting new things.
3   Traditional role as housewife viewed with displeasure and experimentation with new foods done to express individuality not to please the family.
4   Image of Flavourfest suggests exciting and exotic taste. Good reaction to product in terms of taste and appearance. Compatibility between values of user and product image.

B   Light to moderate users (20%)
1   Housewives aged 35–54, large families, children under 12. Middle income groups, mostly live in Italy, Germany.
2   Strong desire to express individuality through cooking which conflicts somewhat with desire to maintain tradition and subvert herself to family desires.
3   Desire to experiment with foods constrained by lack of confidence in results of her experimental cooking.
4   Image of Flavourfest is favourable. Product liked in all respects but confined largely to use with one type of food. Viewed as unacceptable in other uses. Vision limited with regard to new uses for Flavourfest.

C   Non-users (41%)
1   Older housewives, large families, lower income brackets. Mostly live in Portugal, Spain, Greece and northern UK.

2   Strong motive to retain tradition and emotional ties with past; identification with her role as mother and in the home.
3   Conservative, non-venturesome personality.
4   Role as mother and housewife discourages use of Flavourfest which is looked on unfavourably. Image of Flavourfest denotes exotic flavour and modernity which is unacceptable.
5   No interest in new uses and experimentation with Flavourfest, as the product does not represent values of housewives.

Questions

1   On which segment(s) in the Flavourfest case would you concentrate your marketing programme and why?
2   Create no more than fifty lines of advertising copy which you believe capitalizes on the values base of heavy users in the Flavourfest case.
3   What is meant by the terms lifestyle, AIO, personality? In what way are these concepts applicable in the Flavourfest case?
4   In what way would you suggest advertising directed at consumers born before the Second World War might differ from that directed at consumers born after the war? How is this dependent on differences in culture and values of the two groups?
5   Which would you say is more likely to be valuable in marketing research, standard personality tests or specific lifestyle measures? On the basis of what evidence do you make your assertion?

References

Engel, J. F., Blackwell, R. D. and Miniard, P. (1993) *Consumer Behaviour*, 7th edn., Dryden, Fort Worth, Texas
Gunter, B. and Furnham, A. (1992) *Consumer Profiles – An Introduction to Psychographics*, Routledge, London
Maslow, A. H. (1954) *Motivation and Personality*, Harper and Row, New York
Mitchell, A. (1983) *The Nine American Lifestyles*, Macmillan, New York
Novak, T. P. and MacEvoy, B. (1990) On comparing alternative segmentation schemes. *J. Consum. Res.*, **17**, 105–9
Plummer, J. T. (1974) The concept and application of lifestyle segmentation. *J. Marketing*, **38**, 33–7
Riesman, D., Glazer, N. and Denney, R. (1960) *The Lonely Crowd*, Yale University Press, New Haven, Conn.
Roberts, M. L. and Wortzel, L. H. (1979) New lifestyle determinants of women's food shopping behaviour. *J. Marketing*, **43**, 28–39
Wells, W. D. (1975) Psychographics: a critical review. *J. Marketing Res.*, **12**, 209–29

15 *Attitudes and behaviour*

Introduction

How much are people persuaded what to eat by the adverts they see on television? Do people shop in one particular supermarket because all their friends go there too? Which adverts do people remember they saw on television last night? If their favourite sportsperson started taking vitamin supplements would this have an influence on whether they did? Do their friends' attitude towards the environment have an effect on whether or not they buy organically produced food?

These questions illustrate the content of this chapter, which is concerned with attitudes and behaviour. It is commonly believed that attitudes shape behaviour. A person who has a favourable attitude towards French food may occasionally buy Brie or baguettes. The assumption is that a positive attitude will almost automatically lead to a related behaviour.

However, it can be equally true that attitudes are shaped by behaviour. One day a person may spontaneously buy some Camembert, and as a consequence develop a favourable attitude to French cheese. In other words, an attitude may lead to a behaviour, or the reverse, a behaviour to an attitude. The importance for consumer researchers and marketeers is whether knowledge about a person's attitude can enable prediction of their behaviour. If someone says in an opinion poll that they like France and things French, does this mean they are likely to be purchasers of a new type of French food?

The second issue considered in this chapter is attitude change. If there is a link between attitude and behaviour it follows that a lot of marketing effort should be concerned with trying to change attitudes to persuade people to buy something for the first time or to repeat a purchase. This could expand into coverage of the whole of marketing theory. However, the emphasis here is on what is known from research about attitude change. This is taken further in Chapter 17, which examines what types of communication persuade us to change our attitude.

Attitudes and behaviour

Attitudes are a conceptual invention or hypothetical construct so that like intelligence or personality they cannot be seen and located in a particular part of the brain. This being so, they have to be inferred.

We have attitudes towards objects, people, institutions, places. If someone was asked if they would eat snails or chocolate they would have an attitude one way or another. Either they would be against the idea, for it, or ambivalent. In some cases attitudes are strongly held. A person may be strongly for or against the Maastricht treaty and hence European integration. The degree of strength with which an attitude is held is also likely to affect how easily it can be changed. If someone strongly hates fish they are unlikely ever to eat any. On the other hand, if that person was only mildly antagonistic and a friend were to cook a wonderful Dover sole with a tasty sauce, they would probably eat it.

Many of our attitudes have been built up over time. Our family and friends are major shapers of our attitudes, some of which may last a lifetime and are very resistant to change. However, despite this some attitudes do change. Our collective attitude towards Europe, the eating of foreign foods, and factory farming have all changed in recent years. English people now eat snails, pâté and steak tartare which they might have been loth to do thirty years ago.

Hence it is possible to say that attitudes are inferred, vary in strength, are affected by our upbringing and the influence of our peers, and vary in how easily they can be changed.

Although it is not possible to dissect a person to find their attitudes, it is possible to dissect the concept of attitude. Most psychologists agree it consists of three components:

- Cognitive – an element of belief or disbelief.
- Affective – an emotional response; positive or negative.
- Conative – a tendency to behave in a certain way.

Beliefs are assumptions about the probability something actually exists. If a person had never been to Lisbon they could take it on trust that it is there because they have met people who have been, have seen photos of it and it appears on maps. People used to believe that butter was good for them, but now they are not so sure and usually eat margarine. Virtually every move one makes depends in part on what a person believes about the world in which they live. If someone believes fatty meat is bad for them, they will avoid eating it. So beliefs guide behaviour. As originally defined by Plato, beliefs are largely cognitive, that is concerned with knowledge or what a person assumes to be knowledge.

A person's beliefs tell us what they think is true. Their values are what they would like to be true. Values contain an affective or emotional component. Whereas beliefs may or may not guide behaviour, values generally do. A value relates to whether a person wants something and judges their behaviour against whether or not it gets them nearer to their goal. People eat muesli, low fat margarine and avoid fatty food as they value health and believe these products are more likely to make them healthy or keep them healthy.

The strong interaction of belief and emotive response is indicated in Illustration 15.1, which demonstrates the differing reactions to pâté de foie gras of French and British consumers.

If someone values the environment they are more likely to avoid products which seem to damage the environment. The belief about, and evaluation of an object interact to establish a predisposition to act towards it. This is the third component of an attitude. Put simply, our attitude towards a new food product can be summarized in

Illustration 15.1 Pâté de fois gras

The deep south-west of France is foie gras country, the home of ducks and geese reared to produce the artificially fattened livers prized by chefs and gourmets.

British commentators refer to the production of foie gras as the cruellest food of all. In Britain the foie gras market is tiny because retailers fear the wrath of radical vegetarians. By contrast the French produce 600 tonnes of foie gras each year. Although some is destined for top restaurants all over the world, most is eaten by ordinary French people. It is as normal for the French to consume foie gras on a special occasion as it is for the British to eat smoked salmon.

The French find the British attitude of horror at the production of foie gras unbelievable. They see the technique as simply the intensive but progressive fattening of a species which is linked to its physiology. Before migrating ducks and geese store energy by accumulating fat in their livers, so the French argument is that the production of foie gras is perfectly natural. However one of the arguments against it from the British point of view is the unnatural, force feeding. The birds are delivered to the farm at day old and stay outdoors in fields of maize until they are 16 weeks old. At that point they are brought inside to pens in groups of ten. At feeding time a funnel is put down the duck's throat, filled with maize which is then massaged down its throat. In this way over two or three weeks a duck weighing about 4 kg puts on about 1–2 kg by being fed 10–12 kg of maize. A few birds resist, but usually because they do not like being held. In all other respects it could be argued that this farming method is not worse than systems used to produce broiler chickens or battery laid eggs in the UK.

The beliefs of the average British consumer mean they would be just as likely to reject foie gras as frogs legs or pig's brain, which are also eaten in France.

Based on J. Blythman, 'A myth rammed down our throats', *Independent* 6 February 1993

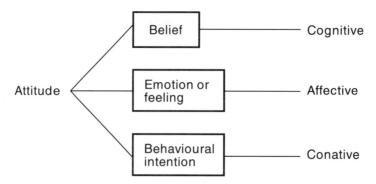

Figure 15.1   *Components of attitude*

Table 15.1 *Measures of attitude components*

Belief measure
Indicate how strongly you would agree with the following statements:
'Peanuts give you a lot of energy'

| Strongly agree | Agree | Neither agree nor disagree | Disagree | Strongly disagree |

Value measure
Do you agree or disagree with the following statement:
'Peanuts are good for you'

Intention measure
What is the probability you will buy peanuts when you next go to the supermarket?

| 0% | 20% | 40% | 60% | 80% | 100% |

---

these three concepts. If we believe a product has certain desirable characteristics (cognitive element), it seems probable we will like the product (affective element) and should an appropriate opportunity arise we are likely to buy it (conative element) (Figure 15.1). Measurements of attitudes usually involve the identification of these different components, as illustrated in Table 15.1.

Table 15.1 also indicates the most usual method of measuring attitudes, which is by use of a Likert scale. This consists of a series of statements about an object. The respondent is then asked to indicate his or her level of agreement with the statement, usually on a 7-, or sometimes 5-, point scale with ratings ranging from strongly agree, through a neutral point to strongly disagree.

Behaviour and attitudes

A great deal of attitude research has been concerned with whether attitudes are directly related to behaviour. Do you like pears? Do you buy pears more than once a week? Do you have any pears at the place where you live right now? Did you buy any pears last time you bought fruit?

This set of questions illustrates the conundrum. It would be extremely useful for market researchers to be able to predict purchase behaviour from knowing attitudes. Indeed the simplistic assumption is that if you can detect a person's attitude you will thereby be in a position to know their behaviour. However, the relationship between attitudes and behaviour is very inexact. This was first illustrated by a famous experiment conducted by La Piere in 1934. During the 1930s he travelled around the USA with a Chinese couple at a time when anti-Chinese feelings ran very high. Of 200 hotels and restaurants, they were refused entry only once. Later La Piere wrote to all these places to ask if they would accept Chinese, and 90 per cent said they would not.

Data in Table 15.2 illustrates the inconsistency between general attitudes towards healthy food and purchase behaviour. People are generally positive about choosing

Table 15.2   *Fastest growing grocery markets (annual percentage change, February 1993)*

Olive oil	44
Pre-cooked sliced meat	26
Chilled desserts	23
Chinese food	22
Dairy spreads	17
Cooking sauces	17

Degree of importance when considering where to shop (% respondents)

	Very	Important	Fairly	Not very	Not	Don't know
Wide range of high fibre products	28	27	20	17	6	2
Wide range of organic food	14	18	19	33	13	3
Wide range of low sugar and low fat products	38	23	17	16	5	1
Wide range of fresh food	65	25	7	3	0	1

Source: Nielsen, 1993.

food stores because of the importance of obtaining heathy foods but at the same time the fastest growing grocery products are mostly very unhealthy.

There are a variety of reasons why attitudes and behaviour do not always tie up. It may be the measures of behaviour and attitude are inappropriate. The same attitude may evoke different behaviour at different thresholds. It could be argued in the La Piere study that it is easier to refuse Chinese in an anonymous letter than face to face. Social pressures also influence behaviour far more than individual attitudes. Habit also has a strong influence. A friend may persuade someone to buy a product which they would not buy on their own.

Research also shows the best correspondence between attitude measures and behaviour is when the former is very specific. If someone is asked if they like margarine this may not predict purchase. However, if asked whether on their next trip to the supermarket they are likely to buy Flora, this is more likely to tie up with actual behaviour.

In summary a majority of studies show some inconsistency between general attitudes and behaviour which may be due to the fact the measures are incorrect, or because situational factors have a strong influence on a behaviour but not an attitude. Where the attitude measured is more specific and the time difference between the measure of attitude and behaviour is small, the relationship holds up better.

Another area of attitude research is the direct reverse of the above and is concerned with whether behaviour shapes attitudes. Cognitive dissonance theory (Festinger, 1957) argues that people strive to maintain consistency between what they do, their behaviour and the attitudes they hold. If someone decides one day to try prawns which they have never eaten before, then two things can happen. Either they will confirm to themselves they hate prawns or they will find that they like them. The attitude shifts

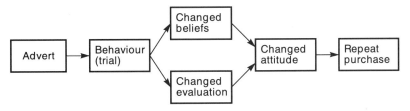

Figure 15.2   *Changes in attitude as a result of behaviour changes*

into line with the actual and subsequent behaviour and they are therefore likely to report an attitude which is consistent with their behaviour, in order to create the cognitive consistency predicted by dissonance theory.

This is an explanation also of the simple fact people can evaluate a product higher once they have bought it, leading to an increased likelihood of repeat purchase. People will also avoid things they do not wish to hear. Their selection of information feeds the attitude they already hold.

The concept is illustrated in Figure 15.2, which shows how trial of a product, a behavioural reaction, can lead to a changed attitude, which in turn is likely to trigger further behavioural response, namely a repeat purchase.

Multi-attribute attitude models

Various researchers, of whom Fishbein and Ajzen (1975) are the most famous, have turned attitudes into a mathematical formula and attempted to measure the components of an attitude. In symbol form the relationship is expressed as:

$$Ao = \sum_{i=1}^{n} b_i \, e_i$$

Where Ao = attitude towards the object
   b_i = strength of belief an object has attribute *i*
   e_i = evaluation of attribute *i*
   n = number of salient attributes

The supposition therefore is that attitude is the sum of a set of beliefs multiplied by the evaluation of those beliefs, in relation to whatever set of salient or significant attributes a particular product may have.

The first part of applying the model is to elicit salient or significant attributes a person uses in evaluating a product. Let us say the product is margarine and the attributes are:

● Whether it costs less than butter.
● If it spreads easily from the fridge.
● If it contains low levels of polyunsaturated fats.

Next, the appropriate belief (*b*) and evaluation (*e*) measures would be developed. An example of an evaluation statement is:

buying margarine costing less than butter is:

very good	___	___	___	___	___	___	___	very bad
	+3	+2	+1	0	−1	−2	−3	

This would be repeated for each salient feature. The belief component represents how strongly consumers believe the particular brand possessed a given attribute.

How likely is it brand X costs less than butter?

very likely	___	___	___	___	___	___	___	very unlikely
	+3	+2	+1	0	−1	−2	−3	

Supposing a survey with these measures is given to 1000 females aged between 25 and 40. An average response could be calculated for each *b* and *e* measure. A set of hypothetical results could be as in Table 15.3.

Table 15.3   *Measures of attitude components*

		Beliefs (b)		
Attribute	*Evaluation (e)*	*Brand A*	*Brand B*	*Brand C*
Cost	+2	+2	+1	−1
Spreading	+1	+2	+2	0
Low fat	+3	+1	+3	+1
Total sum of b, e		+9	+13	+1

In this example low fat is evaluated as the most significant attribute. Brands A and B get a positive rating on all desired attributes, whereas C does not. Obviously advertising is concerned with trying to convince consumers that a brand possesses desirable attributes and avoids negative ones. This sort of market research is necessary to discover if this is so. Although brand A outperforms B and C on cost, B is better on low fat which consumers evaluate as a very significant characteristic of margarine. To estimate overall attitude towards each brand, using the sum of *b* and *e*, each belief is multiplied by the corresponding evaluation score. The score for brand B is highest overall.

Advertisers, using this example, might be concerned to change consumer attitudes by changing either brand beliefs or attribute importance. Brand B could be improved still further by changing its spreading powers or cost differential with respect to butter, but not its fat content, which is perceived as ideal and should not be touched.

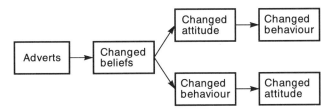

Figure 15.3 *Changing beliefs*

The objective of such a promotional campaign, as illustrated in Figure 15.3, would be to change the beliefs which consumers have about the product with the assumption this would lead to changes in both opinions held and purchase behaviour (Figure 15.3).

Another way is to change attribute importance. In fact margarine producers have made great play of the fact margarine is better for you than butter because of the lower fat content. They also worked hard on the spreading power of margarine when taken straight from the fridge. Early forms of margarine scored badly on this attribute. In this case therefore the attempt is to change the criteria used to make a judgement of a product, again, on the assumption this will change opinions and behaviour (Figure 15.4).

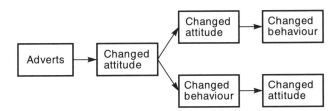

Figure 15.4 *Changing attributes*

The battle between first butter and margarine, and then between margarine manufacturers, as outlined in Illustration 15.2, shows how the different attributes of a new margarine product have been developed to capitalize on the salient properties of both butter and margarine.

Behavioural intention models

Earlier on it was noted that attitude – behaviour relationships can be weaker when behaviour is directly affected by situational or social influences. Fishbein has come closest to identifying that intention, which is the immediate predecessor of actual behaviour, is determined by an attitudinal element and a normative or social component.

Illustration 15.2 Is it butter or a lookalike?

During the 1960s butter consumption in the UK was relatively stable whereas margarine sales were in decline. However from 1970 to 1980 butter and margarine consumption were a virtual mirror image of each other. As one went up, the other went down.

In the early days margarine suffered from an inferior image compared with butter. However, this began to turn around when manufacturers were able to give margarine properties which butter could not emulate. One breakthrough was to make it possible to spread directly from the fridge, another was progress in producing low fat varieties.

However, the belief persisted in the minds of consumers that margarine was a poor substitute for butter.

One of the recent success stories in marketing is 'I Can't Believe It's Not Butter', produced by Van den Bergh, a subsidiary of Unilever, which mimics the taste and look of butter, but is a low fat with good spreading properties.

What is even more ironical is that just as Unilever's new product apes butter, recently rival products have been brought out to ape it. Tesco launched its own low fat spread called 'Unbelievable' which is roughly the same size and shape as Van den Bergh's product with a yellow tub and blue banner on the lid.

Based on 'I can't believe it's not illegal', *Daily Mail*, 26 May 1994, 10

$$B \simeq BI = W_1\,(AB) + W_2\,(SN)$$

where B = behaviour
           BI = behavioural intention
           AB = attitude towards performing behaviour A
           SN = subjective norm
           W_1 and W_2 = weights representing the component's influence

Table 15.3 demonstrated how attitudes towards an object can be measured. The subtle difference here is that Fishbein measures attitudes towards an intended behaviour. This is a much more specific measure and gets over some of the earlier problems caused by measuring general attitude and finding this does not tie well with specific behaviour.

An attitude measure of intended behaviour might be

Buying peanuts is

                   good   ____   ____   ____   ____   ____   bad

The normative component is intended to represent people important to the consumer. It is usually measured by asking what the person thinks other people who are important to them would do with respect to a particular behaviour.

Most people who are important to me think

    I should   ___   ___   ___   ___   ___   should not buy peanuts

A combination of these two measures seems to provide good predictive measures of actual purchase behaviour. The relationships to target behaviour are indicated in Figure 15.5.

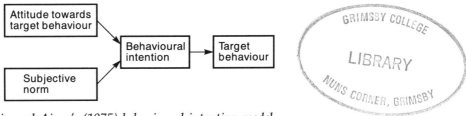

Figure 15.5 *Fishbein and Ajzen's (1975) behavioural intention model*

One of the important outcomes of this model is to show that it is not sufficient to measure global attitudes and to hope from this to predict purchase behaviour. For instance, general attitudes towards health foods would not predict whether a consumer bought an organically grown turnip on their next shopping trip. The measure of attitude would need to be very precise, for instance the consumer's likelihood of buying that sort of turnip in a supermarket on their next shopping trip might then predict his or her target behaviour. This may help to explain why there are many failures of new products even after exhaustive attitudinal surveys by market researchers to test whether consumers would be likely to buy a new product. Unless the attitudes measured are very precisely linked to behavioural intentions they do not give a very good measure of eventual behaviour. Much better is to measure actual buying behaviour which gives a reasonable prediction of future buying behaviour (Foxall and Goldsmith, 1994). Unfortunately, it is expensive to wait this long into the sequence of new product development before finding it is necessary to abort production.

Conclusion

Attitudes are normally considered to consist of three components: an element of belief or disbelief (cognitive), an emotional response, good or bad (affective), and a tendency to behave in a certain way (conative). These three components are usually measured on the basis of responses to a series of attitude statements each followed by a Likert scale ranging on a 5- or 7-point scale from strong agreement to strong disagreement.

One of the most contentious issues in consumer research is whether attitude measurement allows prediction of behaviour, or whether the reverse is true and attitudes are only formed once someone has behaved towards an object. The evidence is that the relationship is tenuous, which may be because of the influence of situational or contextual factors or the use of inappropriate measuring devices.

Fishbein and Ajzen's multi-attribute attitude model argues that an attitude can be measured from a combination of belief and evaluation scores for a series of salient features relevant to a particular object. Advertising might therefore be aimed at changing a salient feature or belief about a product in order to strengthen the consumer's overall evaluation of it.

The behavioural intention model is more specifically concerned with measuring attitude towards a potential behaviour and the strength of reaction expected from people important to the respondent. In combination, these two measures give a much better prediction of eventual behaviour. The reason is the focus is on attitude towards a potential behaviour, which in turn is close to the target behaviour. It suggests attitude measures are only predictive of actual behaviour if what they measure is very precisely focused on the context and not far removed in time from eventual behaviour. This may explain the failure of market research, which measures general attitudes in an attempt to measure buying behaviour towards new products. On the other hand, actual purchase is a relatively good predictor of repeat purchase.

Questions

1 What is an attitude?
2 Discuss whether you consider attitudes precede or follow from behaviour.
3 Develop nine attitude statements to measure the cognitive, affective and conative evaluation which might be made by consumers with respect to a new form of breakfast cereal.
4 Using the formula created by Fishbein and Ajzen referred to on page 173 above, show in tabular form (as in Table 15.3) how three brands of orange juice evaluated on four criteria ranked 1–4, might end up with overall scores of +7, –1 and +10.
5 Explain Fishbein's behavioural intention model by reference to purchase of fast food takeaway meals by teenage boys.
6 Why is it that new products fail even after extensive market research to test consumer opinion before the product is launched?
7 How does cognitive dissonance theory account for the finding that people who may be hesitant about trying a new meat substitute change their attitude once they have tried it?
8 Suppose you were the Marketing Manager of the French producer of pâté de fois gras. Using the information in Illustration 15.1, in what ways would you attempt to change the attitudes to your product of the average British consumer?

References

Festinger, L. (1957) *A Theory of Cognitive Dissonance*, Stanford University Press, Stanford, Ca
Fishbein, M. and Ajzen, I. (1975) *Belief, Attitude, Intention and Behaviour: An Introduction to Theory and Research, Reading*, Addison–Wesley, Reading, Mass.
Foxall, G. R. and Goldsmith, R. E. (1994) *Consumer Psychology for Marketing*, Routledge, London
La Piere, R. T. (1934) *Attitudes versus actions. Social Forces*, **13**, 230–237
Nielsen (1993) *The British Shopper*, NTC Publications, Henley-on-Thames

Part Four

Marketing Influences

Consumers are not only influenced by internal cognitive processes to behave in a certain way but also by the stimulus of the external environment. One estimate is that as much as 20–45 per cent of consumer behaviour is accounted for by situational influences, while individual differences such as personality or attitude account for 15–30 per cent and interaction between individuals and situations for 30–50 per cent (Argyle, 1976).

The retail environment creates a complex set of stimuli which impact on the consumer. Where the food shop is in relation to others, how it is designed, how the products are laid out and merchandized, whether there is music playing, how crowded it is, will all impact on the consumer and affect their purchase behaviour. In addition the type of shops through which food is retailed will have an effect. There are wide differences between food retailing in the UK, which is mostly via large super- or hypermarkets, and the situation in Italy or Portugal where the small independent specialist shop or the street vendor is the usual outlet.

The impact and structure of the retail environment on consumers is discussed in Chapter 16.

Consumers are bombarded each day by up to 2500 adverts for different products. The attempt by advertisers is to change the knowledge, beliefs or evaluations consumers make of products in the hope this will change their attitude and hence their behaviour. A considerable amount of communications research has been concerned with what makes a message credible, the effect of fear, humour and repetition. This is discussed in Chapter 17.

Part Four is therefore concerned with elements of the marketing mix with a particular emphasis on place and promotion and their impact on consumer behaviour.

Reference

Argyle, M. (1976) Personality and social behaviour. In Harre, R. (ed.), *Personality*, Blackwell, Oxford

16 *Retailing*

Introduction

Consumers are influenced in what they buy by what is made available to them. This in turn emphasizes the significant role of retail outlets. The retail outlet where people buy food, and the point of sale or merchandizing material intended to influence their purchase, give retailers a more direct impact on the consumer than those who have produced or packaged the food. Any marketing text will contain extensive treatment of the influence of pricing, packaging, promotion and place of purchase – the traditional 4 Ps – on consumer behaviour. In this chapter the treatment is restricted to the direct influence of the retail operation on the consumer. Besides a brief treatment of the history of retailing, and in particular the evolving power relationship between retailers and manufacturer, this chapter considers the changing mix of retail food outlets, shopping behaviour and the influence of store layout and point of sale material on purchase. Consideration is also given to the development of food retailing in mainland Europe.

History

At one point in our history all our food was produced and made available through markets. Ancient techniques of preserving food were limited so that consumption was heavily influenced by availability, and in particular by seasonal factors.

The industrialization of food processing developed rapidly from the mid 1800s. Traditional techniques of pickling, drying and curing were soon added to by bottling and canning. At the turn of this century small manufacturers geared their output to the specifications of wholesalers who were the link between small manufacturers and small retailers. The power of wholesalers diminished in the 1930s, partly because of the growth of multiple and co-operative grocery stores who bought directly from manufacturers. To counter multiple retailer strength, food manufacturers developed branded goods.

After the Second World War many small food manufacturers were taken over or merged. By 1974 this resulted in the UK having twenty-two of the largest food businesses in the world, as ranked by turnover. By 1979 fifteen of the top twenty-one food manufacturers in Europe were in the UK. This excludes the largest of all, Unilever, which is a global company not limited to the UK (Senker, 1988).

UK food retailing

Besides the sale of food in markets, nowadays most food is sold through some form of retail outlet. There are three major types:

1   Multiples: organizations with 10 or more outlets.
2   Cooperative societies: regional or local societies owned by consumers.
3   Independents: organizations with less than ten outlets, usually single shops.

The main trend has been for the growth of multiples at the expense of independents and co-ops. Over the period from 1976 to 1987 the market share of major retailers increased from 57 per cent to 78 per cent. In the UK the big retailers are opening about eighty new stores a year to add to the 800 superstores already in existence.

We used to buy our food from a large number of small independent shopkeepers. Since 1961 three-quarters of grocers have disappeared. In the UK over 50 per cent of everything we ate in 1990 came from five supermarket groups (Table 16.1). However, the demise of the independent grocer is not so extreme in other parts of Europe (see below).

In the UK the major reason for this development is because of the rise in the buying power and significance of major food retailers which in turn has created large super- and hypermarkets. Sainsbury was the first in the UK to adopt supermarket selling at its Croydon store in 1950. Since then the growth of the multiples has continued, with a decline in the proportion of sales from co-operatives, symbol retailers (such as Spar) and independents. However, independents are attempting to fight back, as indicated in Illustration 16.1. The balance of power also shifted during this period as retailers drove down margins in negotiations with manufacturers and killed off small-fry competition. Their economies of scale on price and labour enabled them to cut their costs and become more powerful in the relationship with their suppliers. (Economic Intelligence Unit, 1992).

Table 16.1   *Market shares of UK retailers, (percentage)*

Sainsbury	15.3
Tesco	13.9
Argyll	9.3
Asda	7.6
Kwiksave	5.2
Gateway	5.0
Marks & Spencer	3.8
Other multiples	8.3
Co-ops	9.5
Independent grocers	6.9
Specialist food retailers	15.9

Source: Based on turnover data from *Supermarketing, Retail Fact File 1993.*

Illustration 16.1 Independents fight back

Once the main sellers of groceries, the number of independent retail outlets shrank by a third in the 1980s while their share of food and drink sales fell from a quarter to a seventh.

Nisa Today, the largest association of supermarkets and wholesalers, organizes discounts with suppliers and promotional campaigns for its 718 members. It has formed a consortium to provide a common front to suppliers. Independents generally compare badly charging as much as 20 per cent more than Sainsbury or Tesco. Independents are trying to get over this by offering to manufacturers to buy more of their branded goods lines as opposed to the heavy emphasis on own label which the large multiples have pursued.

But will the initiative turn the tide of decline which has relegated many small grocery outlets to a precarious position as a source of occasional 'top up' purchases or as suppliers to remote rural communities?

One analyst believes that 'anyone who expects Britain to turn back the clock and start buying most of their food in neighbourhood shops again isn't living in the real world'.

Based on G. de Jonquieres. 'Independents fight back', *Financial Times*, 26 November 1992

This development has been further increased by retailers who have developed own label brands. These started as a cheap and cheerful alternative to branded goods but have given way to own label becoming a flagship product. Sainsbury and Waitrose rely on own label for 50 per cent of their trade, while Marks & Spencer trade is 100 per cent own label.

Marks & Spencer turned what was originally a low quality and cheap own label concept on its head over a decade ago by launching high-quality ready-made meals such as Chicken Kiev. In recent years Tesco and Sainsbury have responded in the same way and also sell high quality own label products.

The rise of own label is closely linked to retail concentration. In the UK its growth is related to the concentration of food retailing in the hands of fewer and fewer multiples (*The Guardian*, 1992). It is also true that own label is strongest in countries with the strongest retailers. So, for example, Portugal, with only around 12 per cent of market share held by the top retailers, has only 1 per cent own label. On the other hand Switzerland, with around 70 per cent market share amongst top retailers, has around 25 per cent own label. These relationships are shown in Figure 16.1 which is based on an analysis by de Jonquieres (1993).

Shopping behaviour

The retail environment provides a complex physical situation which can influence consumer behaviour. This is considered more extensively by Foxall and Goldsmith (1994).

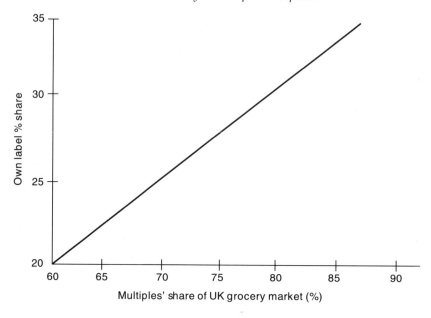

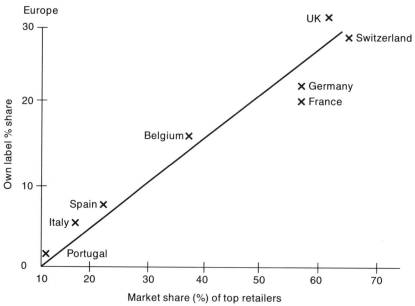

Figure 16.1   *Own label and retail concentration. (After de Jonquieres, 1993)*

Consumers are affected first of all by where a shop is in relation to other shops. Supermarkets and other major departmental stores tend to attract people to a shopping area. The design and layout of a store, for instance ease of parking and width of aisles will influence the level of satisfaction and hence purchase patterns.

The degree of crowding in a shop will affect purchase behaviour. Empty restaurants or underutilized shops are avoided but a heavily crowded supermarket will lead to faster shopping and a low level of purchase. On the other hand people shopping together will stimulate each other to buy more.

If consumers are under time pressure they tend to rely on memory and previous experience and so choose from a limited range of brands and generally decrease their search time. What they choose is also significantly affected by the purpose for which the purchase will be used, whether say for a snack meal or a dinner party.

Relatively few people are consistently loyal to a particular foodstore. As with products they are inclined to pick and choose between a limited set of different stores, perhaps used for different purposes, such as a main shop or as a top up (Kau and Ehrenberg, 1984).

Food shopping for the main bulk purchase is still most common on a Friday (25 per cent) or Saturday (21 per cent), involves travelling of less than two miles (64 per cent), by car as opposed to other forms of transport (70 per cent), and is most often to a large supermarket or hypermarket (63 per cent) (Food Pocket Book, 1992).

It is reported that over 50 per cent of food purchases are on impulse. However, this must be carefully interpreted. It is likely that merchandizing prompts recall by the purchaser of the fact they are out of a particular product at home. Whereas they may not have set out with the intention to buy, the stimulus of the in-store environment may prompt the purchase. It is more correct to say this is an unplanned rather than an impulse purchase.

Store layout

The layout of food supermarkets is not a chance business. The major groups specify from head office to local stores where products are to be positioned. Most entrances are to the left of the frontage as it seems the majority of people feel easier moving from left to right as they shop. Inside the entrance the vegetables and fruit, because of their colour, attractiveness and freshness give a harvest festival image and an air of plenty. Staple items such as bread, sugar, eggs are almost hidden around the store so as to pull customers past as many other items as possible before reaching items which they are almost certain to buy. The alcohol tends to be as far as possible from the entrance for security reasons.

Aisle length is important. If they are too short then customers look down them rather than pass along them and so make few spontaneous purchases. The strong selling areas in a store are the outer aisles, service areas (for meat, bread and delicatessen), the start and end of aisles and the checkout areas.

Merchandizing aims to prompt purchase at the point of sale. Shelf positioning, music, price tickets, bin dumps and displays all aim to increase the visibility of a product with the assumption this increases the probability of a sale.

Shelf space is allocated to different product lines to achieve optimal space utilization but also in proportion to sales; faster selling lines get more space and vice versa. The fastest selling lines are at eye level.

Recent innovations such as data derived from checkout scanning make it possible to get accurate measures of sales and hence restocking requirements. This also enables alterations to be made in product display and space allocation. The concept of category management is explained in Illustration 16.2.

In recent years the design of supermarkets has changed as many have tried to improve their image and emphasize quality. Except in cheaper discount stores, the cramped aisles, and pile it high and sell it cheap philosophy has been replaced by rustic

---

Illustration 16.2 Category management

Category management involves dividing a store's products into categories. A big superstore might have 400 which are each then managed like a small business. Direct product profitability analysis (DPP) allows the calculation via checkout scanning of which products sell and hence the profitability of each product in a store. DPP is then used to determine the correct mix of brands, i.e. what shelf space to allot to each brand. It both maximizes profitability of an overall category, best meets customer demand and triggers re-stocking.

Based on N. Buckley, 'Category Management', *Financial Times*, 15 June 1993

---

buildings, pitched roofs, architectural features, wide aisles and an emphasis on space. At one stage when Asda spread from its northern UK base it employed 32 designers to rework its image to attract more affluent southern customers.

Store produce

As consumer tastes have changed supermarkets have reacted, but they have also helped to shape trends. In 1985 Safeway responded to growing concern about additives by making all their products additive-free. In 1986 Tesco and Sainsbury followed suit by deleting product lines which contained the additive tartrazine, thought to stimulate hyperactivity in children.

The tendency towards a more international cuisine stimulated by increased foreign travel has also been responded to and helped along by supermarkets, which have stocked Italian, Indian and Chinese foods and exotic vegetables and fruit such as kiwis and mangoes.

They have also reacted to consumer antagonism to plastic, highly processed and tasteless products by the introduction of in-store bakeries, pre-prepared salads, fresh pasta and speciality meals.

Safeway started the trend of introducing vegetable and fruit sections where people could help themselves rather than rely on pre-packaged products. The concept of the independent store within the large retail operation selling fish, meat and delicatessen further eroded what had been the traditional source of such products, namely the fishmonger, butcher and speciality grocer.

One of the small counter-trends to the dominance of the large retailer has been made by stores which remain open late at night or on Sundays, such as Circle K and 7-eleven.

Consumer needs

In 1964 manufacturers in the UK lost the right to fix the price at which their goods were sold in shops. Up until the 1980s the UK grocery industry was driven largely by price competition. In 1980 55 per cent of respondents identified price as the most important

Illustration 16.3 Discounts and private label

Traditional manufacturers and retailers are being threatened by the rapid growth of aggressive discount retailers, such as Aldi from Germany, Netto from Denmark and US warehouse 'clubs' such as Costco. Many of these offer only limited grocery ranges but with their high volumes, their low margins and costs they represent a challenge to both manufacturers and other retailers. The US warehouse stores are about three times the size of a typical UK Sainsbury or Tesco at 100 000 square feet, and sell a range of about 4000 lines (against 15 000 in a typical Sainsbury). Typically the margin on products is only 10% as opposed to 25% expected by most multiples. At the same time the growth of retailers' cheap private label brands has eroded the hold of many branded products.

Discounters	*Share (%) of food sales by value, 1992*
Belgium	19
France	2
Germany	25
Holland	11
Spain	6
UK	8

Private label share of grocery value sales (%)

	1980	*1992*		*1991*
Belgium	13	18	Denmark	18
France	16	21	Spain	8
Germany	5	23	Portugal	1
Italy	3	7		
UK	25	29		

At present manufacturers are divided on how to respond. A few international brand leaders such as Kellog, Coca-Cola and Mars refuse to make private label at all. Unilever and Nestlé do so on a limited basis largely to fill spare capacity. United Biscuits, on the other hand, has a large special plant for private label which generates about one-third of its UK sales.

Based on de Jonquieres, 'Discounts and private label', *Financial Times*, 15 June 1993, 6 October 1993

reason for choosing a store compared with 30 per cent for convenience. By 1985 the study showed that convenience was the main reason (59 per cent) and price had dropped to 35 per cent (*The Grocer*, 1985).

In the late 1980s competition between major retailers was mainly based on increasing concern for choice, quality, convenience, service and shopping environment. Retailers in the UK vied with each other on aspects of quality improvement supported by profitable operating margins, generally much higher than those in mainland Europe. In the past decade some of the major innovations have been improvements in store layout, with wider aisles and in-store facilities. Safeway now has eight different trolleys to meet the needs of customers with children or disability (Hosking, 1993). Sainsbury has recently experimented with 'scan and pack' checkouts at which groceries automatically fall into a waiting carrier bag to avoid the customer having to fill it. Safeway is opening crèches in some stores.

However, these additions cost money, which until now British shoppers have been happy to pay in order to buy extra choice and convenience. The recession has fostered a new price consciousness in UK consumers. It has given rise to discount food shops as the fastest growing sector of the UK retailing industry (see Illustration 16.3). From only two discount chains in 1990, the number increased to 14 by 1993. Besides Costco from the USA, much of the incursion has come from other parts of Europe with Netto from Denmark, Aldi from Germany, and Ed, owned by Carrefour, from France.

These stores make money by shifting huge volumes of goods. They are usually on cheap, out of town sites, with little technology. Goods are often sold from cardboard boxes on warehouse racking, with a limited range and few staff. Most forecasters expect further growth in discount operations and some cutback in the opening of further superstores by the major multiples (*Supermarketing*, 1993).

Innovations such as loyalty cards and vouchers given at the point of sale, triggered by actual purchase, are likely to be introduced as the major retailers react to discounters. The losers are likely to be middle of the road stores which do not compete effectively on either price or quality. The number of independent butchers, bakers and greengrocers in the UK is likely to continue to decline. It has already decreased from 116 000 in 1962 to 32 800 in 1992.

The effect of these trends on one middle of the road discounter is indicated in Illustration 16.4.

Illustration 16.4 Price pressure

Lo-cost, the Argyll discounter, is finding it difficult to keep pace with growing competition from Kwik Save, Aldi and Netto.

The concentration on price has resulted in customers clamouring for own label products at the expense of branded goods. Argyll also owns Safeway, and Safeway own label goods have increased their share from a percentage in the high thirties to one in the low forties.

With money tight, Argyll is cutting back on new stores. Just five new Lo-Costs will open in 1993, less than half the usual number.

Based on 'Price pressure', *The Grocer*, 4 December 1993

European retailing

In the UK food retailing is broadly divided between the multiple retailers trading from large superstores and independent retailers with small shops. This is not the case elsewhere in Europe, where the structure of the food retailing trade is different.

The French market is saturated with very large retail operations such as Intermarche and Carrefour, but in fact one-third of all French hypermarkets and a 62 per cent share of the largest stores are run by independents. Leclerc, for instance, is a symbol group made up of independents with an average store size of around $4000\,m^2$. France still also has a large number of small independents selling bread, meat and drink.

In the Benelux countries laws restrict large development which means the small store plays a major role. In Luxembourg 86 per cent of the market is dominated by small stores of less than $100\,m^2$. However, the retail structure in Holland is more like that in the UK with dominance by a small number of multiples with 72 per cent of the market.

In Germany the multiples also have a strong base but so do co-operatives. The number of food retailers in Germany fell by 2700 in 1992, with just under half of these closing in the East (Eurofood, 1993). Aldi, which is a specialist discount operation, has had a strong influence on food retailing, in Germany and now elsewhere. A further 500 discount stores opened in Germany in 1992. Discount stores have become a feature of German retailing, visited regularly by two out of every three households to buy basic groceries. Supermarkets and hypermarkets are visited as the source of fresh produce and more specialized or branded products.

Discount operations have also had an impact in France. Aldi and Lidl moved from Germany into France in 1988 and 1989 respectively. In turn the major French retailers such as Carrefour, Intermarche and LeClerc all started their own discount operations. Aldi also stimulated the discount trade in Belgium when it first moved there in 1973 and now has a 17.3 per cent market share.

In Spain, Italy and Portugal the retail structures are still relatively undeveloped. In Spain the five largest food and drink retail groups represent only 30 per cent of sales. Most of the supermarket chains are confined to only one or two of the 17 autonomous regions of Spain because of difficulties of distribution over long distances (*Agra Europe*,

Table 16.2 *Percentage share of turnover among European retailers, 1986*

	Multiples and cooperatives	Independents
Belgium	59	41
France	64	36
W. Germany	70	30
Italy	26	74
UK	83	17

Source: Food Pocket Book, 1992.

Table 16.3   *Number of hypermarkets over 2500 m², 1986*

France	628
W. Germany	859
Italy	72
Spain	87
UK	460 (800 in 1992*)

*Source: Food Pocket Book, 1992; *Hoskin, 1993.*

1992). In Spain three of the top ten retailers are from France, a cross-border development which is becoming more common. In Portugal 35 000 out of 38 000 retail outlets are small but the proportion of sales at 46 per cent is less than the 81 per cent it was 10 years ago (*Dairo de Noticias*, 1993).

Hypermarkets are developing quickly in Italy from a base of 12 in 1980 to a prediction of 155 by 1996. However, independents and street vendors are still the largest sector of the grocery market, with a share of 50 per cent and 23 per cent respectively (*Supermarketing*, 1992).

The percentage share of turnover via multiples and independents for a sample of European countries is indicated in Table 16.2, with the number of hypermarkets in Table 16.3.

Conclusion

The retail environment provides a complex but important stimulant to consumer buying behaviour. In the UK the retailing of food is now primarily in the control of five large supermarket groups with a dwindling impact of co-operative and small independent grocers or specialist foodshops. This has given these groups power in the relationship with manufacturers and encouraged them to create their own brands. The food shopping environment within the store has a considerable impact on purchases. A crowded shop will decrease sales. Time pressure will cause the consumer to rely on experience and memory and stick to recognized brands. Shoppers are not consistently loyal to one store but shop from amongst a limited set of favourites.

Stores are usually laid out so as to encourage consumers to pass the maximum number of items. Stocking and the shelf position allocated to items is related to the pattern of sales. Innovations in computer technology mean sales information will trigger restocking. There is evidence supermarkets have innovated with the products offered reacting to consumer demand for fresh produce, exotic items and less unnecessary packaging.

The fastest growing sector of the UK food retail industry is discount stores, which originated in Germany. On the continent too they are having an effect.

In the richer more northern European countries, retailing of food tends to be controlled by just a few major multiples. In countries such as Spain, Italy and Portugal the small independent or street vendor still provides half or more of all food bought. However the ascendancy of the large multiple is likely to continue even in these countries once storage and distribution problems have been overcome.

Questions

1   Describe how the relationship between UK food manufacturers and retailers has changed in the past eighty years and what impact this has had on the consumer.
2   Why have own label food products appeared and why have they taken off at different rates in different parts of Europe?
3   Consider whether the growth of hypermarkets has reached saturation point, using France and Italy to make comparisons.
4   How is what consumers are looking for from UK food retailers different this year from what it was in 1988?
5   Why are food discounting stores having such success and how do you foresee their future development in the UK and Germany?
6   Compare two major food retailers from the point of view of what they offer their consumers.
7   What influences where and how often people shop for food?
8   Investigate the merchandising of food in your local supermarket. What influence do you believe it has on unplanned consumer purchases?

References

Agra Europe (1992) 'Spain – a dynamic market for UK food and drink', 6 March

Economic Intelligence Unit (1992) 'Fighting falling margins'. *European Retail*, 13 October

Dairo de Noticias (1993) 'Pequeno retalho cede aos gigantes', 22 February

Eurofood (1993) 'Fewer German food shops', February, Agra Europe, London

Food Pocket Book (1992). NTC Publications, Henley-on-Thames

Foxall, G. R. and Goldsmith, R. E. (1994) *Consumer Psychology for Marketing*, Routledge, London

The Grocer (1985) 30 November, 50

The Guardian (1992) 'Own label and retail concentration', 28 October

Hoskin, P. (1993) 'Store wars; will we all be losers?', *Independent*, 27 February

de Jonquieres, G. (1993) 'Discounts and private label', *Financial Times*, 15 June, 6 October

Kau, A. K. and Ehrenberg, A. S. C. (1984) Patterns of store choice. *J. Marketing Res.*, **21**, 399

Senker, J. (1988) *A taste for innovation: British supermarkets influence on food manufacturers.* Horton Publications Ltd, Bradford

Supermarketing (1992) 'European food retailing', 16 October

Supermarketing (1993) 'Counting the cost of discounting', 17 December

17 Persuasive communications

Introduction

An important purpose of the whole of marketing strategy is to persuade people to buy a product for the first time or to buy it again. Persuasive communications are an attempt to change an attitude on the assumption this will lead to a change in behaviour.

Companies invest vast sums of money in an attempt to modify or reinforce how consumers think, feel and act. Advertising, a salesperson's hard sell, product packaging, point of sale material, and word of mouth information from friends and relatives, are all communications which will impact on a consumer.

This chapter develops from the attitude–behaviour debate considered in Chapter 15 and is concerned with understanding the communication process and how certain elements of a communication can have an effect on the consumer.

Model of communications

The purpose of a communication is for a sender to transmit meaning and information to a receiver. This person will hopefully receive and interpret whatever message is sent as the sender intended. In some cases the receiver will have the opportunity to check whether this is so via a feedback mechanism.

Figure 17.1 shows an idealized system. In the case of one-to-one interaction between a salesperson and a consumer this complete loop is possible. However, at the opposite

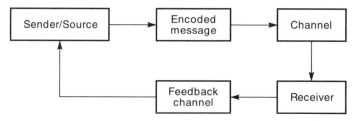

Figure 17.1 *The communication process*

extreme, an advertising message on the side of a building may never be received by the audience for whom it was intended. In the second case, there are obvious opportunities for it to be received by the 'wrong' people or to be perceived in a way never intended by the company who paid for the advert.

Source

The source of a message is very important in determining how influential the communication is. For example, Coca-Cola worried long and hard about ending their ties with Michael Jackson when he was accused in a child abuse case. His endorsement of their product was crucial to them in the creation of their wholesome, exciting, all-American image. If a new supermarket were to open in your area, consider whether you would be more likely to give it a try having seen a TV advert or alternatively if your best friend told you it was the best in the area she had been to. You would probably be more influenced by your friend. Robertson (1971) showed that for food products advertising will first bring a product to the attention of a consumer, but friends and family are the most important source of information about the product and hence most significant in influencing eventual purchase. This is obviously because people feel they can trust their friends or relatives who have no vested interest, whereas the manufacturer or retailer does. A long-standing principle of communication is that the credibility of a source will influence persuasion.

> The more trustworthy, credible or prestigious the communicator is perceived to be, the less manipulative his intent is considered to be, the greater is the immediate tendency to accept his conclusions. (Berelson and Steiner, 1954)

Credibility is a combination of two separate source characteristics: expertise and trustworthiness. A friend is trustworthy but not necessarily expert. The man in the white coat playing the scientist in a TV advert may appear expert, but is not necessarily trustworthy (Hovland and Weiss, 1951).

Illustration 17.1 demonstrates how a member of the public may be bombarded by a variety of sources of information, ranging from articles in scientific journals to advertising by a manufacturer. The message which gets through depends crucially on the credibility of the source.

Branding is obviously all about trying to build a reputation and hence credibility of a manufacturer or retailer. Trademarks and tradenames are intended to give confidence that a new product can be believed in because it has been produced by a company with a long tradition and good name.

The medium in which a message is transmitted will also affect credibility. A prestigious newspaper will have a beneficial influence on any advert which appears in it, compared with a tabloid.

If a celebrity is used to endorse a product then their credibility is important. People tend to agree with someone they like. The danger for the advertiser is that a famous spokesperson may go out of fashion or do something in real life to decrease their credibility, as was the case with Michael Jackson. However, there is evidence that using celebrities, or satisfied consumers with similar characteristics to the market segment being aimed at, will help to persuade new consumers.

Illustration 17.1 Butter or margarine?

A vast amount of research and expression of opinion has arisen over the possible role of blood cholesterol in heart disease and the claimed value of polyunsaturated fats in the diet in reducing the chances of circulatory disease.

The Flora Information Service (funded by Van den Bergh Foods, the makers of Flora, a margarine rich in polyunsaturates) pointed out studies showing the consumption of polyunsaturates reduces heart disease. The Butter Information Council pointed out discrepancies in the research and quoted research with alternative conclusions.

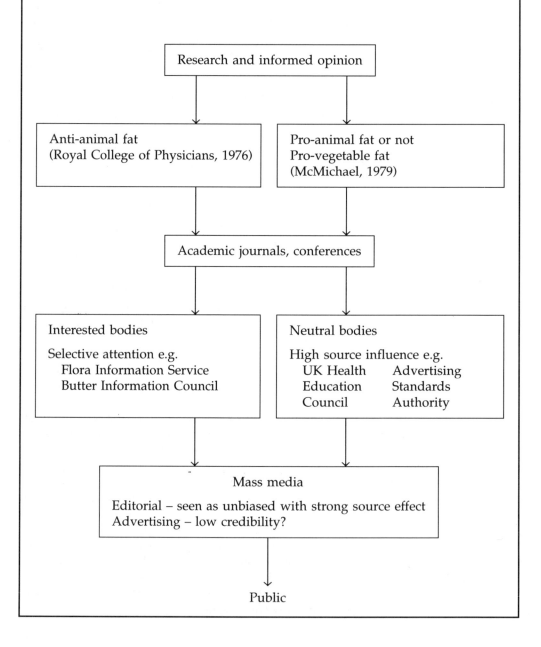

Message

Research has shown that there are various characteristics of a message which can influence its effectiveness. Strong messages, for example, will inhibit negative thoughts about a product and bring out the positive. Strength is particularly related to the relevance of a claim to a consumer, and to its objectivity.

Decoding the second concept, consumers are much happier with the quotation of an actual price rather than a claim such as 'all time low price'. 'Low fat' as a claim for a margarine is less effective than giving the consumer actual calorie information. Claims work much better if they can be substantiated. 'We have the cheapest food prices in town' is a claim which consumers could check if they wished.

Communications research has consistently shown that giving both sides of an argument induces more attitude change than a one-sided appeal. It increases the credibility of the source (Walster, 1966) and inoculates the listener against counter-argument (Lumsdaine and Janis, 1953). The consequence of this is comparison advertising, in which one product is compared with another on a number of criteria, often backed up by independent research data.

Emotional advertising is directed at the affective element of attitudes, designed to elicit favourable or strong feelings. There is some evidence people pay more attention to such adverts but that they are less effective with more intelligent people who respond more to a cognitive or logical message. How consumers receive a message can be more important than what is said. Visuals, sound, colour and pace can be critical. Humour excels in attracting attention but needs to be subtle, relevant to the brand and should not belittle the potential user. Certainly there is evidence that humour increases liking of a product and this increases the persuasiveness of the message. However, there is a danger that humour can displace the product message, and it is the humour which is remembered while the product is not. Successful use of humour involves weaving the two together. Even though abrasive or agonizing messages can be annoying, they still can work merely because the product name sticks in the consumer's mind as they attempt to reject other elements of the advert. Fearful messages indicate to a consumer that harmful consequences will follow if they do not use a particular product or brand.

Very strong fear messages appear not to work, as evidenced by recent scare campaigns about AIDs. This was certainly true of the very first research which showed fear messages are not persuasive (Janis and Fechbach, 1953). However, more recent studies show fear messages work if the source is credible and if the listener is given a way out. A lot of food advertising has played on the fear people have about their health. Advertising of new low fat spreads has played on fear of coronary heart disease (Sternthal and Craig, 1974).

Repeating a message is generally beneficial because of the conditioning effect, but it has drawbacks. Early repetition builds up familiarity but this reaches a peak and then can be counter-productive. This is one problem with using humour in a message; a repeated joke soon wears very thin. However, the right level of repeat promotion increases acceptability. Consumers attribute higher quality to a higher advertised brand. Repetition alone serves to increase liking and hence acceptability of a product.

Some of the all-time great adverts which combined humour, a clear product message, and could stand the test of repetition are in Illustration 17.2.

Illustration 17.2 Smashing ads

Every day consumers are exposed to thousands of adverts but remember very few of them. When the bible of the advertising world, *Campaign*, reached a quarter of a century it celebrated by producing its own hall of fame, twenty-five adverts which were the most memorable or persuasive.

These included the advert for Hovis based on nostalgia: 'It's good for you and always has been'. Hovis was first baked in 1890 and its heritage has been drawn upon to suggest unchanging values and wholesome living.

Heineken refreshes the parts other beers cannot reach. In the 1985 version there was a reversal of the Eliza Doolittle scenario. A Sloane is taking lessons to say in a broad cockney accent 'the water in Majorca don't taste like what it oughta'. Heineken does the trick so she can talk properly.

The Cadbury advert shown between 1973 and 1988 was what made instant mash potato acceptable. It showed Martian robots laughing at us for the laborious way we peel, boil and mash potatoes when Smash could be bought.

Based on W. Fletcher, 'Smashing ads', *Daily Mail*, 17 September 1993

Receiver

The effectiveness of a particular source and message type will depend on where a consumer is on the scale between being first aware of a product and purchase. Various models referring to stages in the life of a product demonstrate a correlation with the most appropriate communication strategy.

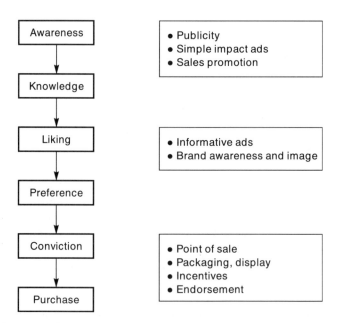

Figure 17.2   *Stages in the communication process*

In the first stage of a communications process the intention is to generate awareness, hence simple adverts with high impact are appropriate. Later the intention should be to inform and create brand awareness. Finally, purchase or repeat sales are more likely to be stimulated by point of sale promotion, packaging and display. The sequence is illustrated in Figure 17.2.

People differ; the same communication will not affect everyone equally. A scattergun approach in which one message is directed at the whole market will not be effective. The basis of segmentation strategies is to identify ways of directing a message which is appropriate to a particular consumer group.

> Communications directed at particular individuals are more effective than those directed at the public at large. (Berelson and Steiner, 1954)

Nestlé Rowntree's chocolate bar Kit-Kat is now sold throughout Europe with the same slogan, 'Have a break, have a Kit-Kat' but in the UK the TV ad features a puppet show, while in Holland the voice-over is by a Dutch humorist. Neither would work in the other country.

Illustration 17.3 shows how one company overcame the problem of promoting the same product in different countries by compromising between a global logo but with individualized messages in each country.

Illustration 17.3 European packing of coffee

In the Ardennes tradition prescribes drinking ten cups of coffee after dinner, while in Turkey the drink is meant to be 'black as hell, strong as death and sweet as love'.

So how does a pan-European supplier market such an inherently nationalistic product?

Sara Lee is a Chicago-based group best known for cheesecake but through a process of acquisition it has bought a dozen European coffee companies. Now it has a market share of 74 per cent in The Netherlands (Douwe Egbert), 27 per cent in Denmark (Merrild Kaffe), 21 per cent in Spain (Manilla) and 15 per cent in France (Maison du Café). While Sara Lee accepts that coffee is a locally determined product, it needed to achieve some coordination and harmonization of its marketing strategy because the 'brands could not be supported properly in every country'.

The result is that coffee still sells under country specific brand names but standardized packaging and a common corporate symbol provides a strong visual identity. The Friesian lady in simple eighteenth-century dress creates an image of authenticity, quality and is fairly non-committal and mid-European.

Advertising strategy emphasized some national identity in the language and name but otherwise the packaging is similar. The visual image and sound track used to advertise the 'Manilla' brand on TV in Spain was used in an advertisement for Hungarian brands.

Based on N. Tait, 'European packing of coffee', *Financial Times*, 14 January 1993

Not all promotional messages are taken in because of the process of selective attention. One estimate is that the central nervous system of an average human being contains 260 million visual cells whereas there are only 48 000 dealing with visual perception, a reduction of 5000:1. To deal with visual information alone would require a brain a cubic light year in size. In short, we filter out a lot of information before we perceive it.

> People tend to see or hear communications favourable or congenial to their disposition. The more interested they are in a subject the more likely is selective attention. (Berelson and Steiner, 1954)

> The people you most want to get at in your audience are the ones you are least likely to get to. (Abelson, 1949)

People actually physically see between 250 and 2000 adverts each day but only recall a fraction of them. Selective perception means only a small proportion are noticed. This implies that marketers should address their messages to current customers and others rather like the present customers.

A related phenomenon is arousal. If an advertising message is stimulating it will cause a person to be physiologically aroused. There is evidence that this will increase the persuasive effect of the message. However, too great a level of arousal such as excessive noise, flashing lights or too rapidly repeating a message, will be counter-productive.

People are also strongly pressurized by group norms. They will react against promotional messages which are counter to the actual or perceived attitudes of their reference group.

> People strongly motivated to retain group membership are most resistant to communications which are contrary to the standards of the group. (Hovland *et al.*, 1953)

A strongly held belief tends to be intimately tied up with a person's self-awareness, ego or identity. It is therefore difficult to change such a belief at all and only possible to change it a little. The only practical way to test this issue is to show potential consumers a range of proposed communications to test which can be believed. However, generally consumers will not change their beliefs if they are strongly held, however effective a promotional message may be.

Promotional activity

In the UK last year the biggest category of TV advertising for food was £84 million on breakfast cereals, followed by £72 million on chocolate confectionery, £23 million on crisps and snacks, and £19 million on ice creams and lollies. On the other hand, frozen vegetables attracted only £10.7 million.

Two years ago the Food Commission spent a week logging every advert beamed during children's TV in the UK. Four of the top five products were American in origin (Kellogg's Sugar Puffs, Coco Pops and Frosties, and MacDonald's), while the fifth was KP Skips, a UK snack product.

Conclusion

Persuasive communications are an attempt by a manufacturer, retailer or even another person to change the attitude and hence the behaviour of a consumer.

The source of a message in terms of both the company or individual who originates it and the channel of communication used will affect its credibility. Credibility is related to the expertise and trustworthiness which the source is perceived to have. Branding and the use of celebrities or experts in adverts are an attempt to create credibility. Research has shown that two-sided messages have more effect than one-sided, particularly with an educated audience. Humour and fear can both increase the persuasiveness of a message if they do not mask the appeal of the product itself. All advertising is more effective if repeated, although care must be taken not to create boredom.

To be effective advertising messages need to be tailored for particular market segments. Even then they may be selected out because of selective perception or because they run counter to the norms of the target audience.

Questions

Read the following case then answer the questions at the end.*

Butchurst, a chain of family butchers who had based their reputation on the sale of high quality meat, were interested in whether branding of meat had any effect on sales. With advice from their advertising agents, Pushits, they financed a promotional campaign, the effects of which were carefully monitored from sales figures and consumer attitude surveys.

The test product chosen was pork, given the brand name of Cracklean, since this had proved a popular name from preliminary group interviews. In fact the pork sold as Cracklean was no different from other pork. Cracklean was promoted in two test areas over a four-week period in November 1972. The test towns chosen were Sunderland and Leeds. Sales there were compared with sales of meat in Butchurst shops in two control towns, Coventry and Nottingham.

The advertising and promotional campaign was mounted on two fronts, one aimed at the retailer, the other at the consumer. In each test area a prize of a free weekend in Paris was offered to the branch manager of a Butchurst shop who sold the highest percentage of Cracklean as a proportion of total turnover in the four-week promotion period.

The advertising aimed at the consumer was based on an Edwardian theme which had previously been used to create the appropriate high quality image for Butchursts. Advertisements were placed in the local press, on posters, and as point of sale material, such as window banners, price posters, product stabbers, carrier bags and the 'Cracklean' logo on pork cuts. The overall copy stressed the product was 'Cracklean pork – the real farmhouse flavour'.

The sales measure used was increase in sales brought about by the promotion. Sales by volume and weight were compared for the two test areas and the two matched control

*This case is based on a study by D. R. Hughes, D. Lesser and D. Renard (1974) 'Consumer perceptions of pork', published by the Department of Agricultural Marketing, University of Newcastle, Newcastle upon Tyne.

areas for six weeks before the promotion, for the four-week promotion, and for three weeks immediately after the promotion.

The consumer survey was conducted by personal interview on the pavement outside the Butchurst shops in the last week of the promotional period, and in interviewees' homes six weeks after the promotion. A total of 1182 questionnaires were administered in the two last areas; 75% of those questioned were Butchurst shoppers. Most of the interviewees were women although there were a few men, one of whom was surprised to be asked by a woman, 'What does Cracklean make you think of?'

Some of the major results from the sales audit and the survey are given as tables below.

Survey data from consumer attitude research on 'Cracklean'

Figures in Tables 1–4 refer to percentage of respondents.

Table 1a   *'What is the first thing the word Cracklean makes you think of?'*

	All respondents	Under 20	Over 20
Pork	53	30	55
Other food	13	23	12
Bacon	3	14	3
Detergents	2	2	1
Don't know/NA	28	30	29

Table 1b   *'What is the second thing the word Cracklean makes you think of?'*

Crackling	16
Crispy	4
Lean	2
Don't know/NA	78

Table 2a   *'What meat did you buy at Butchurst's today?'*

Other meat	59
Pork	12
Cracklean	2
Don't know/NA	27

Table 2b *'When you have bought pork at Butchurst's what did you ask for?'*

Pork	40
Cut on display	2
Cracklean	1
Other	2
Butcher recommended	1
Don't know/NA	54

Table 2c *'What did the butcher say when you asked for Cracklean?'*

The pork is good	6
Other	1
Cracklean	0.5
Don't know/NA	92

Table 3a *'Did you notice Butchurst had been selling Cracklean for the past four weeks?'*

	Butchurst shoppers	Others
Yes	31	21
No	66	76
Don't know/NA	3	3

Table 3b *'Where did you first hear of Cracklean?'*

Shop window	19
Newspaper	4
Poster	3
TV	1
Butcher	1
Don't know/NA	71

Table 3c *'If Butchurst's were selling Cracklean at 1p more than ordinary pork which would you buy?'*

Cracklean	54
Ordinary pork	18
None	9
Don't know/NA	20

Table 3d *'In what way is Cracklean different from other pork?'*

Leaner	17
More crackling	13
Name only	9
Crisper	9
Other	9
Don't know/NA	42

Table 3e *'Is it a good idea to call high quality pork by a special name?'*

Yes	60
No	22
Don't know/NA	18

Table 3f *'Why?'*

Easier to ask for	21
Guarantees quality	20
Best should be named	8
No difference	
Only a name	21
Other	30

Table 4   *Pork sales as percentage of total meat sales*

	Run-up	Campaign	After
Sunderland	29.7	31.9	31.2
Leeds	21.5	23.5	29.7
Nottingham	28.6	29.1	28.8
Coventry	34.5	30.4	29.8

Based on D. R. Hughes, D. Lesser and D. Renard (1974) 'Consumer perceptions of pork', Department of Agricultural Marketing, University of Newcastle.

Questions

1   What effect did the promotion campaign have on sales in the test compared with control areas?
2   What were the main responses to the name Cracklean from customers interviewed?
3   What was the most effective method of communicating with consumers in this case study? What other media could have been used and where would you make your greatest effort in any future campaign?
4   Do you consider the sales incentive offered to retailers was adequate or successful? What other factors do you think would influence housewives' decisions about which meat to buy?
5   What reasons did interviewees give for considering Cracklean was better than pork? How is your knowledge of perception relevant here?
6   What is a price premium? What danger is there in assuming a consistency between attitudes and behaviour? How would you test whether the findings quoted on differential pricing of Cracklean were valid or not?
7   How would you proceed from here with the idea of branding pork?

References

Abelson, H. (1949) *Persuasion*, Springer, New York
Berelson, B. and Steiner, G. (1954) *Human Behaviour: An Inventory of Scientific Findings*, Harcourt, Brace and World, New York
Hovland, C. and Weiss, W. (1951) 'The influence of source credibility on communication effectiveness'. *Publ. Opin. Q.*, **15**, 635–50
Hovland, C. I., Janis, I. and Kelley, H. (1953) *Communication and Persuasion*, Yale University Press, New Haven, Conn.
Janis, I. and Fechbach, S. (1953) 'Effects of fear arousing communications'. *J. Abnorm. Soc. Psychol.*, **48**, 78–92

Lumsdaine, A. and Janis, I. (1953) 'Resistance to counter propaganda produced by a one-sided versus two-sided presentation'. *Publ. Opin. Q.*, **17**, 311–18

Robertson, T. S. (1971) *Innovative Behaviour and Communication*, Holt, Rinehart and Winston, New York

Sternthal, B. and Craig, C. S. (1974) 'Fear appeals revisited and revised'. *J. Consum. Res.*, **1**, 22–34

Walster, E., Aronson, E. and Abrahams, D. (1966) 'On increasing the persuasiveness of a low prestige communication'. *J. Exp. Soc. Psychol.*, **2**, 325–42

Part Five

Outcomes

In the last part of this text the intention is to bring together the range of factors which can have an influence on food purchase. To date, these have been examined as if each existed in 'isolation' and had no interaction with each other. However, in this chapter, using UK sales of chicken meat as the example, it can be shown how over a period of thirty years different factors have risen and fallen in importance as the major influence on purchase behaviour. At various times in that period product availability, price, the level of consumer incomes, scare stories about polyphosphates, the arrival of new technology to enable different means to store and retail chicken, advertising, the introduction of fridge freezers, European regulations, and perceptions of the product compared with others, have all come to the fore as a major influence on purchase behaviour.

This last part also includes a brief overview of the work of Ehrenberg and his colleagues who are rarely, if ever, mentioned in American texts. Their approach provides a very different way of looking at behaviour with little interest in what precedes a purchase. The focus is on patterns of previous purchase behaviour from which it is possible to make predictions about the future.

The analysis of actual versus predicted behaviour shows a good correlation. It serves to emphasise that the pattern of repeat purchase is a valuable item to study. The analysis also shows that many accepted 'truths' in marketing may not be valid. Hence, the text ends with a healthy but critical note in order to encourage the reader to reflect back on the value of understanding consumer behaviour by examining predispositions as opposed to outcomes.

At the end of the day a huge number of new product innovations fail suggesting we have a long way to go in being able to fully comprehend and predict behaviour.

18 *Purchasing outcomes*

Introduction

The opening chapter of this book contains an outline of models of consumer behaviour, all of which indicate that a multitude of factors combine to have an influence on actual purchase and consumption. However, the majority of the text has then been concerned with the evaluation of one influence at a time. This is an oversimplification, which is addressed in this chapter. The means chosen to do this is to examine how a variety of factors have combined to affect the purchase of chicken meat since the Second World War, based on material collected by Senker (1988), supplemented by the author from *Food Trends* (1992) and the *Food Pocket Book* (1992). The assumption still, however, is that in order to understand different categories of consumers, and therefore how best to promote products to them, it is worthwhile examining those factors which precede purchase.

The other area of work examined in this chapter maintains that consumption patterns can best be understood by determining what consumers actually buy rather than focusing on the processes which precede a purchase. The work of Ehrenberg (1972) and his colleagues has made an important contribution to this approach. Not only are the ideas of significance in helping to understand patterns in the purchase of frequently bought items such as food, but also because of the value of the ideas in acting as a foil to the reductionist approach taken so far.

Overall, therefore the purpose of this final chapter is to consider two issues. First, how some of the influences examined in detail in this text combine to affect purchase of one food product. Secondly, how an examination of patterns of purchase can enable predictions about future purchase behaviour.

Purchase of chicken meat

It would have been possible to choose virtually any food product and show how purchase of it varies because of the impact of a variety of pre-purchase influences. Chicken has been chosen because it has been well researched by Senker (1988), who has docmented the history of product development in the UK since the Second World War.

Table 18.1 *Retail purchase of chicken by weight, 1953–1984*

Year	'000 tonnes
1954	51
1964	167
1974	283
1984	357

Source: Senker, 1988; *Food Pocket Book*, 1992

The growth of the chicken meat market has been extremely dramatic. Up until the end of the 1950s the annual consumption of chicken in the UK was less than 50 000 tonnes. It was a high priced luxury item usually eaten only at Christmas, although sometimes eaten cold in the summer. The change in farming methods which led to the intensive rearing of broilers, and changed distribution systems altered consumer buying and eating habits.

There was an almost ten-fold increase in production in the period from pre-war until the mid 1980s, including some increase in imports, particularly from France. Once corrections are made for loss due to evisceration, wastage, processing and produce going to catering outlets then the quantity of chicken reaching retail outlets showed a seven-fold increase from 1953 to 1984 (Table 18.1). Per capita consumption showed a similar rise in the same period. Recently consumption of cooked chicken has increased relatively faster than consumption of uncooked chicken (Table 18.2).

The first factor which had an influence on purchase was price. In 1956 the average price for poultry was higher than for any other carcass meats. In the period up until 1965 the demand for poultry was elastic, as explained in Chapter 4. In 1965 a cut in the price of poultry combined with an increase in the price of beef gave a further stimulus to poultry consumption, which continued to rise steeply until 1971. At this point a fowl pest epidemic both decreased supplies and had a scare effect on consumers worried whether the disease would have any effect on humans (cf Chapter 8).

Much of the increased demand in the 1960s was due to the fall in price. Demand flattened somewhat in the mid 1970s due possibly to the introduction of a European Community scheme to make beef available at low cost to some low income families.

Table 18.2 *Consumption of chicken, 1970–1985*

	1970	1975	1980	1985
Uncooked	100	116	135	133
Cooked	100	83	107	154

Indexed to 1970 = 100.
Source: Senker, 1988; *Food Pocket Book*,1992.

Table 18.3 *Uncooked meat consumption, 1956–1990 (oz per person per week)*

	1956	1965	1975	1983	1990*
Carcass meat	19.1	16.8	15.2	13.9	11.1
Bacon and ham	5.1	5.4	4.0	4.0	3.0
Poultry	0.6	3.4	5.5	6.6	7.1
Total	24.8	25.6	24.7	24.6	21.2

Source: Senker, 1988; *Food Trends*, 1992.

The income elasticity of demand (a concept explained in Chapter 4) declined substantially over time, showing that rising incomes do not appear to have had a substantial impact on demand since the mid 1960s. The rates varied from 0.42 in 1965 to 0.15 in 1980.

There does seem to be some substitution effect between beef and chicken as their relative prices change, although this is more marked between chicken and lamb. Very possibly this substitution effect would be even more marked were it possible to look at the effect of the weekend roast chicken as an alternative to roast beef, lamb or pork. Certainly chicken has changed since the 1960s to be perceived as a viable alternative to other roast meats and therefore was seen as a real meat in the sense explained in Chapter 8. It also must have replaced consumption of other meats since consumption of all meats has remained relatively stable except for some recent decrease in consumption of red meat because of increasing concerns about health (Table 18.3).

As recounted in Chapter 5, technological innovations also had a significant impact on the availability of chicken in the UK. Prior to the late 1950s chickens were only available in a fresh state with a very brief storage time of only one or two days. At that point no frozen product was available. From the early 1960s the large scale processing of chickens, which were frozen and distributed to supermarkets wth large freezer display capacity, stimulated sales. The home ownership of freezers and later fridge freezers increased from 1 per cent in 1970 to 36 per cent by 1985. By 1990 more than half the households in the UK owned a fridge freezer. These developments supported the sale of first frozen whole chickens, and later frozen portions.

Changes in shopping behaviour occurred. With more women in the workforce (cf Chapter 9), the growth of car ownership and the trend towards once weekly rather than daily shopping trips (cf Chapter 16), sales of frozen products increased.

More recently sales of frozen whole chicken have decreased. Partly this is because of a rise in sales of the chilled product which is perceived to have a better taste and does not require thawing out. A boost to the chilled market was also provided by the polyphosphate scare in the early 1970s. Sodium polyphosphate diluted in water and injected into the bird prior to slaughter was said to improve meat texture. However, a senior medical officer claimed it increased the water content of the birds and hence the price. EEC Regulation 2967/76 (cf Chapter 3) ruled that frozen chickens should not exceed 7.4 per cent of extraneous water. From 1981 birds treated with polyphosphate had to be marked accordingly. The effect was that eventually processors gave up the practice of using polyphosphate. Meantime many consumers had switched to the fresh or chilled product.

During the 1980s and 1990s chicken has benefited from the recognition it is a low fat, lean meat which is perceived as healthy compared with other meats (cf Chapter 6).

Advertising campaigns were necessary to persuade consumers to buy frozen chicken when it was first made available (cf Chapter 17). The public took some time to realize it was no longer a luxury item and to buy it for consumption other than as a weekend roast. Promotions were primarily aimed at increased year-round sales and increased mid-week sales by telling people how to cut up a chicken. This seemed to work as since 1958 the sales of portioned chicken have increased. This is partly to do with a longer-term trend of stabilization of the frozen market from around 1970, with a corresponding growth in fresh, chilled and cooked chicken available either whole or in portions.

At present the fastest growing sector is the value-added market which began in the early 1970s. Products such as burgers, nibbles, flavoured portions, special recipe dishes and ready meals provide the consumer with alternative ways of eating chicken and also coincide with the rise in ownership of microwaves (cf Chapter 5) to cook convenience foods.

The fluctuating sales of chicken and chicken products show how the complicated interaction of product availability, price, incomes, scare stories, methods of retailing, advertising, home based equipment, European regulations and perceptions of product quality interact to affect consumer purchase.

Purchasing patterns

Much of the information in the previous chapters makes the assumption that consumers can be segmented on one or more criteria, whether by lifestyle, social class, stage in the family life cycle or degree of innovativeness, and that each segment will behave towards products in a particular pattern. Much of marketing theory is about drawing out and emphasizing the particular characteristics of a product so as to appeal to a particular consumer segment.

The assumption in much marketing literature is that these two concepts of market segmentation and product positioning will result in a particular set of consumers who first select a particular brand and then loyally buy it time after time. The consequence of these ideas is that consumers will stay loyal to a particular brand amongst the set of available products and will only be lured away to an alternative brand by a radical change in price differential or a particularly alluring promotion. Persuasive communication or point of sale merchandising, as elaborated in Chapters 16 and 17, are therefore the means to cause consumers to switch their allegiance. Hence promotional devices must constantly be used to replenish the number of consumers who are switching away from a particular product to alternatives.

An alternative view first advocated by Ehrenberg (1972), reported at length by East (1990) and in abbreviated form by Foxall and Goldsmith (1994), is considered next. The concern is not with the reasons why people do or do not buy particular products but simply a concentration on the patterns of purchase. Consumers vary in how often and at what level they buy products but this behaviour is relatively consistent.

Ehrenberg has shown that repeat buying is much more stable than would be predicted by a model which assumes people are constantly switching around. Consumers tend to form habits, with the consequence that they are relatively stable in their buying behaviour. They purchase one or more products from within a particular set. If a new product is introduced or an existing product is heavily promoted this may have a temporary effect on their purchase behaviour but then they revert back to their old ways and purchase from a set of products which may or may not include the new one.

Many markets are very stable; the number of heavy and light buyers of a product, the degree of repeat purchase of particular brands, and the frequency with which consumers buy any brand of a particular set are all relatively stable. Variations in price, availability and advertising may have a passing but not a permanent effect on purchase behaviour. Hence although this approach does not help to understand individual behaviour, it does demonstrate remarkable consistency of behaviour in a population of consumers and this behaviour can be described by a mathematical model.

Consumers vary as to how frequently they buy a product and how much they buy overall. A consumer who shops at the supermarket every week may buy bread every week and buy three loaves on each occasion. Another, perhaps with a freezer, may buy bread only every other week but buy eight loaves every time. Yet another consumer may buy one loaf only every third week. Some consumers buy more of a product than others do and these heavy buyers buy more from one time to the next. Some heavy buyers of bread do not buy every week. On the other hand, in any particular week there will be other heavy buyers who are buying that particular week. These varying periods between purchase are generally less extreme in the case of food, with many purchases made at consistent weekly or in some cases daily intervals. However, purchase intervals are not necessarily even. East (1990) has described the effect as more like the fall of raindrops. It is not possible to predict the fall of the next one from the fall of the last one. The purchase pattern is quasi-random and fits a Poisson distribution as long as the purchase pattern is examined over a relatively long period of time. Heavy buyers are an attractive proposition to marketers. For a majority of products few people buy the product at all. However, of those that do, a large proportion buy only once in a time period. The important consumer group are those who buy frequently. A substantial proportion of purchases of any particular product are made by a very few heavy buyers. East quotes as a rule of thumb that the heaviest buying half of all purchasers are responsible for 80 per cent of purchases.

Light purchasers simply purchase less often and may also buy less when they do buy. However, they may be no less brand loyal than heavy buyers; they simply do not buy every time.

This analysis leads to a different conclusion than the usual one about the function of advertising. Its purpose is not to cause switching to other brands but to retain purchasers who have not switched to another brand but may simply not buy at every available opportunity. The repeat purchase of a brand depends on the size of its penetration (market share) and its purchase frequency. The probability of a purchase being made in a given period is determined by negative binomial theory, hence the idea is known as negative binomial distribution theory (NBD). These terms are explained in Table 18.4.

The predictions from the theory appear to match actual purchase data well. Repeat purchase of a single brand can be shown to depend mainly on purchase frequency and not so much on market penetration (East, 1990). The concept of double jeopardy is

Table 18.4   *Key definitions in the repeat purchase model*

Penetration	=	the proportion of all potential buyers who buy a brand at least once in a period
Frequency	=	the average number of purchase occasions for those who purchase at least once in a period
Sales	=	penetration × frequency

revealed also. Less popular brands, those with small market shares, are bought by fewer people and those who do buy them do so less often.

Whereas much of the discussion about different consumer segments emphasizes the influences on the consumer before purchase, Ehrenberg's ideas focus much more on behaviour after a purchase. His view is that although awareness of one or more products may prompt some comparison and evaluation, it is only after they have bought and consumed it that any effective evaluation can be made.

An important factor in whether someone buys a new brand of breakfast cereal or salad topping for a second and third time is what they thought of it after the first trial. The purchase can lead to satisfaction or dissatisfaction. Obviously satisfaction is not a one-off event but needs to be maintained if repeat purchase is to be continued or at least until some alternative product either promises or actually delivers greater satisfaction.

Multibrand purchase

Consumers tend not to buy one brand consistently on all purchase occasions. It may be they stick fairly regularly to one type of instant coffee but also experiment with similar products or substitute if their favourite is not available. Customers try several brands in a set, often switching between them but coming back to their original choices rather than rejecting them for ever. Consumers buy from a repertoire rather than one brand consistently so that for instance consumers of Nabisco shredded wheat were shown over a thirteen-week period to also buy cornflakes (33%), Rice Krispies (29%) and Special K (18%).

Without a new radically improved product in the market, consumers as a population are relatively predictable even though individuals may appear to buy in an ad hoc way from week to week.

In some cases a new product revolutionizes the market, so that in the UK Flora margarine went rapidly from a peripheral brand for health freaks to the leading brand fairly quickly because it offered attributes no other brand could (John Dudley, personal communication).

Foxall and Goldsmith (1994) show that from recent research consumers can be categorized according to their buying strategy:

- **Long loyals** buy only one brand regularly regardless of price.
- **Rotators** care little about price but switch brands for variety.

- **Deal-sensitives** switch amongst a small set of brands but always buy the one on offer.
- **Price-sensitives** buy the cheapest brand.

Conclusion

The purchase of any food or drink product is the consequence of a variety of influences acting simultaneously on the purchaser. Whereas these have been examined one at a time in previous chapters, in this final chapter the trends in the purchase of chicken meat in the UK are studied in order to show how at different points in history various of these influences have been paramount. This assumes, as does most of the research reported in previous chapters, that a study of what influences consumer behaviour will help the manufacturer, retailer and advertiser to produce products for which there is demand and to position them correctly in the marketplace.

The assumption in the work of Ehrenberg and his colleagues is that a better prediction of likely future behaviour of a population of consumers is to be gained by a study of their previous patterns of purchase.

Most markets are stable, so that the number of heavy and light buyers of a product, and the degree of repeat purchase of products and brands do not vary much. The level of repeat purchase of a brand depends on the size of its market penetration (market share) and purchase frequency. Predictions of likely purchase patterns for a population of consumers over a reasonable length of time appear to match actual measures of purchase behaviour.

In the case of small items, like food purchase, consumers tend not to stick to one brand alone but buy from within a set, switching back and forth between brands depending on price, special promotions and availability.

Ehrenberg's views have stimulated a lot of rethinking about what were taken to be truths in marketing. Advertising, for instance, may not work so much to initiate sales and cause people to switch their behaviour; instead its purpose is to retain consumers' preferences and therefore to cause them not to switch their behaviour.

The new product developer or advertiser interested in understanding how people might react needs to understand the factors which might influence actual behaviour. However, they are also interested in the consequent actual purchase decisions. The two approaches briefly outlined here are not in conflict, but both help to improve understanding and prediction of the consumer's behaviour.

Questions

1 Using a product of your choosing, identify the major factors which you analyse to have affected changes in consumption in the past twenty years.
2 Examine the relationship between the consumption of chicken and of other meats. What substitution effects can be identified?
3 Collect information on poultry consumption in three other member states of the EU. Identify factors which are common and different in their effect on consumption in the countries you choose.

4 Explain how the behaviour of light and heavy buyers of breakfast cereal differs according to the views of Ehrenberg and his colleagues.
5 Compare Ehrenberg's views of how advertising works with those outlined in Chapter 17.
6 Evaluate your own food shopping behaviour to determine whether it is consistent with the ideas of multibrand purchasing advocated by Ehrenberg.

References

Food Pocket Book (1992) NTC Publications, Henley-on-Thames
Food Trends (1992) Fast Facts Ltd, Walgrave, Northants
Foxall, G. R. and Goldsmith, R. E. (1994) *Consumer Psychology for Marketing*, Routledge, London
East, R. (1990) *Changing Consumer Behaviour*, Cassell, London
Ehrenberg, A. S. C. (1972) *Repeat Buying*, North-Holland, Amsterdam
Senker, J. (1988) *A Taste for Innovation. British Supermarkets' Influence on Food Manufacturers*, Horton Publishing, Bradford

References

Abelson, H. (1949) *Persuasion*, Springer Publishing Co, New York

Actualidad Economica (1992) 'El coste de comer bien', 5 April

Agra Europe (1992) *Spain – a dynamic market for UK food and drink*, 6 March

Allt, B. (1978) 'Husbands and wives and shopping for food' Mirror Group Newspapers Ltd, February

Argyle, M. (1976) 'Personality and social behaviour'. In Harre, R. (ed) *Personality*, Blackwell, Oxford

Arndt, J. (1968) 'A test of the two step flow in diffusion of a new product', *Journalism Q*, **45**

Ashwell, M. (1993) 'Apple juice scare' *BNF Nutr. Bull.*, **18**, 90–1

Avery, N. and Drake, M. (1993) *Cracking the codes; An analysis of who sets world food standards*, National Food Alliance

Bareham, J. (1990) Consuming interests; inaugural lecture, University of Brighton (unpublished), Brighton

Beardon, W. O. and Etzel, M. J. (1982) 'Reference group influence on product and brand purchase decisions', *J. Consumer Res.*, **9**, 183–194

Belk, R. (1975) 'Situational variables and consumer behaviour' *J. Consumer Res.*, **2**, 2

Berelson, B. and Steiner, G. (1964) *Human Behaviour; an inventory of scientific findings*, Harcourt, Brace and World, New York

Blandford, D. (1986) 'The food people eat'. In *The Food Consumer*, (ed) C. Ritson, L. Gofton and J. McKenzie, Wiley & Son, New York

Blythe, K. (1993) 'Twenty years on in Europe after 2012', *J. of Marketing Mgt.*, **91**, 79

Blythman, J. (1993) 'We'll fight them on the beaches of Blackpool', *Independent*, 17 April

Blythman, J. (1993) 'A myth rammed down our throats', *Independent*, 6 February

Bourne, F. S. (1965) 'Group influence in marketing and public relations'. In J. U. McNeal (ed) *Dimensions of Consumer Behaviour*, Appleton Century Crofts, NY, 137–146

Bowen, D. (1993) 'Growing pains, *Independent on Sunday*, 7 February

Bradshaw, D. (1993) 'The science of shopping', *Financial Times*, 8 October

Bralsford, R. (1986) 'Food processing'. In *The Food Consumer*, (ed) C. Ritson, L. Gofton and J. McKenzie, Wiley, New York

Buckley, N. (1993) 'Changes ahead', *Financial Times*, 5 October

Buckley, N. (1993) 'Category management', *Financial Times*, 15 June

Buss, D. (1991) 'The Changing Household Diet', In *Fifty years of the National Food Survey 1940–1990* (ed) J. M. Slater, HMSO, London

Cathro J. (1992) *Trends in the consumer perception of food*. Food Technology International Europe – Review for the European Food and Drink Processing Industry, 29–32

Cattell, H. B. (1989) *The 16 PF: Personality in depth*, Inst. for Personality and Ability Testing Campaign, Illinois

Chesher, A. (1991) 'Household composition and household food purchases'. In *Fifty*

Years of the National Food Survey 1940–1990 (ed) J. M. Slater, HMSO, London

COMA (1984) 'Diet and cardiovascular disease'. *Report on Health and social subjects*, No. 28, DHSS, London

Conning, D. M. (1991) 'Vitamin A in pregnancy' *BNF Nutr. Bull.*, **61**, 3–4

Coughenour, (1972). In *Consumer Behaviour*, Engel *et al.* (1993)

Dairo de Noticias (1993) 'Pequeno retalho cede aos gigantes', 22 February

Davis, H. and Rigaux, B. (1974) 'Perception of marital roles in decision processes', *J. of Consumer Res.*, **1**, 5–14

Davis, J. (1994) 'Richer pickings for the elderly', *Daily Mail*, 23 June

de Jonquieres, G. (1992) 'Independents fight back', *Financial Times*, 26 November

de Jonquieres, G. (1993) 'Clash of the cans', *Financial Times*, 4 March

de Jonquieres, G. (1993) 'Europe's cold warriors', *Financial Times*, 19 May

de Jonquieres, G. (1993) 'Discounts and private label', *Financial Times*, 6 October, 15 June

Dichter, P. R. (1964) *A Handbook of Consumer Motivations*, McGraw-Hill, New York

Dichter, P. R. (1958) 'Typology', *Motivational Publications*, **3**, 3

Douglas, M. and Nicod, M. (1974) 'Taking the biscuit: the structure of British meals', *New Society*, **30**, 744–747

Drummond, G. (1993) 'The whole hog', *Supermarketing*, 15 October

East, R. (1990) *Changing Consumer Behaviour*, Cassell, London

Economist Books (1990) *Vital World Statistics*

Economist Intelligence Unit (1991). 'Using demographic data', *EIU Retail Business No. 403*

Economist Intelligence Unit (1992) 'Fighting falling margins', *European Retail*, 13 October

Edgell, S. (1970) 'Spiralists: their careers and family lives', *Brit J. of Sociol*, **40**

Editorial (1993) 'The Blair House agreement', *Living Earth and Food*, 9 November

Ehrenberg, A. S. C. (1972) *Repeat Buying*, North Holland, Amsterdam

Engel, J. F., Blackwell, R. D. and Miniard, P. W. (1993). *Consumer Behaviour* (7th edn), Dryden, Fort Worth, Texas

Equal Opportunities Commission (1992) *Women and Men in Britain*, EOC/HMSO, London

Erlichman (1993) 'What's in a name', *Guardian*, 27 March

Eurofood (1992) 'European canned foods', September, Agra Europe, London

Eurofood (1993) 'Fewer German foodshops', February, Agra Europe, London

Euromonitor (1990) *Change in eating habits 1989 versus 1988*, Euromonitor, London

Euromonitor (1992) *European Marketing Data and Statistics*, 27th edn, Euromonitor, London

European Marketing (1992) NTC Publications, Henley-on-Thames, London

Eurostat Basic Statistics of the Community (1990) 27th edn, Brussels

Eysenck, H. J. and Eysenck, S. B. G. (1964) *Manual of the Eysenck Personality Inventory*, University of London Press, London

Family Policy Studies (1985). In *Consumer Behaviour*, Rice (1993)

Festinger, L. (1957) *A Theory of Cognitive Dissonance*, Stanford University Press, Stanford, CA

Fieldhouse, P. (1986) *Food and Nutrition; customs and culture*, Croom Helm, London

Findus (1988) *Frozen food report*, Findus, Croydon

Fishbein, M. and Ajzen, J. (1975) *Belief, attitude, intention and behaviour: An introduction to theory and research*, Addison-Wesley, Reading, MA

Fisher, A. (1993) 'Tapping into convenience', *Financial Times*, 11 November

Fletcher, W. (1993) 'Smashing ads', *Daily Mail*, 17 September

Food Trends (1992) Fast Facts Ltd, Walgrave, Northants

Food Pocket Book (1992) NTC Publications, Henley-on-Thames

Foxall, G. (1980) *Consumer Behaviour*, Croom Helm, London

Foxall, G. (1975) 'Social factors in consumer choice; replication and extension', *J. Consumer Res.*, **2**, 1

Foxall, G. R. and Goldsmith, R. E. (1994) *Consumer Psychology for Marketing*, Routledge, London

Foxall, G. R. and Greenberg, A. (1988) 'Personality and consumer research: another look', *J. Mark. Res. Soc.*, **30**, 111

Green, E. (1991) 'Grazing in the land of fast food fantasies', *Independent*, 16 February

The Grocer (1985) 30 November, 50

The Grocer (1991) 'Only 3% fat', 30 October

The Grocer (1993) 'Focus on Frozen Foods', 4 May, 71–98

The Grocer (1993) 'Price pressure', 4 December

Guardian (1992) 'Own label and retail concentration', 28 October

Gunter, B. and Furnham, A. (1992) *Consumer Profiles – an Introduction to Psychographics*, Routledge, London and New York

Hall, C. (1987) 'Youth's middle tier comes of age' *Marketing and Media Decisions*, October, **58**

Halpin, T. (1994) 'The take away', *Daily Mail*, 16 June

Harrison, B. (1993) 'Selling on the sofa', *Financial Times*, 1 April

Harrison, K. (1993a) 'Product management; predictions', *Supermarketing*, 17 December

Harrison, K. (1993b) 'The face of foods to come', *Supermarketing*, 27 August

Hastings, P. (1993) 'Retail chain management', *Financial Times*, 15 June

Henley Centre (1990) *Planning for Social Change: Origins and Prospects*, Henley Centre, Henley-on-Thames

Horney, K. (1958) *Neurosis and Human Growth*, Norton, New York

Hosking, P. (1993) 'Store wars; will we all be losers?', *Independent*, 27 February

Hovland, C. I. and Weiss, W. (1951) 'The influence of source credibility on communication effectiveness', *Public Opinion Q*, **15**, 635–50

Hovland, C. I., Janis, I. and Kelley, H. (1953) *Communication and Persuasion*, Yale University Press, New Haven, Conn

HMSO (1992) *The Health of the Nation*, HMSO, London

Hughes, D. R., Lesser, D. and Renard, D. (1974) *Consumer Perceptions of Pork*, Department of Agricultural Marketing, University of Newcastle, Newcastle upon Tyne

Hutchinson, D. (1993) 'Ginger joins garlic as the great cure all' *Daily Mail*, 21 December

Hyam, J. (1993) 'Snacks: the food of the future', *Supermarketing*, 10 September

Janis, I. and Fechbach, S. (1953) 'Effects of fear arousing communications', *J. of Abnormal and Soc. Psych.*, **48**, 78–92

Katz, I. (1993) 'My boat will be worth £100,000 less at the stroke of a pen' *The Guardian*, 27 March

Kau, A. K. and Ehrenberg, A. S. C. (1984) 'Patterns of store choice', *J. Mkg Res.*, **21**, 399

King, C. W. and Summers, J. O. (1970) 'Overlap of opinion leadership across consumer product categories' *J. Marketing Res.*, **7**, 43–50

Komarovsky, M. (1961) 'Class differences in family decision making'. In *Household Decision Making*, N. Foote (ed), NYU Press, NY

Kotler, P. (1984) *Marketing Management, Analyses, Planning and Control*, Prentice Hall Englewood Cliffs, NJ

La Piere, R. T. (1934) *Attitudes versus Actions*, Social Forces **13**, 230–237

Lang, T., Dibb, S., Cole-Hamilton, I. and Lobstein, T. (1989) 'This Food Business', *New Statesman and Society*, August

Lazarsfeld, P., Berelson, B. R. and Gaudet, H. (1944) *The People's Choice*, Columbia University Press, New York

Lifestyle Pocket Book (1992), NTC Publications, Henley-on-Thames

Lifestyle Trends (1990) *Food and Drink*, NTC Publications in association with Advertising Associates, Henley-on-Thames

Lumsdaine, A. and Janis, I. (1953) 'Resistance to counter propaganda produced by a one-sided versus two-sided presentation', *Public Opinion Quarterly* **17**, 311–318

MacLean, D. (1991) 'Food Policy and the National Food Survey'. In *Fifty Years of the National Food Survey 1940–1990* (ed) J. M. Slater, HMSO, London

Martineau, P. (1958) 'Social class and spending behaviour', *J. of Marketing*, **23**, 121

Maslow, A. (1954) *Motivation and Personality*, Harper and Row, New York

Massey, R. (1994) 'Food junkies', *Daily Mail*, 22 June

Mennell, S. (1985) *All Manners of Food: Eating and taste in England and France from the Middle Ages to the present*, Blackwell, Oxford

Mennell, S., Murcott, A. and van Otterloo, A. H. (1992) *The Sociology of Food*, Sage, London

Micham, R. (1991) *Lifestyle Market Segmentation*, Praeger, NY

Mitchell, A. (1993) *The Nine American Lifestyles*, Macmillan, New York

Monk, J. (1979) *The Philosophy of Social Grading*, JICNARS, London

Murcott, A. (1983) *The Sociology of Food and Eating*, Gower, Aldershot

Murphy, P. and Staples, W. (1979) 'A modernised family life cycle', *J. Cons. Res.*, **6**, 12–22

NACNE (1983) Proposals for nutritional guidelines for health and education in Britain, Health Education Council, London

New York Times (1992) 'Forget the Sauerbraten', 20 July

Nielsen Homescan (1992) In *The British Shopper 1993*, NTC Publications, Henley-on-Thames

Novak, T. P. and MacEvoy, B. (1990) 'On comparing alternative segmentation strategies'. *J. Consum Res.*, **17**, 105–9

Nugent, N. (1991) *The Government and Politics of The European Community*, Macmillan

Pais (1992) 'Hoy Cocino yo', 12 Sept

Pettifer, J. (1993) 'Going Bananas', *The Guardian*, 22 June

Plummer, J. T. (1974) 'The concept and application of lifestyle segmentation', *J. of Marketing*, **38**, 33–37

Pryke, S. (1993) 'Generation grain', *Marketing Week*, 2 July, 46

Rice, C. (1993) *Consumer Behaviour: Behavioural Aspects of Marketing*, Butterworth-Heinemann, Oxford

Riesmann, D., Glazer, N. and Denney, R. (1960) *The Lonely Crowd*, Yale University Press, New Haven, CT

Ritson, C. and Hutchins, R. (1991) 'The consumption revolution'. In *Fifty Years of the*

NFS (ed) J. M. Slater, HMSO, London

Roberts, M. L. and Wortzel, L. H. (1979) 'New lifestyle determinants of women's food shopping behaviour', *Journal of Marketing*, **43**, 28–39

Robertson, T. S. (1971) *Innovative Behaviour and Communication*, Holt, Rinehart and Winston, New York

Scott, R. (1976) *The Female Consumer*, Associated business programmes, London

Senker, J. (1988) *A Taste for Innovation: British supermarkets' influence on food manufacturers*, Horton Publishing, Bradford

Shepherd, R. (1989) 'Factors influencing food preferences and choice'. In R. Shepherd (ed) *Handbook of the Psychophysiology of Human Eating*, J. Wiley and Sons, Chichester

Silverstone, R. (1993a) 'Vegetarianism – food for the future' *Nutrition and Food Science*, **6**, 20–24

Silverstone (1993b) *Healthy Eating*, Macmillan, London

Smith, D. (1993) 'Exorcising those little grey sells', *Marketing Week*, 2 July

Social Trends 22 (1992) Government Statistical Service, HMSO, London

Somers, F. (ed) (1991) *European Economics*, Pelican, London

Stafford, J. (1966) 'Effects of group influences on consumer brand preferences', *J. Market Res.*, **3**, 68–75

Sternthal, B. and Craig, C. S. (1974) 'Fear appeals revisited and revised', *J. Consum Res.*, **1**, 22–34

Supermarketing (1992) 'European food retailing', 16 October

Supermarketing (1993) 'Counting the cost of discounting', 17 December

Supermarketing (1993) Retail fact file, Reed Publishing

Supermarketing (1993) 'A new slant on statistics', 15 October

Supermarketing (1993) 'What price customer loyalty', 17 September

Supermarketing (1993) 'Food additives', 22 October, 8

Tait, N. (1993) 'European packing of coffee', *Financial Times*, 14 January

Tangermann, S. (1986) 'Economic factors influencing food choice'. In *The Food Consumer*, C. Ritson, L. Gofton and J. McKenzie, J. Wiley and Son, New York

Food Pocket Book (1992) NTC Publications, Henley-on-Thames

Twigg, J. (1983) 'Vegetarianism and the meaning of meat'. In Murcott (1983)

Walster, E., Aronson, E. and Abrahams, D. (1966) 'On increasing the persuasiveness of a low prestige communication', *J. Exp. Soc. Psych.*, **2**, 325–342

Walter Thompson J. (1968) In Scott, R. (1978)

Ward, S. and Wackman, D. (1972) 'Children's purchase influence attempts and parental yielding', *J. Marketing Res.*, **9**

Wells, W. C. (1975) 'Psychographics: a critical review', *J. Mkg Res.*, **12**, 209–229

Wells, W. C. and Gruber, G. (1966) 'Life cycle concepts in marketing research', *J. Marketing Res.*, **3**, 355–63

Wheelock, J. V. (1991) 'Coping with change in the food business' *Food Marketing*, **2**, 3

Which? (1993) 'How safe is your food?', June

Whitehead, R. G. and Paul, A. A. (1990) *Secular trends in food intake in Britain during the past 50 years*

Whitehorn, M. (1994) 'Food experts are out to lunch', *Observer*, 17 April

Wright, G. (1988) Consumer Reaction to Food and Health, unpublished PhD thesis, University of Bradford

Young, C. (1992) EC Packaging and labelling law, *Croner's European Bulletin*, November, 3–14

Index